Ben Gurion
State-Builder

Ben Gurion
State-Builder
Principles and Pragmatism
1948-1963

Avraham Avi-hai

A HALSTED PRESS BOOK

JOHN WILEY & SONS, New York • Toronto
ISRAEL UNIVERSITIES PRESS, Jerusalem

Copyright © 1974 by Keter Publishing House Jerusalem Ltd.

ISRAEL UNIVERSITIES PRESS
is a publishing division of
KETER PUBLISHING HOUSE JERUSALEM LTD.
P.O. Box 7145, Jerusalem, Israel

Published in the Western Hemisphere and Japan by
HALSTED PRESS, a division of
JOHN WILEY & SONS, INC., NEW YORK

Library of Congress Cataloging in Publication Data

Avi-hai, Avraham, 1931–
  Ben Gurion, State-builder.

  "A Halsted Press book."
  I. Ben–Gurion, David, 1886–1973. 2. Israel–Politics
and government. I. Title.
DS125.3.B37A97 1974   956.94′05′0924 [B]   74–557
ISBN 0–470–03836–5

Distributed in the rest of the world by
KETER PUBLISHING HOUSE JERUSALEM LTD.
IUP cat. no. 25136
ISBN 0 7065 1418 1

PRINTED IN ISRAEL

For Hannah Adinah with love

Contents

PART FOUR. WITHDRAWAL FROM POWER

Preface

In my early teens I became a Zionist. My interest in Ben Gurion probably began when I heard his radio statement on May 16, 1948, rebroadcast in Canada from Tel Aviv. I recall my disappointment at the high-pitched voice which did not match my idealized hopes for the deep tones of the orator. I set eyes on Ben Gurion for the first time three years later when he visited Los Angeles to launch the Israel Bond campaign in the United States. Shortly after that, my wife and I settled in Israel, and within a few more months, I was fortunate enough to work in a capacity which enabled me to see Ben Gurion briefly but often as he met the press or, later, received visitors from abroad. There was no doubt in my mind that he embodied and personified history. Only with his departure from office in 1963, and my engagement in the cause of an embattled Levi Eshkol, was I able to begin the attempt to view Ben Gurion objectively. That required, however, a period of study in the United States and further research and reflection over the years.

In 1967, at a meeting with Professor Gerson Cohen, then Professor of Jewish History at Columbia University and now Chancellor of the Jewish Theological Seminary, the thought was born that the ideas of leading Israel political figures were a field which deserved further study. In a doctoral seminar at

Columbia University, the idea was further refined, under the criticism of my fellow students and Professors J.C. Hurewitz, Charles Issawi and John Badeau. Under Professor Hurewitz's guidance, I undertook to do a study of Principles and Pragmatism in State-building for which I earned the PhD. degree from Columbia University. I owe much to Professor Hurewitz, and I am happy to acknowledge this debt to him here. His academic challenges and steadfast direction were coupled with great courtesy and understanding. A number of professors in New York and Jerusalem have read all or part of this work in earlier draft. Since they are not to blame for its contents and because I frequently did not give their comments due weight, it would probably be unfair to list their names. I must except Professor Michael Brecher of McGill University and Visiting Professor at the Hebrew University of Jerusalem. In dark moments he cast much light, and made himself and his materials available to me at all times. He and any others I may mention here bear no responsibility for the flaws and errors which may be found in the book.

Since I came to this study via a longer road than most writers, I have many acknowledgements to make. I am grateful to the heads of the Jewish Theological Seminary: Professors Louis Finkelstein, Bernard Mandelbaum, Simon Halkin and Seymour Fox who encouraged me to undertake studies there and at Columbia, to Mrs. Sylvia Ettenberg and particularly to Rabbi Morton Leifman whose friendship, aid and encouragement are recorded with gratitude.

At the Hebrew University of Jerusalem, Professor Nathan Rotenstreich, from the time he served as Rector, was encouraging in many ways, as was Professor Moshe Davis. The President of the University, Mr. Avraham Harman, has been an inspiration and a friend. Mr. Samuel Rothberg showed sincere personal interest. Drs. Dan Horowitz and Shlomo Aronson of the Department of Political Science were good enough to share some of their unpublished studies with me. My senior colleagues at the School for Overseas Students were most cooperative in arranging blocks of writing time. My colleague and good friend, Mr. Roger Hurwitz, has been a fine sounding board for ideas and of great help in many ways, including the pursuit of elusive data. Mr. Harold Manson of the American Friends of the Hebrew University of Jerusalem was also most helpful. Miss Sheila Rabin helped check references. My dear friend and former secretary, Mrs. Miriam Guini, rendered valuable and diverse aid, in good cheer and with dedication. Mrs. Chani Danziger Weichselbaum typed more drafts more efficiently than one would believe possible from such a happy soul.

Mr. Haim Yisraeli, Director of the Minister of Defence's Bureau, a fine and honorable civil servant who won the confidence of three defense ministers — Ben Gurion, Eshkol and Dayan, a not inconsiderable feat — opened many doors. Mr. Yehudah Erez, who edited most of Ben Gurion's writings and has worked on his archives, was exceedingly kind. Mr. Yitzḥak Navon, M.K. provided useful information and Minister Shimon Peres and Mayor Teddy Kollek kindly clarified a number of questions. I was able to conduct two lengthy interviews with Mr. Ben Gurion in 1968 and 1969 for which I gratefully record my thanks. Dr. Michael Heymann, Director of the Central Zionist Archives, and his staff were kind and helpful.

The head of Keter Publishing House, Mr. Yitzḥak Rischin, and Dr. Geoffrey Wigoder were anxious to publish this book quickly, a fact which I hope the readers will appreciate as much as the author. Mr. Robert Amoils' fine advice and efforts as editor are highly appreciated, as are the work and useful suggestions of Mr. Derek Orlans. I am also grateful to the Memorial Foundation for Jewish Culture and the Canadian Foundation for Jewish Culture, which expressed their encouragement through modest grants. The dedication of this book to my wife covers more than I would care to detail; our daughters, Shoshanah, Tovah and Dror Lee, are involved fans and supporters.

Jerusalem
Kislev, 5734; November, 1973   Avraham Avi-hai

CHAPTER ONE

Principles and Pragmatism in State-Building

The reestablishment of a people as sovereign in the land once ruled by its ancestors, after a lapse of 19 centuries, has aroused varied reactions. These range from profound interest, wonder and partisan support to fierce opposition, forced acceptance and, rarely, indifference. This is another way of saying that Israel's rise merits careful study. In particular the role of one man clamors for analysis.

The creation of the modern State of Israel was due, beyond all other individual contributions, to the leadership of this man. The state's first 15 years were under the star of David Ben Gurion, so much so that one of his severest critics wrote:

> The policy of Israel and the form of its regime in this period were determined to a critical extent by his person- ality and by the prestige and authority of the leadership he had won for himself . . . . [He] ruled absolutely in his party and in Israel's political life so that even those among his comrades who questioned his path and methods negated their will before his, and recognized his almost sole auth- ority to make decisions in defense matters, and conse- quently in foreign affairs as well. Among wide classes and circles he was accorded popularity bordering on worship.[1]

1

The use of extreme language notwithstanding, the citation nevertheless draws the outlines of a powerful, perhaps charismatic, leader who shaped policy at home and abroad with unusual authority in comparison with most democratic leaders. By 1948, Ben Gurion had completed 13 years of leadership of the quasi-governmental Jewish Agency for Palestine, and he then embarked upon a further 13 years of ministry at the head of Israel's cabinet.

From 1948, Ben Gurion was engaged in a process of state- and nation-building, in which he applied with pragmatism the principles he espoused. Under the impact of reality, some principles changed, and under his impact, a new reality evolved.

This study will examine three interrelated theses which are based upon the early Israeli experience. First, the argument will be advanced that effective national leadership stemmed from the pragmatic solution of major state problems and crises in accordance with the fundamental aims and principles of the leader. The key words here are principles and pragmatism. Decisions and action will be viewed along a continuum ranging between these two concepts. The coincidence of principles and pragmatic action, it will be shown, tended to make for effective leadership. To the leader, some principles may never be forsaken, regardless of the circumstances; others may be bent or adjusted as the situation dictates.

This thesis will constitute a continuing strand, to be applied throughout the study. For clarity's sake, here is one example which should suffice at this particular point. Zionist ideology and Ben Gurion's own belief posited an eternal claim by the Jewish people on all of *Eretz Yisra'el* (Palestine). In 1937, at a Zionist Congress, Ben Gurion said, "The integrity of the homeland and our full right to the homeland is engraved . . . on our heart."[2] Nonetheless, he favored accepting the partition of Palestine, and the creation of a Jewish state in part of "western Eretz Yisr'ael" (cis-Jordanian Palestine), since this would lead to "*speedy* strengthening of our power in the land" through increasing Jewish immigration and land settlement, and in general improve the demographic balance in favor of the Jews.[3]

The principle emerged diminished in scope, for pragmatic reasons, in the realization that part of something is more than nothing.

The word "pragmatic" will be used in its common, everyday sense, which is close to its Greek root meaning, a deed. In other words, in this sense, to be pragmatic is to be concerned with doing, with achieving, with practice. The Hebrew word closest to conveying this is *bitzu'a,* literally, to carry out, to apply or execute a plan or policy, to get things done, to act pragmatically. Ben Gurion's use of the term in 1941 presents a clear example: "The test of Zionism is in its application (bitzu'a), not in its formulation."[4]

Effective leadership will be measured by two indicators: the maintenance of leadership, that is, the perpetuation of the leader in his role; and, second, the advances made toward realizing the aims which he had established and which his constituency had accepted in elevating him and choosing him as leader. The roles in Ben Gurion's case were those of prime minister and minister of defense, and to a lesser extent, party leader.

The second thesis under examination will be that the state leader, particularly in a postrevolutionary situation, tends to maximize the power of state institutions and to minimize that of rival frameworks in order to achieve his aims of state-building. The road to a Jewish state was built by the Zionist movement, the Zionist political parties, the labor movement in Palestine, and the military and paramilitary forces maintained or fostered by them. After the creation of the state, these institutions continued to exist. It will be shown that Ben Gurion attempted to unify them under state control, as in the case of rival military organizations or competing "trends" in the educational system. When unification was not possible, that is, in cases where Ben Gurion had to recognize the legitimate right of the institutions to exist, he attempted to arrogate to the state some of their major functions or at least to establish the primacy of the state over the older institutional frameworks. One example was the attempt to nationalize part of the functions of the *Histadrut* (General Federation of Labor), such as its employment bureaus or labor exchanges, and its sick fund, or health insurance system. Another example was the relationship between the World Zionist Organization/Jewish Agency and the state apparatus. In both cases, ideological differences and questions of power and control merged.

The third thesis lies in the realm of the relations between the political system and the individual leader. Ben Gurion forged a political system based on the parliamentary tradition of proportional representation which had obtained in the prestate national forums: the World Zionist Organization and the representative bodies of the Palestine Jewish community, the *Yishuv*. Political systems impose limitations on the power of the individual leader. Conflicts between the leader and the system, it will be argued, lead to an eventual loss of will on the part of the leader and the loss of support on the part of his followers. This may be seen as the waning of charisma and the victory of the system over the individual. In this study it will be shown that increasing discord between Ben Gurion and his coalition partners and the growing friction within his own party brought about the loss of effective leadership and the withdrawal of support, leading to his resignation in June 1963.

This thesis may also be viewed along the continuum of principle-pragmatism. As Ben Gurion continued to foster certain principles which he believed were vital for Israel's future security or internal well-being, he refused to bow to the pragmatic internal political realities, the counter-policies advanced within the coalition and his party. These points of friction are embodied, for example, in his pursuit of a policy of reconciliation with West Germany, over the opposition of his left-wing coalition partners and some of his own Labor Party colleagues; his clash with the orthodox religious faction over the definition of "Who is a Jew? "; or in the intra-party dispute over the disposition of the Lavon Affair of 1960-61. These points will be examined in due course in the framework of this study. The principle-pragmatism continuum is also inherent in the thesis of the maximization of state power. Here the principle of state primacy coincides with the pragmatic desire or need to wield maximum power.

METHOD

To indicate this continuum, and analyze the mixture of principle and pragmatism or the primacy of one over the other in various areas of public policy or in the realm of institution- and state-building, I shall try to isolate the statement of principle and compare it with the end action or result. In Ben Gurion's addresses in parliament and cabinet statements, in his other writings of the period, as well as in public appearances at a host of forums, he laid down his basic tenets and aims. In some cases, the aims changed with the evolving reality; in others, he helped change the reality, the history of the period. To examine this interplay, major policy statements, recurrent expressions of principle, and major historic developments or policy decisions will be examined, working from available sources. Reminiscences will only be used if they coincide with statements of the period, or if they sum up the thinking of the time.

Although official documents of the period under review, 1948-63, have not yet been released to the public, not only decisions, but sometimes actual cabinet proceedings or minutes have been published. This has usually occurred at a time of coalition crisis, when the contending factions leaked information to the press, and the record was cited by one or both sides to gain public sympathy and support.

To prepare this study, I had to comb Ben Gurion's collected speeches and articles, happily published to a great extent in a number of volumes, his other books, as well as the *Knesset* (legislature) and Zionist Congress proceedings, and similar primary sources. The lack of a standard political history of Israel or of post-state Zionism has made it necessary to include some descriptive or narrative accounts of the period, in order to elucidate the framework of events in which the analyses are set.

The study, aside from its opening or introductory and its concluding, evaluative chapters, is divided into four parts. First, the setting for state-building is discussed. This theme is sub-divided into chapters covering Ben Gurion's growth to leader-ship and his training in the use of power and the control of institutions as instruments of policy, his world-view, and the political culture he helped form for the state.

The second and third parts deal with state-building in an attempt to demonstrate the thesis of maximizing state power against the background of pragmatic applications of principles. State-building will be studied on two axes: domestic and foreign affairs. Maximization of state power will first be demonstrated in relation to four domestic issues: the labor movement and capital; the religious establishment and the educational systems of the state; the defense establishment; and the Arab minority in Israel. Externally, relations with the neighboring Arab states, the securing of arms (including some treatment of foreign rela-tions, particularly in this context), and the primacy of Israel over the Zionist establishment and in world Jewish affairs will be studied.

In the fourth part, the friction and clashes within the politi-cal system — in the coalition and the Labor Party — will be viewed from the dual vantage point of the waning of pragmatism and of charisma.

Thematically, the study covers a wide range of basic issues or crises around which major policy decisions were taken. It in-cludes consideration of the following: Israel's political system and the lack of a full, formal constitution; the relationship with the labor movement and attempts to nationalize part of its functions and to influence the *kibbutz* movement in line with the government's overall immigration policy, and the encouragement of capital investment. Also considered are the unification of the educational systems and some pragmatic accommodations to the Jewish religious establishment and political groupings.

The unification theme is pursued in the study of the creation of the Israel Defense Forces, the disbanding of rival military organizations, the conduct of defense affairs, and the use of the army as an educator and state-builder. Continuing the security theme, the Arab minority in Israel and its control by military government, the maximization of state military power, and the destruction of Arab strength are treated. The security approach to statecraft is concluded with an analysis of arms supply policy and its impact on foreign policy. Major issues such as the decision to create ties with Germany, and the concomitant crises, the Franco-Israel arms arrangements, the attitude toward the UN and concrete examples of ignoring its decisions, as in the case of making Jerusalem the capital of Israel, are considered. Israel's basic orientation toward the West and Ben Gurion's attitude to Great-Power intervention in the Middle East are also touched upon.

The question of state primacy over the Zionist movement is considered both from an organizational point of view as well as from the standpoint of ideological change. This change is dealt with at some length, consideration being given to its impact not only upon Israel but upon the entire Jewish people. In other words, Ben Gurion's decisions and actions in this area have an effect extending far beyond Israel's borders, which must be investigated and clarified. The role of immigration to Israel is important from both points of view — the organizational and the ideological — as well as from the standpoint of internal demographic balance vis-à-vis the Arabs and for increasing defense capabilities. The concluding discussion of the waning of pragmatism and charisma in the crises within the coalition and party has been outlined above.

It may seem to some readers that the scope of this study is too wide; others may feel that some areas were unnecessarily excluded. The task of selection is at best arduous and dangerous. It is, of course, at the nub of any type of study such as this. In selecting the themes mentioned above, the criterion was to isolate the major areas of public policy or the main public institutions in the specific Israeli context. In this context, state-building relies less upon sweeping foreign policy decisions and, as far as possible, is inward-looking, dealing with the instruments at the disposal of the state for enhancing its growth, increasing its population, strengthening its defense structures, and maintaining its political system and autonomy.

POLITICAL BIOGRAPHY AND
POLITICAL THEORY

The classic distinction between political biography and political theory needs no definition. There is a wide range of both, going back to Plutarch and Plato, and the output has shown no signs of diminishing in recent years. In a steady stream, studies are published on the lives of statesmen, and on the theories set forth by thinkers and political figures. There are, however, few attempts, if any, to study specifically the theories advanced by an important political leader of a state and their actual application in his day-to-day leadership. This work essays to analyze the political theories of an individual leader of a specific state, as put into practice by him in that state. To some extent, political biographies such as those of Lenin, Nehru and others treat the subject. But works dealing solely or basically with the nexus between principles and pragmatism are rare, if at all extant.

The last few decades have seen new attempts to study leadership as a social, political and psychological phenomenon. A wide and growing bibliography examines facets of leadership, and attempts have been made to apply these new approaches to the study of leaders.[5] These range from probes into more definite categorization or typology of leaders, an approach exemplified by Lewis J. Edinger's work on Kurt Schumacher, to the more psycho-historical studies of the genre of Erik Erikson.[6] The state of the science (or art, as one may argue) is at its beginnings.

At any rate, the present work is not conceived as a broad survey of leadership, nor as a case study using the tools of these newer attempts. It is rather limited to one man, one political system, one set of circumstances, in a specific period. Some challenges to thought result from the interaction of the newer approaches with the material presented below. A few thoughts on leadership and particularly its loss will therefore be raised. However, the essential thrust of the work is to see the principles and pragmatism along a continuum, to weigh the state-centered primacy Ben Gurion created in Israel, and to study how friction between him and the most important component of the political structure — his party — led to his withdrawal from leadership. More skilled and practiced minds than the writer's may then, if they find it useful, apply other tools of analysis to this work.

PART ONE

The Setting

CHAPTER TWO

The Road to Leadership

What was the background from which David Ben Gurion grew, and what were the phases in his career until his attainment of preeminence in the renaissance of the Jewish state? The road led from Eastern Europe at the turn of the century, through work in the new Jewish settlements in Palestine, to organization of the small community of idealistic laborers who came to that country in the first decades of this century. It carried him to leadership of the labor movement and Jewish community in Palestine, and of the World Zionist Organization.

David Green was born on October 16, 1886 in Plonsk, a small manufacturing town with a majority Jewish population of 6,000 some 60 kilometers northwest of Warsaw, in Russian Poland.[1] Avigdor (Victor) Green, his father, was a literate man, versed in the byways of Russian bureaucracy and legal procedures. He is reported to have filled the role of informal legal counsellor, who presented petitions on behalf of the less skilled Jewish and non-Jewish residents of the area and represented them vis-à-vis the authorities. David, who after his arrival in Palestine at the age of twenty adopted the Hebrew last name by which he is known, was the sixth child. He studied in an "improved" ḥeder, that is, a traditional private school in which Hebrew prayers, Bible, Talmud and some arithmetic were

13

taught with no great pretence at modern didactics. The "improvement" consisted of more stress on the Bible, as distinct from the Talmud, and greater care to teach Hebrew as a language, and not only as *the* holy tongue.[2]

The 19th century was a period of rapid demographic growth for Jews, their number quadrupling to ten million by the end of the century. The majority of Jews lived in Europe, and most of these in Eastern Europe and the Balkans.[3] In Poland, the process of impoverishment of these Jews resulted from their being squeezed out of agricultural factoring. Owing to the competition with non-Jewish labor and the lack of Jewish industrial skills, the nascent industrialization in Europe did not provide them economic refuge. This struck hard at the urban centers in which the Jews lived, often comprising a majority in the townlets, sometimes as much as 80 to 90 percent of the total population.[4]

In 1905, according to one study, there were barely 2,809 families engaged in agriculture and 4,198 in specialized agricultural pursuits, out of a total Jewish population in Poland of over 1,300,000; Jews comprised 14 percent of the total population of Russian Poland, but 40 percent of the urban population. Twenty percent of the Jewish families lived in abject poverty, the breadwinners lacking all skills, engaging in woodcutting, portering, and the like.[5] These demographic and social changes came at a period of intense ideological innovation.

The Enlightenment *(Haskalah),* a movement to open up Jewish communities to West European thought and attitudes, had penetrated into Jewish Eastern Europe late. In the West, it had held out the hope of civic acceptance on the basis of equality (with concomitant assimilation and the abandonment of Hebrew as the medium of communication), the lessening of the sense of being the outsider, the stranger in exile, and therefore led to the displacement of religion and tradition. These hopes and processes did not obtain in the East, at least not to anything like the same extent. In unenlightened Czarist Russia, in Rumania and the Balkans, the Jews' sense of difference remained. The traditional patterns were deep-rooted, a protective shield against persecution and hopelessness. The Hebrew Enlightenment turned back upon itself, trying to revive the ancient and never-forgotten language in new forms, for modern usage in literature and publicistic journalism.

Through its medium, as well as from the ambient non-Jewish environment, the twin forces of nationalism and social radicalism entered the Jewish towns, villages, and cities. The Jewish intelligentsia was riven, toward the end of the 19th century, between the old-generation "enlighteners" *(maskilim)* who were either experimenting traditionalists or leaned toward some form of cultural assimilation and, on the other side, the sons, inspired by socialism. At the same time, Jewish nationalist sentiment and institutions began to grow. The analyses of both rabbis and secularists tended to show that assimilation was either undesirable or impossible.

The new nationalism, trying to build on the foundations of the "eschatological tradition," found its expression in the popular movement *Hovevei Tziyyon* (Lovers of Zion) in the later decades of the century. And before the turn of the century Theodor Herzl gave the stirrings and rumblings a focal point, a flag, and a slogan. The World Zionist Organization gave Western form to Eastern content. "The popular organization which Herzl established had one paramount aim and activity: to serve as the representative of the Jewish people and in this capacity to obtain recognition for Jewish nationalism."[6]

Victor Green was active in Hovevei Tziyyon, and later in the Zionist movement. Though punctilious in religious practice, he no longer wore the old gabardine of the ultra-orthodox. David Green grew up in the heady atmosphere of ideological change, discussions, debates, and organizational work. Having lost his mother at the age of 11, the slight, intelligent boy lent his imagination and threw his efforts into organizing his peers into a club whose aims were Zionism and the use of the Hebrew language.[7]

Zionism in Eastern Europe developed a "life-style," and new myths. The 1882 pogroms had led to the organization of self-defense groups. By the end of the century, Herzl was seen as a new redeemer, as "King of the Jews." Tradition underwent modification; new stress was laid on the religious holidays — emphasizing their national and social content. An attempt was made to transform Hebrew education in order to provide both writers and readers for the reborn and evolving ancient tongue. The movement tried to influence Jews not to fall into the historic pattern of flight, and to repudiate assimilation. The Enlightenment had failed, the emancipation had aborted.[8] The choice was then threefold: to flee, as individuals, and find a new life in Western Europe and, particularly, in the New World; to assimilate or to fight the battle for emancipation and socialism in the land of birth — that is, not to emigrate; to build a Zionist community which would reshape its culture while helping to reconstitute Palestine as a Jewish Home and eventually a Jewish state.

Within the Zionist camp itself, in Ben Gurion's formative years, attempts were made to wed socialist theory to the nationalist analysis. Socialism without Zionism had made great inroads among the Jewish proletariat, especially through the Jewish Social Democrats, the Bund. But beyond the ideology was the fact of Jewish emigration from Eastern Europe; it was a mighty flow pouring out westward. A small trickle though had turned east, and had given the biblical term *ḥalutz,* he who goes "first, before the camp," its new content: volunteer, pioneer, worker of the land. Used in the new sense a few years before Ben Gurion was born, it helped shape his thinking.[9] He welded his intense Zionism, socialism and ḥalutz-inspired youthful activism into the decision to cut loose from the debates and wordiness of Russia and Poland. He opted for the "doers" in Zionism, the practical Zionists.

In a fine study of the ideas in the air at this time, a scholar has described the "practical" and the "political" Zionists. The latter believed that the recognition of the Jewish claim to sovereignty in Palestine had to precede "an effective demographic concentration." The former felt that settling the land would make possible and sustain the thrust toward sovereignty.[10]

The eighteen-year-old Ben Gurion left Plonsk. First he

worked as a Hebrew teacher in Warsaw for two years. He helped build the Labor-Zionist group called *Po'alei Tziyyon* (Workers of Zion), and finally emigrated to Palestine. His move was against the general trend. Skeptics among the Jews claimed that Christianity would never permit a Jewish state in Palestine, that the land itself was barren and waste, and that Jews lacked any experience or knowledge of farming. The Zionist movement was not fostering immigration into Palestine; it was in a confused and disorganized state. Zionism had weathered Herzl's flirtation with the idea of building a temporary Jewish way-station in Uganda; it was still staggering under the impact of his sudden death in 1904. Disillusion came from the left as well: the revolutionary fervor of the young socialists had been dampened by the failure of the 1905 revolution following the fiasco of the Russo-Japanese War. In the wake of the particularly ugly Kishinev pogrom of 1903, Jewish self-defense groups mushroomed.[11]

In early 1905, a Russian immigrant-pioneer in Palestine appealed to Jewish youth in the Diaspora for personal realization of practical Zionism. The romantic language of the stark entreaty shows not only the spirit of its framer, Yosef Vitkin, but also the temper of the times, and therefore merits citation.

> Awake, awake, young men of Israel, arise to the aid of the nation! Our people is dying, our land will shortly pass beyond our reach forever, make haste, speed to its aid! Organize, assume strong discipline, discipline of life and death! Awake, forget all dear to you until now, leave them forever, with no shadow of regret . . . . Prepare to make war upon nature, sickness and hunger, [to fight] people, enemies and friends, strangers and brothers . . . . Make haste and come, heroes of Israel . . . for otherwise we may soon be lost.[12]

In the summer of 1906, at the age of twenty, Ben Gurion arrived at Jaffa (there was no Tel Aviv, and Haifa harbor had yet to be developed). He made his way to a camp of his com-

rades in Petaḥ Tikvah, a farm town whose name means Gate of
Hope. His recollection of the period and of his own mood was
that of hopelessness.

> I came to the land . . . out of total and absolute despair of
> the Diaspora, Zionism and socialism as they were in those
> days . . . . When the revolution broke out — a vacuum
> formed in my heart, for I knew that the revolution might
> free Russia, but not the Jewish people . . . . I believed that
> here was the only and last place of refuge. Then perhaps
> this faith was a kind of madness. The Bund and the
> socialists told us this was a land of "corpses" and
> graves . . . . They also tried to show us that what we were
> about to do . . . was reactionary and opposed to the laws
> of "economic science" — for according to this "law"
> people were going from the village to the city and not
> from the city to the village. The Zionist leaders also held
> us in scorn, not one of them encouraged us. Our comrades
> in Po'alei Tziyyon also opposed this immigration to Israel
> [saying] . . . it should come about of itself and not through
> voluntarism.[13]

THE ROAD TO LEADERSHIP: LABOR

Ben Gurion worked in a number of places in Palestine. But
his oratory, energy and sense of purpose pushed him to political eminence in short order. A veteran pioneer has reminisced
that at one of the first meetings addressed by the newcomer, his
rhetoric and unusual command of the language were so powerful as to leave an indelible impression. "What did he speak on?
I do not recall. I only remember, will never forget, how he
spoke. Inflammatory. And, most important — in Hebrew! And
what Hebrew! "[14]

Ben Gurion spent the next few years wandering and working
in the new settlements in Palestine. He was also obliged to
return to Plonsk to present himself for induction into the Czarist army; failure to do so would have placed his father in jeop-

ardy. Ben Gurion was eventually elected, along with Ben-Zvi and the latter's wife-to-be, Raḥel Yanna'it, to the editorial board of the labor periodical *Ha-Aḥdut* (Unity). He moved to Jerusalem in the summer of 1910, and rounded out his limited livelihood from the Po'alei Tziyyon Party with private tutoring. An indication of his interests may be found in his translating into Hebrew Sombart's *Socialism and Social Movements in the Nineteenth Century. Ha-Aḥdut* carried his trenchant articles, which show no signs of publicistic grace and nuances of style. They make their point by clearly conceived, outspoken criticism and blunt demands: the centrality of the practical work in Palestine, impatience with overseas or Diaspora debating societies and Diaspora-centered activities, the hope for the liberalization of the Ottoman Empire and the future of Zionist building in that political milieu.[15]

Until the outbreak of World War I, he spent a few years in Salonika and Constantinople, studying law and serving as secretary of the Jewish Students' Organization. In this period, he began his career as delegate to the Zionist and Po'alei Tziyyon international conferences he was to attend regularly and with rising prominence.

There were fewer than 2,000 Jewish workers in Palestine at that time, finding their organizational legs and building institutions to serve their needs and interests. While this was going on, Ben Gurion and a few other young "Palestinians" were seeking to increase their self-Ottomanization. Some Zionists, in common with other minority groups in the sprawling Ottoman Empire, adopted this policy in order to advance their specific ethnic cause in the Empire, which they hoped would in time become more liberal and open to their programs. Victor Green in Plonsk helped pay for his son's Turkish education, and the son pondered on whether he would eventually become a farm laborer or lawyer.[16]

The outbreak of World War I found Ben Gurion returning from Constantinople to Palestine for the summer vacation. (Fifty-five years later he still recalled that he had benefited on the ship from a half-fare student reduction.)[17] Ben Gurion continued his pro-Turkish line, but the authorities viewed the immigrant Jews in Palestine as a potential source of disaffection. Ben Gurion and Ben-Zvi were arrested and held in the *Kishleh,* the lock-up near Jaffa Gate in the Old City of Jerusalem. The discipline was rudimentary and Ben Gurion continued his communal activities from jail. He recognized at that time that the encounter with the Arabs of Palestine, which had seemed a conflict between the traditional and the modernizing, as well as a clash between the land-owning and the land-purchasing, was actually a collision of two nationalisms. A Palestine Arab fellow-student from Constantinople met Ben Gurion in the prison courtyard, and expressed his surprise at seeing him in those circumstances. Ben Gurion explained that he was under arrest for being a Zionist and was greeted with the following reply: "As your friend, I am sorry; as an Arab, I am glad."[18]

Ben Gurion and Ben-Zvi were expelled to Alexandria, arrested as enemy aliens by the British, and finally made their way to New York. From the summer of 1915, they worked to propagandize and organize the Jewish ghettoes of North America, spreading the idea of physical labor in Palestine. They published a number of books, including a detailed study of the Land of Israel, its geography, history, and demographic structure. The Bolshevik Revolution, the American entry into the war against Germany, and the Balfour Declaration — all in 1917 — seemed to open new possibilities. Ben Gurion and Ben-Zvi joined the British bandwagon and in early 1918 began recruiting volunteers to fight the Turks. (The U.S. was not at war with Turkey.)

At last Ben Gurion's old yearning to wear the uniform of a nation whose voice mattered in Palestine was satisfied.[19]

The foreign recruits posted to the 39th Battalion of the Royal Fusiliers arrived in Egypt after General Allenby had conquered Jerusalem. Ben Gurion reached Palestine only at the end of 1918. By the time he was demobilized from the 40th Battalion to which he had been transferred, the cornerstone of the

Hebrew University had been laid, the Zionist Commission led by Dr. Chaim Weizmann, the leader of world Zionism, had come and gone, and the British administration was under way. Most striking, and serious, the Jewish population had been drastically reduced by famine, disease and deportation during the war.

The reduced labor community, still organized and alert, received reinforcements from an Eastern Europe in the throes of postwar chaos, the collapse of empires, and the birth of new states. The newcomers lived on the myths of the ḥalutzim who had preceded them, and the promise for the first time by a Great Power to help realize the Zionist ideal. There were three main streams of Labor-Zionist organization in Palestine: *Po'alei Tziyyon*; *ha-Po'el ha-Tza'ir,* which took a less doctrinaire position on class struggle and class organization than its rival; and a group of influential "non-affiliated" or "apoliticals" *(bilti-miflagtiim)* who were labor in spirit but refused to join either of the two parties. One of the leaders of the last group was Berl Katznelson, who was to work closely with Ben Gurion for a number of decades. Another was Yitzḥak Tabenkin, who became Ben Gurion's colleague, later rival, and finally opponent.

In a retrospective summary of his early political career, Ben Gurion recalled in rather objective terms how he had gained the lower rungs of leadership and learned how to construct the ladder at the same time. He viewed his political apprenticeship as beginning long before the setting up of the labor federation; actually as "a schoolboy" in Plonsk and Warsaw he had begun his political action. Political activity, he said, was a step-by-step process: first, "subscribing to ideas which are right and just"; convincing others to accept the same views; organizing them into a political force, and then using this force "to secure the fulfilment of your ideas."[20]

As life returned to normal, after the war, the parties were approached by the three regional unions of farm workers to establish a single workers' union and party. Ben Gurion, Ben-Zvi, Katznelson, and Tabenkin were four of the six committee members who brought Po'alei Tziyyon and the "non-affiliated" to join a new grouping. Ha-Po'el ha-Tza'ir was to remain independent for another decade. The organizers of the new party, tiny in numbers, but counting on reinforcements from the teeming Jewish communities of Eastern Europe and even America, proposed the resounding name — The Unification of the Workers' Class in the Land of Israel: *"Aḥdut ha-'Avodah"* (Unity of Labor). Ben Gurion opened the founding conference in the spring of 1919. In keeping with his views cited above, he saw in the new unity a force which would begin to realize its ideal, and transform the society and the land.

> Different views brought us from the Diaspora, but the reality of the Land of Israel, the recognition of that which exists and that which does not exist in the Land, has given birth in us to a new cognition . . . and we now wish, through the unification of all our forces, to establish its rule over the future of the country . . . .[21]

The organization's name as finally adopted sums up its platform — The Zionist-Socialist Unification of Workers of the Land of Israel: "Aḥdut ha-'Avodah." By not adopting a narrow interpretation of Zionist-Socialism and by refraining from use of the word "party," the new body attempted to keep its ranks open and accommodate fairly wide ranges of opinion. Aḥdut ha-'Avodah at its founding numbered only 1,871 members.

Not much larger was the organization resulting from the next step in unifying the labor movement. Under pressure from a fresh element, the recently arrived ḥalutzim from Eastern Europe, both Aḥdut ha-'Avodah and ha-Po'el ha-Tza'ir agreed to call a joint convention of all workers in Palestine to found a national, non-party federation of labor to deal with economic, welfare and educational questions common to all groups. Not quite 4,500 men and women cast their ballots in the election; of the 87 delegates elected, Aḥdut ha-'Avodah had 38, ha-Po'el ha-Tza'ir 27, New Immigrants 16, and the proto-Communists

6.[22] The convention ended on December 9, 1920, amidst sentimental reconciliations, singing and dancing, with the decision to
create the General Federation of Hebrew Laborers in the Land
of Israel, known by the initial word for "organization," Histadrut, but called "Federation" in English. At the end of 1921,
Ben Gurion became secretary-general of the Histadrut, that is,
its chief executive officer, to borrow a fitting term from
another and quite different culture. Just prior to this, Ben
Gurion had added another facet to his international experience,
fostering relations with the international labor movement and
with Zionist groups abroad. He spent most of the preceding two
years in London, on behalf of Po'alei Tziyyon. In this period,
he traveled extensively in Europe, engaged in movement affairs.
He, Paula, his Russian-American wife, and their son and daughter spent some time as well in Plonsk.

The progress toward labor unity was a dream shared by Ben
Gurion and others; this should be obvious, otherwise it would
not have been achieved in the atomistic and individualistic ideo-
logy-ridden atmosphere of the second decade of this century.
Yet Ben Gurion had a clear conception of what he wanted. His
plan, as expressed in 1917, was to unify the labor movement
and make it dominant in the Yishuv and the Zionist movement.
This leading role for labor would give it hegemony in the struggle to establish statehood and in the future state.

> The Zionist Organization has become the legal instru-
> mentality of the Jewish people for erecting the National
> Home. The conquest of this instrument by the Jewish
> workers will guarantee the national and social character of
> Eretz Yisra'el . . . .[23]

The beginning of the 'twenties was marked in Palestine by
clashes between Arabs and Jews. These came as a Jewish
Defense Organization, *Haganah,* was being formed. It was based
on demobilized Jewish troops from the British army and the
original secret defense groups which had been organized in
Ottoman times *(ha-Shomer),* and was part of the labor group-

ing. In 1929, another series of riots and the massacre of the Jews of Hebron took place. In the interim period, between 1920 and 1929, the political and economic relations between Arabs, Jews and the British Mandatory changed considerably.

The British were learning the contradictions of their Mandate: the need to foster the Jewish National Home, and the countervailing Arab influences and demands. Transjordan had been removed from the terms of the Mandate, and 'Abdallah had become ensconced in 'Amman. The Zionist lobby in London was able to put pressures on the colonial administrators, place parliamentary questions, and reach the top echelons in the government and opposition, but never to the complete satisfaction of the movement.

The Yishuv grew, but economic setbacks, limited Zionist funds, and economic crises — both local and international — held back the pace of immigration and development. However, the kibbutzim, and the economic enterprises of the Histadrut, which conceived itself as a work-creating force and a future "society of workers" rather than as a defensive trade-union movement dealing with improvement of wages and conditions of labor, continued to expand and develop. The Histadrut produced a daily newspaper, *Davar,* edited by Berl Katznelson, and its health, education, welfare and mutual aid arms provided a broad front of contact with the members on a number of levels. The experience of working together in the Histadrut and the mounting external and internal political problems drove the two labor parties toward each other. At the beginning of 1930, following years of negotiations and months after a document of unity had been signed, they united in *Mapai* (acronym of *Mifleget Po'alei Eretz Yisra'el,* literally Party of Workers of the Land of Israel). The first speaker at the founding convention was Ben Gurion — again a sign of his leading role in creating the united party.

The early Ben Gurion tried to weld Zionism and socialism into one inseparable process, based on his belief in the need for labor as a way of redeeming both the individual Jew and the Land. This belief, almost mystical, was shared by most Labor

Zionists in Palestine. Thus, in 1920, Ben Gurion said that:

> . . . labor settlements whose social value is no less than
> their national importance, have proved that not only is
> there no contradiction between Zionism and socialism, but
> on the contrary, they are bound together as one form and
> matter. [24]

The very attempt to combine the two as "form and matter"
demonstrates the conflict between the two concepts: one dealing as it does with nations, the other with class and society. In
Ben Gurion's thinking, the combination is dynamic, leading
from a state- and nation-building labor *élite* which would be the
base and the motive force for the entire nation and enterprise, to
nationhood, to a state whose citizens would form a working
people. In practice, this meant that the national element was the
major goal, while the labor or socialist idea was both a secondary
aim and a means to the national end.

The citation above is from a collection of speeches and
essays, whose name itself is indicative of Ben Gurion's outlook:
Mi-Ma'amad le'Am (From Class to Nation). At that time, in the
1920s and '30s, he did not view the class struggle, cardinal for
orthodox socialists, "solely as a war of class interests." The real
issue, he said in 1932, is to debate and determine the best path
for realizing Zionism's aims, not class war but

> . . . a war between the emissaries of self-realizing Zionism
> and its . . . enemies. The strength revealed by the Jewish
> worker . . . is drawn not only from his class organization or
> social vision, but from the national mission he has
> assumed . . . out of the recognition that behind his work
> and battle stands the historic need of a nation struggling
> for its existence and awaiting redemption. [25]

Two major issues which took shape in the 1920s and continued to attract interest and stir up controversy in the following decade were the exclusive employment by Jews of Jewish

workers, and the escalating Arab-Jewish dispute. The first, called in the jargon of Zionism "Hebrew Labor," was based on the assumption that Jewish citrus-growers and factory owners would prefer to continue to employ the cheaper and less demanding Arab workers. The majority labor position demanded pride of place for employment of Jews to build a Jewish economy. This would also create absorptive capacity for new immigrants: ". . . it is impossible to imagine a Jewish Yishuv whose work is done by others [i.e., by non-Jews] . . . . The question of 'Hebrew Labor' is the question of our very existence in the land, and this question cannot be measured and weighed by any economic standard . . . ," Ben Gurion stated in 1931. [26] The Arab worker would find employment in the Arab economy in Palestine and, following the example of the organized and conscious Jewish worker, would launch similar demands for improvement of his lot, he believed.

Political proposals emanating from the Jews on the issue of the conflict or a future accommodation with the Arabs of Palestine varied in accordance with the changing circumstances and the relative strength and needs of the Jewish community in Palestine. Ben Gurion's basic position was "cooperation between the entire Jewish people and the Arab residents" of Palestine. [27] The Jewish claim was national, the Arab was individual, centering on civic, religious or community rights — but it was not national. Ben Gurion at that time favored the concept of local and regional Jewish (and Arab) autonomy, together with joint representation for minimal services on the municipal or national level. He sought to ensure territorial self-government, on every possible level, including the municipal. This idea eventually led to acceptance of a "smaller" Jewish state in a partitioned Palestine, once Arab opposition to any form of cooperation was made manifestly evident by the riots of 1929 and the revolt of 1936-39. On the other hand, Ben Gurion firmly opposed the binationalist solution as being vague and because it led some of its proponents to agree to limitations on Jewish immigration.

THE TURNING POINT: NATIONAL AND INTERNATIONAL PROMINENCE

Ben Gurion had established his leadership in labor: he was the secretary-general of the Histadrut and a leading figure in Mapai. In the early 1930s, he made the transition from labor to the national and international Jewish stage. Before treating this, it is necessary to summarize the developments of that decade.

The years 1930-40 saw important qualitative changes in Palestine. The weight of the Jewish settlers in the country and of the Zionist movement increased drastically. There were a number of reasons for this: the growing strength of the Yishuv, as well as the mounting pressures on Jews in Eastern Europe and, particularly following the rise of Hitler, in Germany. The upsurge of Arab nationalism within Palestine and the struggle for independence in the neighboring Arab states also changed the nature of the triangular Arab-Jewish-British relations. The intrusion of Nazi and Fascist influence into the Middle East, the approaching World War, and the strain this placed on the British Empire were complicating factors in the triangle.

Over the decade 1931-40, the proportion of Jews to Arabs in Palestine, the latter including Muslims and Christians, doubled. According to official British figures, Jews made up about one-sixth of the total population in 1931, or 175,000 out of just over one million. By the end of 1939, the British set the figure at about 30% of the total of over 1,500,000, but Jewish estimates, which included the "illegal" immigrants, placed the Jews at about one-third of the total inhabitants, that is approximately 500,000. Thus, though the Arab sector had grown in absolute numbers, the Jewish growth was marked indeed. [28]

Two major families dominated the Arab scene in Palestine: the Nashashibis, who were relatively moderate in their attitude toward the Jews and the British; and their less accommodating rivals the Husaynis, whose leader was al-Hajj 'Amin al-Husayni, chief mufti (religious Muslim official) of Jerusalem. The traditional elements in Muslim society were, as they still are today in many parts of the Arab world, stronger than the modern. Yet the beginnings of ideological parties based on nationalism (and even some with Communist influence) were being made in Palestine, including a party called *Istiqlal* (Independence). Beyond these three elements, local and regional alliances of families and interests posed in the guise of country-wide political parties. The existence of small groups put a premium on extremism, which was fed by inflammatory speeches, sermons, and the popular press.

The Anglo-Iraqi treaty of 1930 proved an example irresistible to other Arab nationalists. In 1935 and 1936, Egypt was struck by a wave of nationalist agitation, leading to the Anglo-Egyptian treaty ratified in fall 1936. Palestine's immediate neighbors to the north, Lebanon and Syria, were under French mandatory tutelage. Civil unrest and disturbances there led to particularly grave incidents in 1936. These forced the French, who had vacillated between repression and accommodation, to seal a treaty with Syria, following the assumption of power in France by the government of Leon Blum. The treaty was to have been implemented three years later. Only Transjordan and Saudi Arabia seemed insulated from the nationalist fervor which reinforced the Arab struggle in Palestine.

In the first half of the decade, Jewish immigration grew in tandem with economic development of the Jewish sector. In 1933-36, immigration totaled about 120,000, including the peak year of 1935, when 62,000 legally certified immigrants arrived. The Jewish National Home was growing at a pace which far surpassed the hopes even of many ardent supporters.[29]

There was a radical change in the nature of Jewish immigration following the Nazi rise to power. This, though contemporaneous with extreme economic repression and social discrimination in Eastern Europe, led to a constant increase in the proportion of immigrants from Germany and Central Europe. In 1933, they made up only five percent of Jews entering Palestine, by 1935 they were 18 percent, and by 1938-39 over half. The proportion of newcomers from Poland dropped from 40 percent in the earlier part of the decade to 10 percent in 1939. The German immigrants brought with them a high Western level of educational and technical proficiency of great social and economic importance to the growing Yishuv.

The political structure of the Yishuv was geared to assuming as much autonomous rule as possible, owing to the limited governmental role of the Mandatory power and the Zionist preoccupation with self-rule. The "elaborate machinery of Jewish quasi-government in Palestine" has been more than adequately described and analyzed.[30] The Yishuv's National Council dealt with social, religious, educational and health matters. The Zionist Organization—Jewish Agency apparatus (the latter including at different times non-Zionist participation of varying intensity) had taken upon itself external representation (foreign affairs), finance, immigration, and land settlement. Quasi-military organizations, especially the Haganah, were fostered directly by the Histadrut and indirectly by the national bodies. The Histadrut had undertaken fairly large development projects, and had built economic enterprises and cooperatives, as well as other services mentioned earlier. Its tightly-knit, centralized organization overrode immediate trade-union interests, and its small but highly mobilized kibbutz membership provided it with political (and eventually military) shock troops.

The legislative and executive bodies of both the Yishuv and the World Zionist Organization were based on proportional representation, which led to the multiplication of ideological parties, each with a detailed program for the future independent state or commonwealth. "The Jewish multiple-party system in Palestine, similar to that of France in the late 1930s, was distinguished by a highly organized, vocal and mutually hostile left and right, and a weak, disorganized center."[31] However, the need to maintain a coalition executive, in view of the chronic disability of any one party to obtain a clear-cut majority, led to a wider, consensus type of governance than might have been expected.

Early in 1931, there were just over 30,000 Histadrut members in the country; a dozen years later the number had quadrupled.[32] Its power, and that of affiliated groups in the Diaspora, began to be felt in the World Zionist Congresses, held fairly regularly in the crisis-ridden decade. The Zionist Congress of 1931 was the scene of heavy attacks on the Organization's president, Dr. Chaim Weizmann, who, ever since the Balfour Declaration of 1917, had been the key figure in the movement. He was accused of compromising with the British on basic Zionist ideals. His rival, the talented orator and writer Vladimir (Ze'ev) Jabotinsky, leading the Revisionist Zionists, demanded that Zionism show its true colors: the *Endziel* or final purpose, the creation of a Jewish majority state on both sides of the Jordan. Ben Gurion, with the majority of Zionists, felt at that time that this would be an empty political gesture which would ensure the opposite effect. Weizmann withdrew until 1935 when he was re-elected president of the World Zionist Organization. The threat to Weizmann and his labor allies came from the Revisionist right.

Ben Gurion entered the lists; he toured the centers of voting power in Europe before the 1933 Zionist Congress; the labor bloc received almost half the votes, and came to play an even more prominent role in the Executive. Ben Gurion won credit for this accomplishment. In 1935 he was elected chairman of the Jewish Agency Executive in Jerusalem, while Weizmann, as stated, returned to the presidency. The Revisionists left the Organization in that year and founded their own separate New Zionist Organization, following an attempt by Ben Gurion and Jabotinsky to resove their differences, which had been rejected by the Histadrut. The threat from the right had been crushed. Ben Gurion's role in the world movement became more pronounced. He was the ranking figure in Zionist Palestine and began to share the stage with the prestigious Weizmann.

The turning point in the history of nascent Jewish statehood was the years 1936-37. The debate between Arabs and Jews as well as within the two communities over the composition of a British-sponsored legislative council erupted into attacks on Jews and counterattacks on Arabs, with casualties and anger mounting. Initiatives by the Jewish Agency and by informal groups to reach a compromise with various Arabs made no headway. In April 1936, the Arab Higher Committee, whose function in Palestine is encompassed in its name, launched a country-wide general strike, aimed primarily at halting Jewish immigration and purchase of land. By autumn of that year, the threat of severe British repression and their economic losses led the local Arab leadership to engineer an appeal from outside of Palestine, designed to end the battles and to save face. The pattern of external Arab intervention in Palestine affairs was set. "Their Majesties and Highnesses, the Arab kings and Amirs" called upon "the noble Arab nation in Palestine to resort to quietness and to put an end to the strike and disorders."[33]

By November the (British) Royal Commission on Palestine, headed by Lord Peel, began its work in that country in an attempt to extricate British policy from its confusions and contradictions. It completed its hearings in January 1937, and half-a-year later published its findings. Some 30 years later Ben Gurion reminisced:

> In 1937 I had a private conversation with some members
> of the Peel Commission. They were fair people and the
> report was an excellent description of the Yishuv. It
> became clear to me that they would report the Mandate as
> "unworkable." Before the Commission's report was pub-
> lished, I reached the conclusion that the Jewish state must
> be created immediately. [34]

The British Royal Commission proposed partition of Palestine. The Zionist movement was split over the issue, as was Mapai. Ben Gurion, once repudiated over the attempted rapprochement with Jabotinsky, again met with opposition, and once more from his own labor leadership. Katznelson refused to sanction a dismemberment of the Promised Land; Tabenkin did not trust the British. The Zionist Congress of summer 1937 split sharply over the issue, with Ben Gurion supporting Weizmann.

> I regard the British government's declaration in favor of a
> Jewish state as one of the greatest acts in history. This is
> the beginning of redemption for which we have waited

2,000 years. We have established a great new political
fact . . . .[35]

The man who knew how to convey his thoughts in apoca-
lyptic oratory also understood the workings of power. "A Jewish
state in part of Palestine will help in the realization of Zionism
more than a British state in the whole of Palestine."[36] At a
meeting that summer, the Congress found a formula for endors-
ing partition "in principle without saying so directly" and a
second formula which bridged the gap between Zionists and
non-Zionists.[37] As the Zionists negotiated with the British,
further rioting broke out in Palestine — stage two of what has
been called the Arab revolt.

> The sponsors of the Arab revolt had . . . won two major
> political victories by the fall of 1938. After the first phase
> of the uprising, London admitted that the Palestine
> Mandate was unworkable . . . . Now the second phase of
> the rebellion was followed by the scuttling of the partition
> scheme.[38]

The British published a White Paper in May 1939 whose operative sections drastically limited Jewish ability to purchase land
in Palestine and curtailed immigration to 75,000 over a five-year
period. With the deepening of the crisis in Europe, the British
preferred to protect their Mediterranean and Eastern flank as
well as the Suez Canal. On the other hand, the threat to the
Jews in Europe was imminent, though at that stage it was hard
to conceive of as final a solution as was in fact effected.

The Zionists, like the British, saw the Nazis as the number
one enemy. Ben Gurion formulated the majority position at a
meeting of Haganah leaders a few days after Germany invaded
Poland. "We must help the British in their war as though there
were no 'White Paper,' and we must oppose the 'White Paper' as
though there were no war."[39] From this position, stressing the
primacy of immigration into Palestine and its economic development as the key Jewish demands, the inevitable con-

clusion was that statehood should be made the immediate aim.

> The World War of 1914-1918 brought us the Balfour
> Declaration; this time we must bring about a *Jewish state*
> . . . . The Balfour Declaration was only a formula, not
> well-formulated, not ideal, but important and giving many
> results. Our aim cannot be a formula . . . we must strive
> toward creating a fact: *the fact of the Jewish state*. [40]

Ben Gurion pointed out that a Jewish army was a necessity to defend Palestine and increase the might of the Jewish people. American Jewry would become increasingly important as Britain recognized that the United States "holds the key to victory in this war of Gog and Magog."

In the summer of 1941, Katznelson, the Mapai ideologue and close colleague of Ben Gurion, gave support to Ben Gurion's earlier analysis. In the winter of 1942, Weizmann published his demand for control by Jews of immigration into Palestine and the establishment of a state.

In the war years, Ben Gurion decisively established his pre-eminent right to leadership of the future state. This was accomplished by bringing — or helping to bring — US Zionists and non-Zionists to support the aim of creating the Jewish state as soon as war conditions permitted, and by staking his leadership at home on this, at the cost of splitting Mapai. In this period, the leadership of the Zionist movement had passed entirely into the hands of the Palestinians. The Zionist Executive had been made accountable to the Inner General Council. This body, composed of representatives of the various Zionist parties, in accordance with the results of the elections for the 1939 Congress, nonetheless had an all-Palestinian membership. "Final policy-making authority was thus vested in the Yishuv," and Ben Gurion was at the center of that authoritative body. [41]

Ben Gurion moved the Zionist Executive and Council to a redefinition of aims. His thesis was that mass immigration and economic development of land and water resources (including the Jordan and the Yarmuk rivers), and the provision of credit for financing these would require "state authority and state bureaucracy." [42]   To obtain the backing of the American Zionists, Weizmann, based in London, Ben Gurion and European Zionist leaders who had fled to the New World met with 600 US delegates at the Biltmore Hotel in New York, in May 1942, at a conference called by the American Emergency Committee for Zionist Affairs. The Biltmore Program adopted on that occasion demanded that the Jewish Agency be vested with control of immigration into Palestine and with the necessary authority for "upbuilding the country" and that "Palestine be established as a Jewish Commonwealth integrated in the structure of the new democratic world." [43]

Although partisans of various Zionist leaders will debate the relative weight of Weizmann and Ben Gurion at Biltmore, the specific credit allotted to each is not germane to this study. [44] Ben Gurion, as immediate head of the Yishuv, doubtless added a dimension no one else could provide. Once the Biltmore Program had been adopted as doctrine by the US, and successively by other Zionist movements, Ben Gurion moved to "sell" it to the Yishuv. He succeeded with the General Zionist and religious (Mizrachi) wings, but, again, ran into difficulties with his own party. A "leftist" opposition had evolved in Mapai, centered upon the larger and doctrinaire kibbutzim organized in the *Kibbutz ha-Me'uḥad* (United Kibbutz) federation. The opposition called itself *Si'ah Bet,* that is, Faction Two. Its leader, Tabenkin, had originally opposed partition in the 1936-37 debates. It now similarly felt that "the immediate, open espousal of statism . . . could only lead to the partition of Palestine." [45]

Though the Inner General Council of the Zionist Organization backed Ben Gurion on the Biltmore proposals, by a vote of 21 to four, the three representatives of Faction Two abstained. This was in November 1942. Their opposition was echoed, but from a different point of view, by the left-wing *ha-Shomer ha-Tza'ir* (Young Guard) kibbutz movement, which favored a binationalist solution for Palestine. A number of intellectual figures in the country also adopted or reasserted a binationalist position. The mounting opposition to statehood (i.e., to par-

tition) and to Ben Gurion personally came to a head in 1944.
The second faction in Mapai split from the mother-party. Ben
Gurion called for elections in the Histadrut, which more or less
coincided with elections for the Palestine National Council (of
Jews). The pro-Biltmore parties gained 58 percent of the votes
cast in the labor federation ballotting and 66 percent in the
general community. Mapai, though weakened in both bodies
following the defection of part of its membership, still maintained a plurality in both.[46] At the cost of splitting his own
party, Ben Gurion had received the vote of confidence of the
labor movement and the Yishuv. This was probably the most
crucial point in Ben Gurion's career, one which guaranteed him
the premiership of the state-to-be provided that the war-to-
come would end victoriously.

Ben Gurion had crowned his experience as a leader of the
Yishuv. He carried the Palestine Zionists to a new position, in
which the demand for a Jewish state or commonwealth became
pressing and imminent. He had established himself in world, and
especially American, Zionism as *the* key figure in Palestine, and
would later use these and other overseas contacts in the crucial
military supply area. From the Palestine power base he challenged Weizmann, and would later use it to overshadow him.

The years between 1945 and mid-1948, when Israel proclaimed its independence, were a time of constant political
struggle: with the British, in the United Nations, within the
United States, and within the Yishuv itself.

At the World Zionist Congress in December 1946, Ben Gurion was again elected chairman of the Jerusalem Executive of
the Jewish Agency. He assumed the defense portfolio and devoted all his energies to preparing for the battle for independence: political and military. The November 29, 1947 decision
by the UN General Assembly on the partition of Palestine led to
open hostilities which preceded the actual establishment of
Israel: there was a little war being fought, and arms had to be
procured and men trained for the larger war still to come. The
hundreds of thousands of Jews who had been lodged in the
displaced-persons camps in Europe were finally beginning to

move and a clandestine network was organized to transfer them to Palestine, in the face of British opposition, but with the tacit help of other allies, as well as of the vanquished such as Italy. [47]

At the center was Ben Gurion, and in the final hours of the Mandate, it was he who stood firm for proclaiming statehood when his colleagues, influenced by a vacillating US policy and gloomy predictions of military defeat, considered postponing it. [48] In 1948, Ben Gurion completed 13 years of leadership of the Jewish Agency Executive. He was to embark on another 13 years as prime minister. His apprenticeship of over four decades had served him in good stead.

CHAPTER THREE

The World of Ideas

It is clear that Ben Gurion played the critical role in defining Israel's policy and image. "Indeed," a specialist has written, "the towering position of Ben Gurion is the decisive fact about Israel's High Policy Elite from 1948 to 1963."[1] Before studying in detail Ben Gurion's actual leadership, his principles and their pragmatic application, it would be desirable to understand his world-view, his conceptual framework and approach to Israel and the Jews in general. These shaped his actual handling of situations and problems. Furthermore, the idea-world of Ben Gurion, as the supreme spokesman of reborn Israel, introduced both Israelis and non-Israeli Jews to new ideational approaches. Because of this wide impact, an outline of some of Ben Gurion's ideological premises, approaches, and historiography of Judaism is given here.

At a press conference in 1959, Ben Gurion was asked: What is a Jew? His reply was casual, conversational and almost off-hand:

> You see, we were Jews without definition for the last 3,000 years and we will remain so . . . . By one definition the Jews are a religious community . . . a nation . . . . There are Jews without any definition. They are just Jews.

> I am one of them. I don't need any definition. I am what I
> am. [2]

This is not an exercise in political dodging, nor even a para-
phrase of God's reply to Moses. Ben Gurion was stating exactly
what he was — a Jew who refused to tack on hyphens of any
sort to the term. Its meaning to him is rooted in Jewish history.
In many ways, this *Weltanshauung* is not much different from
that of other Eastern European Jews who took the Zionist
option. Ben Gurion, however, has delineated it with great sharp-
ness, and did apply it to a much wider extent, because of his
power, than his contemporaries.

At the turn of the century the milieu of Eastern Europe
(Jewish Poland, Russia and Rumania) and consequently of
Palestinian Labor Zionism was an ideological one. It was cus-
tomary in some measure to legitimize action by reference to
basic tenets. According to Ben Gurion, this being a view shared
by many contemporaries, the Jewish people has found itself
under a duality of authority: that of the state powers in their
countries of residence, and that of the Jewish heritage.[3] Jewish
history is to him the history of a ceaseless, tremendous battle
by the Jews to withstand the physical and spiritual pressures of
the non-Jewish environment.[4] True freedom for the Jew is the
freedom to be himself.

> I know not one country in which the Jew is truly free to
> follow his heart's desire — even if the law formally does
> not discriminate against him . . . . The freedom of action
> of the Jews is limited in every single place, either by the
> law and the police, or by the political and social reality.
> The Jews in the Diaspora do not control the forces which
> surround them, and they are unable to do what they wish
> to do as Jews.[5]

The reestablishment of Jewish independence in Palestine is a
leap over 2,000 years of Jewish history, to recreate the status of
Jewish authority over the Jews. This therefore prompted Ben

Gurion to gloss over the importance of the Diaspora period — almost to the extent of ignoring the 19 centuries of exile. The Jews today are the heirs of the ancient Jewish people, as it once was, in its own land. There were four major events in Jewish history: the Exodus from Egypt, the theophany at Mount Sinai, the conquest of the Promised Land by Joshua, and the establishment of the State of Israel.[6] Jewish unity in 1948, on the creation of the State of Israel, exceeded even that prevailing at the revelation and law-giving of Sinai.[7] The creation of the state goes back into the totality of Jewish history, and not only to the beginnings of political Zionism toward the end of the previous century.[8]

Jewish history may be summarized as the battle of quality versus quantity.[9] The Jewish revolution of this century is not a revolution against a regime, but against the Jewish people's historic fate.[10] The true revolution of the Jews will be measured in terms of maximal concentration of the people in the Land, that is, "ingathering the exiles." In this sense, the "Third Commonwealth" or modern Israel surpasses its two predecessors, in that the ingathering is greater numerically.[11] Elsewhere, he wrote that the arrival of the first million immigrants in Israel is the greatest event in Jewish history since the Hasmonean revolt 22 centuries ago.[12]

There are two poles to this basic tenet: what is done in Israel to strengthen Israel, increase its population, build its economy, enhance its prestige, power and viability — all this is positive, central, vital, and necessary. These are acts of great historic sweep, countering a miserable past. That which is done in Jewish life outside of Israel, on Israel's behalf, so to speak, is transitory and eventually harmful because it detracts from the main thrust of the revolution. It is an offshoot of all that transpired in the Diaspora and is therefore secondary and second-rate, produced by people not free, people fettered in mind and soul.[13] He rejects the Diaspora, and his eventual opposition to the organized Zionist movement, which was not sufficiently Israel-centered for him, is given legitimation by this principle. Therefore, he said:

Exile in which Jews lived and still live is to me a wretched, poor, backward and inadequate form of life. We must not be proud of it — on the contrary we must reject it utterly and completely . . . . The pseudo-Zionism of today helps Jews to be naturalized and more deeply rooted in a non-Jewish environment and in the processes of assimilation which endanger the future of Jewry in the Diaspora. [14]

From this Israelocentric (or, earlier, Yishuv-centric) point of view, 'aliyah (immigration of Jews to Israel) becomes the main purpose of Zionism. In the early days of independence, Ben Gurion saw the state as a means of realizing this vision of mass immigration. [15] This was one of the main reasons for adopting the program of doubling Israel's population in the first four years of statehood through unlimited and non-selective 'aliyah. [16] (The pragmatic defense consideration, to increase available manpower, will be discussed elsewhere.)

This monistic view of Zionism is marked by a total impatience with Zionists who are incapable of seeing this truth as Ben Gurion saw it. On the other hand, men who claimed not to be Zionists could not be accused of the same "crime" as the Zionists, and thus cooperation with them and mutual understanding were much easier. Whether it was America's sociological difference from Eastern Europe, or the weight of potential supporters for Israel whom Ben Gurion did not wish to offend, the American scene was treated to some extent as an exception; Jews were rooted there. [17] Similarly, Ben Gurion's search for hypocrisy led him to attack the declared believers, the orthodox Jews, who were enjoined by rabbinic law to make their home in Israel. [18]

Over the course of years, and undoubtedly under the impact of his immediate responsibility — ensuring the continued existence of Israel — Ben Gurion's point of view changed. Once, in the early years of his premiership, he could say that 'aliyah takes precedence over the state itself, because it encompasses everything: "security . . . renaissance . . ., ingathering, and there is nothing without it." [19] Later, the state as a means to an end became an end in itself. Defense became central to all other considerations. The ineffectiveness of the United Nations and the arming of Egypt by the Soviet Union led Israel's leaders to an obsessive desire, undoubtedly fed by recalled visions of pogroms, massacres, and the Hitlerian ugliness, to prevent any possibility of a repeat performance. This emphasis on defense and security, *bitahon* in Hebrew, led to the coining of a special Hebrew term, *bithonism*. Though hybrid and ungainly, it describes what may be called a security complex or syndrome: complete preoccupation with Israel's physical survival. From this evolved the first-strike theory, to eliminate Israel's geopolitical vulnerability, a doctrine practiced militarily in 1956 and in 1967 (if one ignores the political elements of the discussion as to the *casus belli* provided by the Arab states). This security syndrome became the dominant attitude governing not only relations with the Arabs, but all of Israel's foreign policy. For security one needs not only an army, but arms, and this called for suppliers both of armaments and technology. From this point of view, an eventual orientation toward America was inevitable, not simply as a supplier of arms — these could be procured from others such as the French, or US arms could be obtained via a third party, such as Germany. Apart from this consideration, Israel would necessarily be attracted by America's technological sophistication.

This explains Ben Gurion's great stress on science and technology. Not that there was not a fascination with science unrelated to military technology. Ben Gurion was a subscriber to *Scientific American* and expressed his desire, "if he could do it over again," to study the physical sciences.[20] His concern with scientific excellence was related to the "quality versus quantity" idea, the preoccupation with the size of Israel, the people, and the Land. One of his most potent essays begins with the quotation from Deuteronomy, "Not because you were more numerous than any other people did the Lord . . . choose you, for you are the smallest of all nations, but because of the Lord's love of you . . . . "[21] The size, the struggle to continue the chosenness, the need for survival — these are encompassed in the citation.

THE BIBLE

In Ben Gurion's historical view, the Bible plays a major role. It is the great Jewish achievement, one which influenced the entire Western world, at least. It is difficult in the normal typology of the West not to categorize as religious someone who claims to be guided by the Bible. Certainly, if by religious is meant formal observance of religious tenets and ritual, the term cannot be applied to Ben Gurion. On the other hand, in the Jewish literary and social reformation following the 19th-century Enlightenment and emancipation, the Bible, no longer interpreted as a guide to strict religious observance, played a unique role as a source of inspiration, as *the* document of the Jewish people, the well of its uniqueness and proof of its chosen-ness, even if that choosing was done by man rather than by God. Thus, though Ben Gurion would be classified as a secularist in that he placed positive law above theology, his own attachment to the Bible, his (sometimes "heretical" to the orthodox) studies of it, and his use of it for oratorical and didactic purposes, tend to show that the Bible is of utmost importance to him. Without entering the field of psychohistory, this is as far as the objective investigator can go.

However, on subjective ground, going beyond meetings, discussions and careful reading of his statements to their evaluation, one is left with the distinct impression that the Bible is central to Ben Gurion in a direct and sincere fashion. It shaped his thinking as a child, and when other gods failed — socialism and organized Zionism — the Bible provided an ideational and historical frame of reference. It was consonant with his needs and able to provide a source for moral values; it lent itself to social and historic interpretation applicable to the situations in which Ben Gurion was leading himself and his people.

On the absolutely conscious level, to revert to the objective plane, Ben Gurion knew that he and his government were molding the image of a new or transcendent people, and their sense of uninterrupted and direct rootedness in the source-book held great romantic and unifying appeal. Such a history-rootedness is common to renascent nationalism and the Jews were luckier than most in having such a history and such a Book to draw upon.

Ben Gurion has a keen sense of history. He can thus speak of the army in terms of restoration of past glory, much as could any nationalist leader, and beyond that give the Jewish perspective of time and continuity to new processes. "The Israel Defense Forces . . . have renewed Jewish heroism in all its glory . . . such as has perhaps never been since the days of Joshua son of Nun and King David."[22] He does not overlook the gains in terms of *realpolitik* and public relations resulting from military victory:

> The Sinai Campaign raised Israel's prestige in the world . . . . The State of Israel is for the first time on the map of the world as an important factor. The world recognizes we are not a negligible force . . . . I doubt if there is an army more praised in world public opinion than the IDF.[23]

His historiography carries him time and again back to the earlier glories. Students of nationalism know that nationalist leaders select certain historic themes which suit their present purpose while rejecting other, less suitable motifs.[24] What did not suit Ben Gurion's purpose was the lachrymose view of Jewish history which saw only the pogroms and pillaging, from the destruction of the Second Commonwealth through the Crusades to the Nazis. He wished to recreate the link with independent Jewish existence, beginning with Abraham the Patriarch who fought not for gain but to protect his own, through the entire biblical experience of conquering the Land and carving out the kingdoms. The navy is not merely ships, but a recreation of the tradition of the Judean kings. It not only protects the sea lanes for defense and immigration; it is as important as making the desert bloom.[25] The great leap back over 1,900 years and more of history to the biblical period of heroism, independence, and freedom from foreign rule, on the one hand, and the messianic leap forward on the other were the twin points of his historic compass, which enabled Ben Gurion to steer through the present (see below, "Messianism").

Ben Gurion does not characterize himself as religious. Others have. Recently, the liberal (in a sense almost 19th-century rationalist) American Jewish theologian, Mordecai M. Kaplan, divided Israeli society into three camps: traditional-religious, modern-religious, and secularist. Ben Gurion was held up as the archetype of the modern-religious.[26] Ben Gurion himself has said, "I do believe in the existence of a spiritual, eternal, all-embracing superior being . . . . " His thinking requires a prime mover or source, and he related this to the credo of Spinoza and some modern scientists (Einstein, Bohr) who believe "there is something" behind the energy, or behind the cosmos.[27] Ben Gurion uses the Hebrew terms for God and Lord in his biblical citations, but seldom if ever in his own statements. In a radio address on Israel's first anniversary of independence in 1949, Ben Gurion stated: " . . . . The hearts of all of us are over-flowing with praise and thanks to the Rock of Israel." The terms has a euphemistic quality, an avoidance of religiosity, for which reason it was used rather than "God" in the Declaration of Independence, but it also conveys an undefined sense of the historic God of Israel in which he believes.[28]

The Bible appears consistently at the center of Ben Gurion's public pronouncements. In the description of the Jewish people moving from the dualistic codes of law and life which govern them in the Diaspora — the legal system of their countries of residence and that of the Jewish heritage — toward the single code to prevail in Israel, Ben Gurion said, at a meeting of professional people in January 1949, that

> . . . the State of Israel will not be tested by its strength or economy alone — but by its spirit. We have inherited a great heritage, and it is binding. We have revolted against all regimes, religions, laws . . . which the powers of the world have attempted to impose on us . . . . [The State of Israel] will be tested by the moral image it will lend its

citizens, by the human values which will determine its internal and external relations, by its faithfulness, in deed and word, *to the supreme command of Judaism: "Thou shalt love thy neighbor as thyself."*[29]

In the cold light of pre-election oratory, this citation seems as commonplace perhaps as any normal platitude in any normal country. Spoken with conviction by a prime minister of a newly independent Jewish state — he still retaining the overawing charisma of the victor, the state still dew-covered and fresh — the statement cannot but have made a greater impact than its dry reproduction can now convey. This moment of participation and identification with the speaker cannot be left out of any equation of leadership. The fact that the leader dips into the old, and then tries to give it new relevance, enhances the sense of historic continuity. Past and present fuse into an orientation toward the future which in a sense conveys the excitement of immortality. The leader, the audience, and its individual members become welded in a bond which promises that they will face down mortality by living that which long preceded them and may, should, shall live beyond them.[30] This Ben Gurion did later in the address by projecting the "supreme command of Judaism" into a rudimentary guide-line for future legislation and for the social aims of the country.

On another early occasion, in 1950, Ben Gurion counseled careful perusal of Exodus XXIII:28 ff. for advice of "great political wisdom." The verses referred to deal with the need to settle the Land "little by little" after the original Canaanites (the Arabs of today, so to speak) leave the country piecemeal, lest it fall prey to wild beasts and desolation.[31] This tendency to relate the quotable and relevant parts of the scriptures to current affairs unites the two trends in Ben Gurion: the attachment to the Bible and the Isaelocentric attachment to the Land. True understanding of the Bible, and not just detached exegesis, will be possible on condition that these two themes combine in the people who inhabit the Land.

Only to the people which settles anew in its Land, and
co-mingles with the landscape which shines out of every
page of the Book of Books — and the language of the Book
will become its natural language, in which it will think and
dream, knowingly or unknowingly — only to this nation
will the Book unfold the secret of its heart and its inner
soul, and the soul of the Book will become one with the
soul of the People. [32]

This is not to say that Ben Gurion was closed to other cul-
tures. At a reasonably (or perhaps unreasonably) advanced age
he began to learn Greek in order to read Plato in the original, to
study Spanish for a better appreciation of Cervantes, and he not
only read widely on Buddhism, but even made a retreat to a
Buddhist monastery during his visit to Burma in 1961.[33] Early
in statehood, Ben Gurion contributed to the Hebrew University
of Jerusalem a prize he had been awarded by it, to finance an
essay competition on Plato's influence on Jewish thought. His
interest in science has been mentioned earlier and was given
expression in fostering scientific development in general and in
the defense establishment in particular. All this notwithstanding, the biblical motif is perhaps the strongest one in his
life, especially that part based on the "literary prophets," who
themselves recorded their own prophecies. Of these, the two
who share the same vision of the "end of days" or "the latter
days" (both are translations which irritate Ben Gurion), Isaiah
and Micah, are probably the most important.

MESSIANISM

What is the messianic vision? Stripped of its personification in a
personal or physical Messiah, a concept which both Judaism and
Christianity shared at one time, the vision is of an era in which
the redemption of mankind will be preceded by the redemption
of the Jewish people, restored to their own Land. There reestablished, Jerusalem will become a center of teaching of world
morality and Zion will be the focus of "the Word of the Lord."

Eternal peace will reign: "Nation will not lift up sword against nation; neither shall they learn war any more."[34] As Ben Gurion recently pointed out, not only will war be outlawed, but military science will be prohibited.[35]

According to Ben Gurion, it was this messianic vision, the vision of a restored Israel, gathering in its own and restoring the ancient creative glories of the Bible, which kept Jews alive, which drew every single immigrant to Israel, even if at the same time he was being forced out of his place of residence by persecution. The theme is so recurrent, persistent and unchanging that it traces a central path through all of Ben Gurion's speeches and writings in the post-state period.

In a debate with Martin Buber in 1949, Ben Gurion rejected Buber's thesis that there were two classes of immigrants: the voluntary idealistic immigration of "the cream of the crop" or ḥalutzim, and, on the other hand, the ordinary folk. He said:

> . . . the immigrants from Morocco are not just refugees,
> they are not plain and simple refugees. Their 'aliyah to
> Israel is also accompanied by the dream of redemption. So
> too the Jews of Yemen, and so too the immigrants from
> the displaced-persons' camps in Germany. Need and vision
> have always been intertwined in immigration to the Land
> . . . . A Jew leaves the Diaspora out of need, and comes
> here out of vision.[36]

The entire question of the physical Messiah is to Ben Gurion — now speaking as the dreamer, the visionary, the man of spirit — immaterial. It is the anticipation of the Messiah which is important, the "days of the Messiah" or messianic era. Once you can find the Messiah's address in the telephone directory, he ceases to be the Messiah. "For the days of the Messiah are more important than the Messiah, and the Jewish people lives in the days of the Messiah, anticipates, believes in the days of the Messiah, and this is one of the major reasons for its existence . . . . "[37]

Ben Gurion was able to make this messianic faith a reason and an end. In atypically moving style, in a Knesset debate at the end of 1949, he spoke of the fear that the waves of immigrants being flown from Yemen to Israel would have to be slowed down, since the large proportion of aged, ill, and weak adults and children among them could have overtaxed the limited facilities of the year-old state. He sent an investigator to the immigrant assembly point at Aden, who reported that the exodus from Yemen was "wondrous, messianic." In response, the then finance minister, Eliezer Kaplan, and Ben Gurion, "the practical man and the dreamer," ordered a speeding up of the aerial exodus. Ben Gurion explained to the members of parliament why this decision was taken. "Better he should die here in his Land, among his brethren, and not in that foreign place." In staccato and emotion-laden phrases, he described those who finally arrived and died of illness and exhaustion at the airport in Israel; the children too tired and weak to cry or even to eat.

> This was one of the most frightful pictures I have ever seen in my life. Only in their eyes did the light of life shine . . . . I was left trembling and shaken by this great and awesome sight. Yes — these are the birth-pangs of the Messiah.[38]

Messianism was the cause of the immigration and of the need to absorb the immigrants, chaotic and improvised as the arrangements would be. Ben Gurion also made it an end: messianism and the great ingathering of "the exiled." Citing a talmudic sage, Ben Gurion could say, in one of his most dramatic election speeches in 1951, that the Jews had been redeemed from the bondage of foreign rule, and entered upon "the days of the Messiah." Together with these days came the "birth-pangs of the Messiah" and only the other political parties could promise "redemption" without these pains. Rejecting what he describes as the solution of the left, subordination to the USSR, or of the right, liberalization of currency restrictions, he climaxed his speech with association-laden traditional terminology, modernized and relevant to its new context.

In whom shall we believe? For whom shall we work? The workers of Israel will have to decide: the Kremlin — or Jerusalem. The entire nation which dwells in Zion will have to decide: the Golden Calf — or the Messiah . . . .[39]

Ben Gurion did not rest content with messianism as a reflection of the past. He knew it was future-oriented and used it as a goal to be projected into the days ahead. "The eyes of all [ancient] nations were turned back toward the past . . . while the eyes . . . of our people were lifted forward, to the vision of the end of the days."[40] This vision demands of the Jews in their reestablished independence the creation of a unique state. Relying both on Spinoza and Herzl, who had stated this in differing terms over a span of centuries, Ben Gurion said in 1951: "These are variant definitions of the same thing — the dream of the later days of the prophets of Israel." These prophets, who are also "the prophets of the nations and of the world," hold out a vision of "Jewish redemption which is intertwined with universal human redemption." These must be the wellspring, he said, for Israel's becoming "a light unto the nations and a salvation for our people."

The theme of "light unto the nations," taken from Isaiah XLII:6, is a central thread in Ben Gurion's thought — an ultimate justification for Israel's existence and an ultimate goal for its future development. In that passage, the prophet explains that the light is "to open the eyes that are blind, to bring out the prisoners from the dungeon, from the prison those who sit in darkness." In the later years of statehood, Ben Gurion spoke less of the "days of the Messiah" as a reason for immediate difficulties, perhaps because he had tired of the theme, or possibly since it had lost its gloss. It was probably hard to believe one was living in the "days of the Messiah" and at the same time haggle over cabinet portfolios. Whatever the reason, these references decreased, but the centrality of the messianic dream and the future-orientated challenge of being "a light unto the nations" continued undiminished.[41]

UNIVERSALISM AND PARTICULARISM

If, as Ben Gurion believed, the creation of the State of Israel was the "beginning of the redemption," the final stages would be the shaping of Israel into a model state and a source of moral and societal light for others.[42] This redemption was to be both particular and universal: of Israel, and of all mankind. The two are inextricably woven together. Just how did Ben Gurion view the universal-particular continuum?

"In essence, we are the most isolated people, and the most universal. This seeming paradox is that which singles out the Jewish people, as well as the State of Israel."[43] In the context of this statement, Ben Gurion does not expound his solution to the seeming paradox. From other statements, though, it is clear that the universalism is in Israel's prophetic message, which was for all mankind, while its particularism is in its uniqueness, or chosen-ness. "During a long period, the Jewish people saw itself as the Chosen People, and it had sufficient cause for this view."[44] In a sense, every nation has the subjective right to see itself as "chosen," each has its own unique history and accomplishments.[45] Jewish uniqueness is to express itself in that "the Jewish people will show the true way to rectify [or reform] the world, for which purpose it was created."[46]

From Sde Boker, in 1954, Ben Gurion launched two articles which were entitled "An Exemplary State — Means or End" and "A Unique People." In the articles he unites the means and the end: in order for Israel to realize its dream of ingathering, it must be attractive to the Jews of the free world, it must be an exemplary state. The people of Israel at the present time are far from being the Chosen People, from having created the way of life which would demonstrate the chosen-ness.[47] In a third article, "Between Israel and the Diaspora," he wrote:

> In order to be a unique people, not only are a historic will and unique spiritual qualities required, but also the state framework which will execute the will of the nation . . . .
> A unique people is only possible in an exemplary state.

Both the fate of the Jewish people in its entirety as well as
the fate of the State of Israel depend on both of these —
which are really one.[48]

In other words, the universal aims of the Jews can only be
achieved through the realization, within the framework of a
state, of the particular Jewish aim of ingathering and social justice.
"There is no universal human mission, without national state
existence."[49] There is an echo of Rousseau's *volonté générale*
in his discussion of the national people's will, with the assumption that he and his state give it expression. This is his ultimate
legitimation. *Mamlakhtiyut,* which in this sense means state-
building and the primacy of the state over other institutions, is
the embodiment of this will and purpose.

This aspiration to create a model state, Ben Gurion said, is
the reason for his objection to the way the cabinet handled the
Lavon Affair (see Chapter 13). Though partisans tend to question Ben Gurion's motives in this case, it is difficult to find any
other explanation, except in the realm of psychology. Certainly
Ben Gurion was aware of the state's role as an educator. In a
number of decisions, he acted as an instructor, for example: the
Eichmann trial; the order to place the army at the disposal of an
archaeological expedition to the Judean Desert to uncover a
hallowed national memory — the resistance to Rome's legions;
Ben Gurion's removal to Sde Boker — all these spring readily to
mind. "Government," Justice Louis D. Brandeis observed half a
century ago, "is the omnipotent, omnipresent teacher. For good
or for ill, it teaches the whole people by its example."[50]

In the weaving together of messianism and particularism, Ben
Gurion came to see the state — as it could be and should be — as
the instrument, and eventually as the end. This is not the
abstract State of Hegel, but rather the State of Israel. According
to Ben Gurion, this state is not total, but is the supreme educator, the provider of means to build and to absorb immigrants,
to realize the vision of ingathering, of Jewish and eventually
human redemption, and the creation of social justice in Israel,
and by example, throughout the world. No other Israeli leader

had such far-sighted vision, and at the same time, no other single person in Israel had the power to move the people and state toward these goals.

WILL — THE POWER OF THE SPIRIT

In his world-view, Ben Gurion rejected the Greco-Christian separation of spirit and matter, and accepted the psycho-physical unity of man, which he related to biblical teachings. Nonetheless, it is the superiority of the will and the spirit which typified the Jews in history, and in the rebirth of Israel.[51] "The State of Israel did not arise by authority of decisions of the UN, but out of Jewish strength of will and the heroism of the Israel Defense Forces."[52] (There is certainly psychophysical unity in this formulation!) Thus *halutziyut* (pioneering) is so important; it is the active personification of will. This is true voluntarism.

Ben Gurion attempted to infuse the sense of voluntarism even into the drab instrumentalities of any state — into the army, into scientific research, into the entire educational system. "The state can coerce its citizens — and it does so coerce — to perform pioneering deeds, even if the citizen is not a pioneer."[53] In this sense, the state receives an additional legitimation, that of being able to perform pioneering tasks and of transforming citizens into pioneers. This seems to strengthen the impression Ben Gurion conveys of ignoring paradoxes by merging them: socialism and Zionism in his early thinking are an organic unity; universalism and particularism are one, through the medium of the state; even voluntarism and étatism are intertwined. The factor which can synthesize the antitheses is will. This too is an echo of Rousseau.

The will, the desire to do, to achieve, overrides expertise and its balanced judgment. In a Zionist Council debate on land settlement, Ben Gurion said that if the "expert" succeeded in his experimentation on a plot of ground, and things grew there, "I will accept his opinion, for experience bears him out." If he reports back that the land is uncultivable, "I will not accept his opinion, because all that the experience proves is that *he* failed, but there is no proof that another will not succeed."[54] There is of course some arrogance in the summary dismissal of expert opinion. However, it should be recalled that the statement was made not quite two years after military experts had told Ben Gurion the new Israel would be overwhelmed by Arab arms. Other experts — financial — were then telling him that Israel would not sell its bonds overseas in amounts of any significance; they too were to be proven wrong.

A recollection by a long-time colleague, and later president of Israel, Zalman Shazar, is pertinent. Writing an accolade on the occasion of Ben Gurion's 70th birthday in 1956, he recalled that a couple of decades earlier Ben Gurion had been under attack by "experts of every kind" at a Zionist conference. Ben Gurion "got up and said in his strong and absolute way: 'I am not an expert on irrigation or finances or world politics. There is only one field in which I am an expert.' The opposition delegates demanded to know the field. 'Zionism — that is the subject in which I am an expert.'"[55]

In mid-1950, Ben Gurion informed the Knesset that "We have a 'weapon' unknown to Russia and America, and I am not prepared to reveal it now. By means of this secret weapon we can enhance Jewish power."[56] In an interview almost 20 years later, Ben Gurion revealed the long-held secret. He was referring to his expertise, no longer classified as Zionist. "I knew Jews." He believed in their superiority vis-à-vis the Arab enemy, their strength of will and ability to learn, which, he said, would enable them to master in a few days the military drill which the British had given him over a period of months in 1918.[57]

Ultimately then, in spite of his pragmatic understanding of the need for power, for material bases, for economic achievements, there is room in Ben Gurion's philosophy for idealism: The will and the idea are no less important than the material. This holds true for the Jews, but applies equally to all mankind.

> Men have fought for their opinions no less than for their
> power or property, and since man began to think, the
> contest of ideas has not ceased. And in the history of our

people, this occupies a place wider, perhaps, than in that
of any other.[58]

STYLE

There is a marked difference between Ben Gurion's style of
speaking and his style of acting. In thought and word, he was
farseeing, sometimes visionary. In action, he was guided by the
need to adapt his views to reality, wherever he could not change
the reality. Often, when necessary and in spite of the image he
created and the view others had of him, he was caution personified. At the same time, he carried the policy of creating *faits
accomplis* to the point of a fine art.

His public addresses shortly after the creation of the state
feature words like saga and adventure *('alilah, harpatkah)*. He
would often shrug off international criticism and UN censure
with the slogan, "It is not important what the *goyim* say, what
is important is what the Jews *do.*"[59] On the other hand, Ben
Gurion did carefully avoid a military confrontation with the
British in 1948 and January of 1949. Nor did he launch the
Sinai Campaign in 1956 until he was sure of French cooperation
with Israel, and of Franco-British intervention in Egypt.

His concentration on the aim to be achieved or on the "direction" to be followed is a variation on the theme of pragmatism.
Hence, he could say, "there are acts which in their day were
revolutionary and in the course of time, with changing situations and conditions, become conservative deeds which delay
and defer."[60] This is another way of saying that he had a good
grasp of the "strategic" and the "tactical." As far back as 1936,
Ben Gurion had written a long strategy memo to Justice Louis
D. Brandeis about the importance of the Negev and Eilat to the
future Jewish state. A decade or so later, he was speaking of the
need to build a Jewish city in the Negev, something which came
about first in Beersheba, and later in other places in the Negev
in the '50s.[61]

Ben Gurion was well aware of his own pragmatism, although,
like every leader of an ideological movement, he made the shifts

in accord with his general world-view, even to the point of changing the view to a more general statement, rather than a specific prescription; for example, the departure from the socialist ideal to the broader social view of the prophetic tradition. The two following citations demonstrate the conscious pragmatism he displayed:

> When one climbs a mountain, it is not enough to look at the high peak and keep one's eyes steadily upon it. One must see the paths which lead to the peak and make sure there are not pits and holes and wild animals on the way. And if there are, one must overcome them or avoid them, otherwise one will not reach the peak. [62]
> . . . we do not see every detail in the Basic Principles [of government] as binding law from Moses at Sinai. If matters should evolve in a way we are unable to anticipate in advance, we do not decree that with dogmatic attachment we adhere to each jot and tittle of the plan, and with a clear mind we shall face new problems and seek new solutions if necessary. [63]

NATIONAL IDENTITY

Just as acute was Ben Gurion's awareness that he was engaged in forging national identity. Mention has already been made of the Bible and the messianic drive. Though these stem from deep down in Ben Gurion's private scheme of things, they could also be universally accepted by wide parts of the general public. That this was not the sole consideration is apparent from his insistence on downgrading the Diaspora experience, which brought considerable criticism from certain religious and intellectual circles. Nonetheless, as a secondary consideration, even as an unconscious one, it merits discussion.

Ben Gurion strongly felt that Israel was "not yet a nation." This was not, he thought, an ideological, or philosophical or sociological question. He was referring to "nation" in the sense of "a community united, rooted in its homeland, culture, unity,

able to defend itself to its last man and last drop of blood." [64]
This was in 1949. In those early years, he used his public
appearances and broadcasts as an object lesson in Jewish history, seeking to link the events of the present with those of the
past, particularly through the medium of Jewish festivals, which
were widely, though differently observed by most segments of
the population. Thus, Independence Day is joined in his and the
people's consciousness with Passover, the feast marking the
Exodus or freedom from Egyptian rule, and with Ḥanukkah,
the Maccabean uprising against Hellenist Syria.

Though always short with the extreme right and left — Ḥerut
and the Communists — and in the later years using rather un-
parliamentary language in reference to them, Ben Gurion on
occasion stated that he used the Knesset forum to demonstrate
democratic techniques. Thus he welcomes, again in 1949, the
debate called by the opposition on the signing of the armistice
agreement with Syria. Even if the claim of the "pessimists" was
true, that parliamentary debates are worthless since the vote, by
parties, is predetermined, "there is educational value to these
debates, since . . . the people listens to them and evaluates and
decides . . . ." [65]

Ben Gurion's decisions to engage the state in demonstrative
acts of a deeper educational nature have already been mentioned (see p. 51). One of his finest formulations as an "educator" came in 1955, on his return from Sde Boker. Although
no national leader can file a patent on the idea (President Kennedy used a similar phrase six years later), Ben Gurion took his
people to task with the following words: "I saw . . . too many
demands from the state, and too few demands from [our-
selves]." [66]

Ben Gurion made many demands on the youth of the country, and personally helped recruit members of kibbutzim and
moshavim (cooperative smallholders' villages) to assist new
settlements, particularly those in the Negev. The link with the
youth seems to be related to his stress on science as part of his
future-oriented view of Israel, and as a counter-balance to the
immense quantitative difference between Israel and the Arab

states. He constantly stressed, along with halutziyut, the role of science and technology, and certainly invested great sums of public money in military and, to a lesser extent, civilian scientific research and development. In November 1949, he announced that a Government Scientific Council had been established, a plan discussed by the Provisional Government shortly after the creation of the state.[67]

Similarly, Ben Gurion used his position to stress the advancement of the Oriental Jews. Addressing himself to the unspoken question posed by European Jews, and, one supposes, by Oriental Jews to themselves, Ben Gurion said, in summer 1949: "But there is no basis for the assumption that the Jews of North Africa, or Turkey, Egypt, Persia or Aden are different in their essence from the Jews of Lithuania, Galicia or America."[68] During his years in office, he often called for the day when there would be a Yemenite general, and appointed a North African Jew his advisor on "Communal Affairs," whose job was to provide official "pull" for the Oriental Jewish communities, and to recruit such Jews into the state and public service.[69]

By constant repetition, through personal appearances, Knesset addresses, press conferences, radio talks, and meetings with overseas Jewish figures and organization delegations, Ben Gurion ceaselessly propagated his world-view, his interpretation of Judaism, and his understanding of Jewishness. His words, as spoken by the prime minister of Israel, surrounded by his own charisma, as well as that of the state — the latter wearing the dual laurels of the tiny victor in the war against the Arab Goliath, and of the 3,000-year-old interwoven leaves of liturgy and longing — had great effect. Their echoes can be heard in many Israeli homes and schools, especially in that school called the Israel Defense Forces, as well as in Jewish institutions outside of Israel. In spite of the country's rejection of Ben Gurion in 1965, with the majority following the Eshkol-Sapir-Meir lead, and notwithstanding his rift with the organized Zionists, his central themes have become the doctrine of the Israel establishment, of the army, and of most world Jewish religious and political organizations. Even though among the last this often applies more to the theory than the practice, their world of ideas nevertheless bears the imprint of Ben Gurion's influence. It extends far beyond Israel; the "world people" of Israel, that is, the Jewish communities throughout the world, have had to fashion their image on Israel's or to redefine their form and content in relation to Israel. A religious activist from the United States and an American Jewish historian have both given expression to this new relationship in trenchant and concise formulations. "The most influential leaders of the Jewish people are the political leaders of the State of Israel." [70] "The State of Israel is in our days weighed against the Jewish religion" as a factor for Jewish survival. [71]

Broadly speaking, the centrality of Israel is accepted as essential for Jewish survival and creativity. The preeminence of the Israel government is taken for granted in the order of precedence of Jewish organizational frameworks. The restressed prominence of the Bible, messianism and the Hebrew language is accepted as a new quasi-religion. This is perhaps Ben Gurion's most important impact outside of the narrowly-defined field of politics and international affairs. He has provided new forms and expressions of Jewishness, which, even if not wholly original, are the fruit of his own synthesizing, and whose spectrum has been defined through his prism. [72]

CHAPTER FOUR

Political Background and System

Both the political culture of the State of Israel and its political system derived from the Zionist ideology and organization of the pre-state period. The political aims of Zionism and of the Zionist leadership in the Yishuv were to maximize Jewish control over a territorial base, eventually to become a Jewish commonwealth or state, large-scale immigration, and development of natural, economic and human resources.

The century-old Jewish experience of creating voluntary institutions which were self-governing had furnished the psychological background and ability to build institutions for clearly defined purposes. In the premodern period, these included courts, educational systems, rudimentary welfare and charity institutions, burial societies, etc. As ideology and political movements entered the Jewish European world, an explosion of political groupings occurred, with more experience in self-government ensuing. It was this ability which was one of the reasons for Zionism's success.

The Zionist settlers of Palestine brought with them political attitudes and organizations. These reflected the wide trends in Zionism as expressed in the World Zionist Organization. On the eve of statehood, there were two overall representative Jewish bodies in Palestine, sanctioned by public law and recognized by the Mandatory. One was the World Zionist Organization — Jewish Agency Executive in Jerusalem, the other was the elected body of the Yishuv, the Assembly of Delegates *(Asefat ha-Nivḥarim)* and its executive the *Va‘ad Le'umi* (National Council). [1]

THE PARTIES

Within these frameworks there were ideological movements as well as political parties. The difference between the two is pointed out in a study of Israeli politics: one, the movement, is an "ideological persuader"; the other, the party, is an electoral competitor. [2] The main ideological trends within Zionism were: General Zionism, religious Zionism, and Labor Zionism. Beyond the pale, for some time at any rate, were the more extreme nationalist Revisionist Zionists. Two groupings remained outside of organized Zionism: the ultra-orthodox Agudat Yisra'el and the anti-Zionist Communists.

In order to define Israeli political parties from an ideological stance, we must view them along three axes: nationalism, social views, and religious attitudes. The fourth axis is that of time: the parties shifted ground both in word and in deed over the years of statehood. An attempt will be made, however, to aggregate their stance along the time axis in the following description whose purpose is to view the general background against which Ben Gurion worked.

On the Israeli political scene the consensus on national issues very often has cut across social ideology, to no small extent due to the pragmatism of Mapai, the labor party which has had a plurality in pre- and post-state institutions since 1933. The exact definition of each party's stand is less important than the key issue which each smaller party emblazons on its flag. Only Mapai has been a truly national party, bearing total responsibility for coalition unity. The other parties have been more sectarian, with a more limited and sectoral appeal.

Loyalty to the movement or party, particularly in the pre-state and early-state years, often preceded loyalty to the state. [3] The central institutions (Jewish Agency Executive and Va‘ad

Leu'mi; the Knesset and cabinet at a later stage) were forums for the parties to meet on a minimal basis. The parties antedate the state and they contained in miniature many elements of national services: press, housing, education systems, cultural centers, health and medical insurance and so on.

Under these circumstances the political system prevailing in the Yishuv under the Mandate and in the World Zionist Organ-ization, i.e., proportional representation, continued with state-hood. The system had the effect of giving continuity and permanence to political fragmentation.[4] For this reason, it would be best to introduce the parties before the general structure.

From the chart on p. 64, one may easily but incorrectly assume that if the Communists are one extreme, the right-wing end of the spectrum is equivalent to the "typical" European right: anti-democratic Fascists or their like. In fact, in 1973, it would be hard to describe Herut and the General Zionists or Liberals as anything but center-right parties, just as it would be difficult to place Mapai as much beyond left-center.

Below, in brief, will follow a description of the parties' major characteristics.

Mapai is *the* party of the ruling coalition, Labor Zionist, i.e., a combination of Zionism and mild democratic socialism. The party is the largest of Israeli political groupings, pragmatic, and power-orientated. The name is an acronym of Labor (Workers') Party of Eretz Yisra'el.

Ahdut ha-'Avodah is a spin-off from Mapai (1944); the party has aptly been described as "left nationalist". It is more doctrinaire than Mapai both on social issues and on defense activism (retaliatory raids) as it was on the question of partition in the pre-state era; Ahdut ha-'Avodah (The Unity of Labor) is centered on the Kibbutz ha-Me'uhad (The United Kibbutz) feder-ation of collective settlements. Its history has shown it to be more sectarian in its interests and appeal than Mapai. In 1948 its disillusionment with Mapai, its stronger socialist emphasis, and its leanings toward the Soviet Union brought it into a merger with another kibbutz-based party.

Mapam (acronym of the United Workers' Party) was formed

in 1948 through the union of Aḥdut ha-'Avodah with ha-Shomer ha-Tza'ir. The latter had consistently seen itself as an ideological rival of Mapai and the moderate Labor Zionists. Ha-Shomer ha-Tza'ir grew out of East European youth movements and combined a Marxist interpretation of the Jewish position with pioneering Zionism. More pro-Soviet than Aḥdut ha'Avodah, it remained true to Stalinism, when the former could no longer stomach the "doctors' plot" and other manifestations of Stalinist anti-Semitism: the Slansky trial in Prague, and the breach of diplomatic relations with Israel by the USSR in the early 1950s. Mapam split in 1954: Aḥdut ha-'Avodah reverted to its previous name and separate organization, while ha-Shomer ha-Tza'ir retained the name Mapam, and a small group joined the Israel Communist Party. All parts of Mapam shared a strong anti-German bias.

All three labor groups, Mapai, Mapam and Aḥdut ha-'Avodah, flaunted the banner of ḥalutziyut — national-social pioneering — which has been described as one of Israel's central myths. This concept will be discussed further on in this study.

The other potential coalition parties theoretically came from the "right" or the religious groupings. To the right of Mapai were the *Progressives* (later to call themselves Independent Liberals) and the *General Zionists* (later to be known as Liberals). Originally constituting one party with the General Zionists, the smaller pro-labor Progressives had formed a separate grouping at Zionist Congresses. The larger General Zionists were generally based on the land-owning farmer class, citrus exporters, and whatever bourgeoisie there was at the time. To its right stood *Ḥerut*. It developed out of the the the Revisionist-inspired *Etzel (Irgun Tzeva'i Le'umi* or National Military Organization), the small underground force formed to pursue a more active anti-British line than that of the "official" Haganah in the last decade of the Mandate. With the disbanding of Etzel in Israel's first half-year of existence, Ḥerut became a legitimate political party. Its economic platform was close to that of the General Zionists—Liberals: a welfare state floor with a pro-"free enterprise" ceiling. On the issue of territory, the party was irridentist, calling for an Israel covering not only Western Palestine, but Transjordan as well.

It should be noted at this juncture that Ben Gurion ruled out the possibility of a coalition partnership with Ḥerut, this policy being due in particular to the bad blood left by the rivalry over political control of the contending underground organizations and the unifying of the post-underground armies after statehood. In a 1949 radio address following the first elections, Ben Gurion said: "The (party) lists to be considered [for forming a coalition] are those which are true to the basic principles of Zionism and democracy."[5] The first obviously excluded the anti-Zionist Communists; the second in Ben Gurion's interpretation eliminated Ḥerut.

The religious parties took as their platform the adoption of Torah law as the legal code of the country. However, the Zionism of the Mizrachi (contraction of *Merkaz Ruḥani,* Spiritual Center) and its constant sharing of responsibility on the world Zionist scene had by statehood created a tacit partnership with Mapai. This was enhanced by the unusual rapport between Ben Gurion and the Mizrachi leader, Rabbi Y.L. Maimon (Fishman), whom Ben Gurion held in great respect. The Mizrachi effectively settles for public observance (or lack of breach) of the Sabbath, of *kashrut* (dietary laws), of orthodox interpretation of Jewishness, and monopoly orthodox control of the so-called *rites de passage.* The more orthodox and originally anti-Zionist *Agudat Yisra'el* is less accommodating to the secular parties. Both religious groups have their kibbutz and labor-oriented subgroupings, which, in the case of Mizrachi labor(*ha-Po'el ha-Mizrachi*) was larger and more significant than its parent group. The religious parties formed various united fronts at different elections, and the labor and non-labor Mizrachi merged in 1956 to form the National Religious Party (NRP). Both Mizrachi and Agudat Yisra'el maintain large educational networks of primary and secondary schools.

In addition to these major groupings, there were small splinter parties. These included ethnic lists, especially of Arabs under Mapai influence, and Communists whose anti-government

NATIONALIST

LESS ⟶ MORE

Communists	Mapam	General Zionists Progressives	Mapai	Mizrachi (Religious Zionists)	Ahdut ha-'Avodah	Revisionists (Herut)

SOCIAL ATTITUDES

LEFT ⟶ RIGHT

Communists*	H.H.*	A.H.*	Mapai	Progressives (Independent Liberals)	Mizrachi (Religious Zionists)	General Zionists (Liberal)	Revisionists (Herut)
	(Mapam)**						

H I S T A D R U T

(Limited agreement with Histadrut on trade union affairs; or joined Histadrut in recent years.)

RELIGIOUS ATTITUDES

Anti-Religious			Neutral (Biased anti)			Neutral (Biased pro)	Orthodox	
Comm.	Mapam	A.H.	Progres-sives	Mapai	General Zionists	Herut	Mizrachi	Agudat Yisra'el

* The three groupings furthest left were at varying stages extremely pro-Soviet; the awakening occurred for each at varying dates until 1967, with a Communist splinter retaining loyalty to Moscow to date.

** 1948–54

H.H. – ha-Shomer ha-Tza'ir

A.H. – Ahdut ha-'Avodah

line also attracted a sizable Arab vote, as a kind of anti-Israel protest.

THE SYSTEM

Israel's unicameral Knesset, elected by proportional representation, is in theory based on the principle of legislative supremacy. The cabinet is responsible to the Knesset, though over the years the power of the executive has grown considerably and often overshadows that of the legislature. The president of the state fills the role of supreme non-partisan representation, an uncrowned constitutional monarch, elected by the Knesset to a five-year term. His functions as head of state are limited to formal and contentless acts. The prime minister, as head of government, wields much more power. For one, he is the leader of the largest party. Second, his resignation brings in its wake the resignation of the entire cabinet; though the resignation of an individual minister or ministers does not.[6]

On the other hand, the authority of the prime minister is limited by the very fact that his party has never commanded a majority in the Knesset and has rested on a coalition agreement. The agreement consists of two parts: the "Basic Principles" of the government, that is, the minimum program upon which the coalition partners agree; and the distribution of portfolios among the party representatives or ministers. The watchdog nature of cabinet and Knesset committees further curtails his power. The cabinet can fall if enough parties withdraw their support, particularly on a key issue brought to a vote of confidence.

The coalition principle is based on collective responsibility, a point enshrined in the first cabinet's "Basic Principles" by Ben Gurion in 1949. Yet the principle was honored in the breach often enough, and will be discussed in Chapter 12, "Coalition Partnership." Necessity may be perceived as a virtue, and in this case the coalition technique has been described as a way of uniting Israel's people. In 1953, Ben Gurion wrote to President Ben-Zvi that he knew

. . . perhaps better than any other person, the difficulties
of a coalition. I headed a coalition for 15 years in the
Zionist Executive, and for over five years in the state. Even
if there were a solid and stable majority in the nation —
and such a majority is in my opinion a vital need — even
then it would be incumbent to unify all the Zionist forces
in the state [and people] and to have them share in the
responsibility and burden.[7]

The constitutional principles are a mixture of precedent and
specially enacted "Fundamental Laws." Ben Gurion prevented
the adoption of a written constitution, a subject which will be
discussed in Chapter 12. The judiciary, appointed by the
president, has traditionally been independent of the executive.
The executive owes responsibility to the legislature, and consists
of ministers who usually head offices (hold portfolios) and come
from the legislature. In fact, the proportional-representation
party-list system, in which the nominating party and its central
institutions control its Knesset members closely, has led to
considerable dependence of coalition party MK's (Members of
Knesset) on the cabinet.

The intertwining of Mapai's power in government, control of
the bureaucracy and of the major public institutions such as the
Histadrut and the Jewish Agency has led to its preeminent
pervasion of the entire system. Mapai's central leadership has
managed to run the party effectively from above, while
preserving the forms of free intra-party elections. Its power has
been great, though limited by institutional and personal rivalry
(see Chapter 13).

The partners Mapai and particularly Ben Gurion chose in the
governments formed between 1948 and 1963 almost always
included the religious Zionists (Mizrachi—ha-Po'el ha-Mizrachi;
later NRP) and the Progressives (later the Independent
Liberals). Until 1955 the General Zionists, i.e., the moderate
right, were partners in some of the coalition cabinets. From late
1955 the cabinet also contained the two left-wing groups,
Aḥdut ha-'Avodah and Mapam.

KNESSET ELECTION RESULTS 1949–1965

Party	First 25.1.49 %	Seats	Second 30.7.51 %	Seats	Third 26.7.55 %	Seats	Fourth 3.11.59 %	Seats	Fifth 15.8.61 %	Seats	Sixth 2.11.65 %	Seats
Electorate	506,567		924,885		1,057,795		1,218,483		1,274,280		1,449,709	
Valid Votes Cast	434,684		687,492		853,219		964,337		1,006,964		1,206,728	
Mapai	35.7	46	37.3	45	32.2	40	38.2	47	34.7	42	44.6	55[a]
Ahdut ha-'Avodah	14.7[g]	19	12.5[g]	15	8.2	10	6.0	7	6.5	8		
Mapam					7.3	9	7.2	9	7.6	9	6.6	8
Herut [b]	11.5	14	6.6	8	12.6	15	13.6	17	13.7	17	21.3[h]	26
Liberals [b]	5.2 / 4.1	7 / 5	18.9 / 3.2	23 / 4	10.2 / 4.4	13 / 5	6.1 / 4.6	8 / 6	13.6	17	3.8[i]	5
National Religious Party	12.2	16[c]	8.3	10	9.1	11	9.9	12	9.8	12	8.9	11
Agudat Yisra'el			3.7[f]	5	4.7	6	4.7	6	3.7	4	3.3	4
Po'alei Agudat Yisra'el									1.9	2	1.8	2
Communists	3.5	4	4.0	5	4.5	6	2.8	3	4.1	5	3.4	4[j]
Arab Lists [d]	3.0	2	4.7	5	4.9	5	3.5	5	3.5	4	3.3	4
Others	10.1	7[e]	0.7		1.9		3.4		0.7		2.9	1[k]

[a] The Mapai–Ahdut ha-'Avodah alignment, with 36.7% and 45 seats, and Rafi (7.9% and 10 seats).

[b] Figures for first four Knessets refer respectively to General Zionists and Progressives, who merged in 1961 to form the Liberal Party. See also notes h and i.

[c] In 1949 these parties constituted the United Religious Front.

[d] Associated with or affiliated to Mapai.

[e] Four Sefardim, one Yemenite, one WIZO (Women's International Zionist Organization) and one of the Fighters' (Lehi).

[f] In 1951, 1955 and 1959, these constituted the Torah Religious Front.

[g] In 1949 and 1951 Mapam included Ahdut ha-'Avodah.

[h] Herut–Liberal Bloc (Gahal).

[i] Independent Liberals.

[j] Three – New Communist List (Rakaḥ) and one – Israel Communist Party (Maki).

[k] Ha-'Olam ha-Zeh.

Source: *Facts About Israel 1970*, Keter Publishing House Jerusalem, Ltd.

COALITION PARTIES 1948–1963
Based on Ervin Birnbaum, *The Politics of Compromise:*
State and Religion in Israel,
(Fairleigh Dickinson Press, 1970), p. 309

May 14, 1948 – Provisional Government March 10, 1949	Mapai,* Religious Parties, General Zionists, Progressives, Sefardim
March 10, 1949 – February 14, 1951	Mapai, Religious Bloc, Progressives, Sefardim**
October 8, 1951 – December 19, 1952	Mapai, Religious Bloc
December 23, 1952 – December 7, 1953 January 26, 1954 – June 29, 1955	Mapai, Mizrachi (both wings), Progressives, General Zionists
June 29, 1955 – December 31, 1957	Mapai, NRP, Progressives
November 3, 1955– December 31, 1957 January 7, 1958 – July 5, 1959 December 17, 1959 – January 31, 1961	Mapai, NRP, Progressives, Aḥdut ha-'Avodah, Mapam
November 2, 1961 – June 16, 1963	Mapai, NRP, Po'alei Agudat Yisra'el, Aḥdut ha-'Avodah

---

   *   Mapai plus Arab lists.
 **   Ethnic splinter group.

PART TWO

Internal Affairs

CHAPTER FIVE

From Socialist to Nonsocialist

Two movements swept across Europe at the turn of the century. Nationalism and socialism penetrated, as only ideas can, social and ethnic groups across Eurasia, not bypassing the cities, towns and hamlets into which millions of Jews were packed in the Czarist Empire, Austria-Hungary, and Rumania. David Green had to come to terms with these two ideas. Like other young Jews in Eastern Europe, he was committed to putting them into practice not merely on the ideological-organizational level, as a party member subscribing to an idea, but as one ready to revolutionize his way of living in order to change radically the life style of the Jewish people.

In reconstructing the development of Ben Gurion's ideas along the axis of time, one finds that he increasingly emphasized the national element of the enmeshed and inseparable national and social revolution in changing the status of the Jewish people. He originally saw in the working class the emissary of the Jewish people in realizing its national aims. With his accession to state power, even greater stress was placed on the achieving of national aims at the expense of the pre-state voluntaristic labor organization tools: the Histadrut and the kibbutzim. The internal needs to foster rapid economic development, and to find employment for the new immigrants were

71

matched by a parallel desire to give preeminence to the fledgling state apparatus, jealously to increase its prestige and power, which were both inextricably bound to Ben Gurion's own.

The internal situation was complicated, particularly until 1956, by the pro-Soviet line of part of the labor movement, and the consequent mergers and splits in its left wing. The changing reality and the new state power, as well as disappointment both with local socialists of rigid ideology and with foreign socialist parties, all combined to bring Ben Gurion to introduce a major change in his lexicon. He finally dropped the word socialism from his pantheon of ideas, substituting the Hebrew prophets' national-social-human vision.

STATE PRIMACY

When Israel achieved statehood, the labor movement had at its disposal a number of relatively powerful instruments. The Histadrut membership then numbered about one-quarter of the Jewish population. Its strength was enhanced by a concentration of services: health, social, cultural and educational, as well as a conglomeration of industries and enterprises controlled by its holding company. The communal and cooperative settlements (kibbutzim and moshavim), particularly the former, provided a pool of manpower readily mobilized, ideologically motivated and action-oriented, at the general disposal of the entire movement. The kibbutzim were organized into ideological federations, but the members and the federations themselves owed allegiance to the Histadrut. Although the trade-union organization wielded a certain measure of coercion through its ability to provide jobs, and through the ancillary benefits and services mentioned above, basically the Histadrut must be seen as a voluntary organization. With the creation of the state, the legitimate instruments of coercion were in the hands of the official leadership, headed by Ben Gurion.

The elements of the national-social "mix" can therefore be measured fairly readily once all these voluntary and coercive institutions were at Ben Gurion's disposal. Of course, the power of a leader is limited by both institutional and personal considerations, but — to reason tautologically — a strong leader can lead strongly. And there is no doubt that Ben Gurion was strong-willed and possessed a general map of the future. This was a national historic vision:

> Full redemption of the Jewish people, [both] national and social . . . and for this purpose, ingathering the exiles, changing the structure of the people from one detached from real life and dependent on the economy of others to a working people returning to its natural sources, vitality and historic heritage, and creating . . . its goods and values . . . . [1]

A few cases illustrate the primacy of national aims and needs during his leadership, and his placing the interests of the state and its apparatus above those of the rival labor federation.

Ben Gurion had served as the first secretary-general of the Histadrut, and, as has been shown, saw the labor movement as the key to capturing the leadership of the Zionist movement (see Chapter 2). This would be the base for state power. Until the achievement of statehood and the possession of its instrumentalities, the labor movement was an embryo state within the state-in-the-making. Its economic enterprises, industrial as well as agricultural, provided it with immense muscle in a capital-poor country.

From 1935, Ben Gurion's political interest in the world Zionist scene removed him from close contact with the Histadrut. This tendency was all the more pronounced after 1948. He was aware of the need for changing the relative weight of institutions like the Histadrut whose post-state role was to be quite different from its pre-independence function.

At the first Histadrut convention after statehood, in May 1949, he said:

> With the political revolution which has occurred in our day [the creation of the state], the old instruments are not out of date . . . [they] must now increase their pioneering

endeavor and settlement activity in order to carry out, in
cooperation with the historic force which has arisen [the
state], the great task . . . .[2]

The convention was still too close to the recent war and the
country was reeling under the impact of mass immigration. Ben
Gurion's address tackled this problem by making specific
demands on the kibbutz, which will be discussed below. The
internal rift in the labor movement, between the threatening,
pro-Soviet Mapam and his own party, took up much of his
second speech. Yet he did devote part of his opening address to
the question of economic independence as a national aim. He
spoke not as a sectoral leader, but as prime minister, urging that
more land be cultivated, that industrial production and exports
be increased.[3] Symbolically, he followed the convention from
afar, appearing only at its opening and closing stages. State
business occupied him and his thoughts.

It was eight years later, at the following Histadrut
convention, that Ben Gurion took the opportunity to assess the
movement's adaptation to the changing circumstances. The
Histadrut, he said, was no longer what it had been. In part, this
was because "the light of vision of the working public had
dimmed, its unity weakened, its pioneering drive
diminished . . . the strength of partial interests — personal,
professional, economic . . . had grown."[4]

Furthermore, the state had not superseded the Histadrut in
those areas in which the labor federation had acted as a proxy
for the state-to-be in Mandatory times. He therefore called for
the establishment of state-operated labor exchanges, to replace
those of the Histadrut, and the nationalization of the
Histadrut-sponsored Mekorot Water Company. "The Histadrut
is neither the rival nor competitor of the state, but its loyal aide
and dedicated supporter." He laid down the principle that the
state must supply every service which is required for the entire
public. He hastened to add that this did not necessarily call for
nationalization of these services. The Sick Fund of the
Histadrut, which provides medical care and hospitalization for

Histadrut members, may continue to provide its services to those paying for them, while the state would look after non-members. He attacked the false concept "that requires provision of all services by the state bureaucracy."

He outlined two major tasks for the Histadrut: the shaping of the image of the state (its social relationships), and undertaking pioneering tasks in the fields of education, the economy, and society, "which cannot be achieved by the force of coercion and law or by the government bureaucracy alone." Although he was the helmsman of the state, he was cautious about it totally supplanting voluntarism. He had made this point in the 1949 address as well. Nonetheless, he clearly placed the supreme national interest above the voluntary act of will and conscience.

Ben Gurion's statement that the Histadrut is *neither the rival nor competitor of the state* indicates that he feared it might be, at least to some extent. He proposed for it a role definitely secondary to that of the state, to be its loyal aide and dedicated supporter. The problem Ben Gurion faced regarding the Histadrut was both ideological-emotional and organizational-political. The Histadrut had been the midwife of the state, just as the Zionist movement had been its mother. The strength of the labor movement, its membership figures, budgets, control of the Haganah — all these had been built on labor ideology and organization. Tied to this was Ben Gurion's rootedness in the labor movement, his ideological home in which he had spent his apprenticeship in leadership.

For these reasons, as well as the pragmatic necessity to preserve his labor following in the large machine controlled by the Histadrut executive and labor council secretaries throughout the country, Ben Gurion settled in the middle of the principle-pragmatism axis. The principle of state primacy tempered by the ideological-emotional sediment was adjusted to the pragmatic recognition of the danger inherent in overly weakening the labor movement's extensive power. The compromise was to nationalize one part of the Histadrut function — the labor exchanges — and to sanction the continuation of the Histadrut-run Sick Fund (health insurance).

The latter was one of the main attractions for joining or remaining in Histadrut. Only labor union members and their families could benefit from the full range of services it provided: free medical care, hospitalization and medicaments. Even the most popular "nationalization" proposed was aimed only at providing coverage for those who were not members of the Histadrut or other such funds.

State labor exchanges were opened following the adoption of the relevant law in 1959.[5] The law depoliticized the job-seeking process by establishing a State Employment Service to which employment seekers and prospective employers were exclusively bound. However, the vested interest of the Histadrut has so far proven stronger than the will of Ben Gurion and others to establish a national health insurance program.

Ben Gurion's attitude on state primacy is illustrated in the crisis over unified state education which had arisen a few years earlier. The crux of the matter was a symbol, the red flag of labor, and Ben Gurion's disposition of the case is symbolic of his approach.

In 1953, the General Zionist members of the coalition resigned over the issue of the Histadrut flag being flown at schools of the labor trend on the first of May. Mapai's Central Committee backed the right of the workers to fly their flag, though Ben Gurion agreed with the General Zionists, and opposed segmentary symbols.[6] Under his pressure and the threat of a coalition crisis, the Central Committee found a face-saving formula for retreat. Ben Gurion resolved the crisis by flatly promising the Knesset that once unified state education was introduced, in which but two trends would exist, religious and "secular", only the state flag would fly over the schools.[7] The State Education Law went into effect the following school year, 1953-54.[8] The red flag was struck.

THE KIBBUTZIM AND IMMIGRANT EMPLOYMENT

Ben Gurion experienced greater difficulty, and met with a singular lack of response in his dealings, immediately after statehood, with the cohesive social structure of the kibbutzim. His espousal of national primacy over sectoral loyalties remained, to a great extent, an exercise in exhortation. The case in point was the struggle between Ben Gurion and the kibbutz movement over the employment of hired labor in the kibbutzim. The background to the struggle was Ben Gurion's 1949 policy to double the size of the Jewish population of Israel, about 650,000 when the state was established, in a four-year period. (The target was reached within three-and-a-half years.)

At the time, agricultural settlement was seen as the easiest and speediest means both of absorbing the immigrants into the economy, and of insuring the occupation of desolate areas or abandoned sites. Ben Gurion appealed to the settlement organizations, to the federations of kibbutzim and moshavim, to take in the newcomers, or at least to provide them with work. Since many of the new immigrants were former inmates of concentration camps, who did not welcome communal living, or newcomers from Arab countries bound to a traditional, family-centered way of life, there was no great possibility of attracting them to become full members in the kibbutzim. The alternative was that the kibbutz hire newcomers from the neighboring tent cities and transit camps as day laborers. The socialist principle not to employ hired labor clashed with the national need to find employment for the tens of thousands of potential breadwinners pouring into Israel with no place to win their bread. In exasperation, Ben Gurion announced to the Histadrut national convention in mid-1949, "There are those who fear that the light of the state will dim the beauty of the kibbutz and the moshav."[9]

In this speech Ben Gurion employed all his polemical and oratorical talents. Immigrant absorption, he said, was "the question of questions." Its importance ranked with winning the war: "We shall not continue to exist if we do not absorb mass immigration." He described the immense financial burden imposed on the state by the cost of providing housing for the newcomers. He explained the policy of dispersal of population to avoid a "Carthage" situation developing along the coast. He pointed out that, unlike the situation prevailing under the Mandate, land was plentifully available. The task was to bring the immigrants to the land, particularly via the agency of the kibbutz.

> We must preserve the values and the way-of-life of the kibbutz and moshav, and must not impose hired labor upon them as a permanent arrangement, but we must demand that they take in temporary workers as a need of the times.

Ben Gurion's closing words at the 1949 convention are illustrative of his approach, his grasp of change, his impatience with sacred cows.

> We will preserve and realize the values of our endeavor — and not by freezing things, and converting [the kibbutzim] into closed monasteries, but, on the contrary, we will open them wide for every Jew. Vision has not come to an end . . . let the scoffers scoff — I believe that the vision will be realized in our day. [10]

Ben Gurion could not bend the kibbutz movements to his will, to become a major instrument of immigrant absorption, but they did comply to the extent of employing some hired labor. However, with the use of national capital and the organizational machinery of the moshav movement, many new moshavim for immigrants were established in the 1950s.

Ben Gurion's criticism of the kibbutz was mitigated by his appreciation of its national and social goals. Toward the end of 1952, Ben Gurion spoke of the kibbutz in glowing terms, as concentrating all the content of national and individual redemption. On both retirements from office — in 1953 and 1963 — he chose to make his home at Sde Boker, which by its nature as a kibbutz, and its location, in the Negev, symbolized his attitude to the social content of the kibbutz and, probably more important to him, the national need for settling the Negev. Significantly, Sde Boker was then apolitical, an anomaly in the politicized kibbutz movements.

REDEFINING GOALS

The wider range of power placed in Ben Gurion's hands with statehood coincided with his measure of disappointment and impatience with the existing socialist groups and bodies, which were slower in mood and in pace to grasp the elemental changes which were taking place. These changes required a redefinition of a key idea in the Labor-Zionist lexicon: ḥalutziyut, which was closely linked to the kibbutz ideal. It is usually rendered as "pioneering," but this is typical of the poverty of translation from a language like Hebrew with its biblical and historical overtones. The word, borrowed from the Book of Numbers and usually mistranslated there as "armed," was revived in the second half of the 19th century.[11] It embraced the idea of a young immigrant to Palestine who would work the land in one of the new settlements. Since this often involved defense as well, there was a secondary connotation of daring and risk. In brief, it presented an ideal picture of the new Jew, independent, working the land jointly with others, and prepared to shoulder arms to protect himself. The Labor-Zionist youth movements adopted the ideal; one quite naturally took the name *he-Ḥalutz*.

In April 1949, less than a year after the proclamation of independence, Ben Gurion presented a list of activities "of a scope and intensity which we have not known until now." Though the list is lengthy, it shows the adjustment to the new element of statehood in the definition of ḥalutziyut.

Settling the Negev, settling Eilat with fishermen, farmers, boatmen, pilots and industrial workers; laying roads in the 'Aravah and on the shores of the Dead Sea; conquest of the oceans and skies with shipping and air transport, commercial and military; founding fishing villages along

the entire length of the Mediterranean coastline; erecting a
chain of settlements along the borders and the Jerusalem
corridor; scientific research, both pure and applied;
managing government offices; training immigrants in trades
and in agriculture and industry; building workers' villages
combining agriculture and industry, physical and mental
labor, which will serve as centers for absorbing immigrants
and as strongholds for the defense of the state . . . . [12]

As important as the list is his definition of the cardinal
element of halutziyut — work, and first and foremost, work on
the land.[13] This facet, agricultural labor, was included in the
Defense Service Law as part of the regular military duties of
conscripts, but was dropped under the pressures of specialized
training (see Chapter 7). It shows how deeply entrenched was
the Labor-Zionist concept of productivization of the Jews,
which is simply "work" in Ben Gurion's language. It underlay
the redefinition of pioneering due to the new circumstances
arising from statehood.

More than five years later, in July 1954, Ben Gurion further
sharpened his definition, or, more accurately, broadened it. At a
youth gathering, he decried political cleavage of the kibbutzim,
alluding to the ha-Kibbutz ha-Me'uhad organization which had
split along a right-left axis. He further accused the movement of
permitting its forms to become "petrified, they neither reflect
the needs of our time, nor the needs of merging the ingathered
communities, nor the needs of settling the wasteland." The five
major tasks of young people were, he said, "1) stressing
common [i.e, unifying] factors; 2) settling the borders; 3)
merging the ingathered communities; 4) purity of (public)
behavior; 5) a new society."[14] Here is "desocialization" *par
excellence*; "a new society" has universal appeal beyond class
borders.

In the final analysis, Ben Gurion conceived of halutziyut as a
state of mind. Here is the answer he gave in October 1954 to
the rhetorical question he posed at a meeting of the Teachers'
Union.

What is ḥalutziyut? It is recognition of the historic
mission, and placing oneself unconditionally . . . at [its]
service . . . it is the talent . . . to live every day in accord
with the dictate of conscience and the demand of the
aim . . . it is the demand a man makes of himself, it is
personal realization of the aims and values in which a man
believes. Ḥalutziyut is the ability to create anew from the
very beginning. [15]

Such a broad definition could fit the word patriotism, or even
the concept of personal morality.

THE IDEOLOGICAL FRAMEWORK AND THE LEFT

Ben Gurion's basic commitment to the cause of labor began in
the revolutionary framework of Russian Jewry at the turn of
the century. Yet, except in its earlier stages, it was never rigidly
ideological, nor directly influenced by Marxism. The ideal of
labor in the sense of work was more important to the Jews for
national reasons, he believed, than the question of property
relations from the social point of view. In fact, his socialist
ideology had become quite watered down by the early 1950s.

One may say, in general, that socialism is basically the
opposite of capitalism: the economy does not rule the
workers, but the workers . . . rule over the economy.
Socialism is the supremacy of labor [work] in society and
the state, as opposed to the supremacy of property . . . . [16]

To return to an earlier period, the ideological break between
Labor Zionism and the Marxist Communists had become
sharper after the Russian Revolution and the pronounced anti-
Zionism of the revolutionary government. Marxism did exert a
strong influence on part of the Labor Zionists, especially
through Ber Borochov, a Russian-Jewish theoretician who
produced a synthesis of Marxism and Zionism. [17] His ultimate
ideological destination was never reached since he died shortly

after the Revolution, at the age of 36. Borochov became, posthumously, one of the ideological influences on the ha-Shomer ha-Tza'ir kibbutz movement and the left Po'alei Tziyyon, which eventually merged into the Mapam Party.[18]

Over the years, Ben Gurion had consistently fought the Communists for their blind echoing of Moscow doctrine. At one Histadrut debate, he simply said, "I do not wish to debate anything with the Communist Party: a) since I have no common Jewish background with them; b) one does not debate with phonograph records, even if they are living people."[19]

Mapam, and its kibbutz element, posed a more complex problem. Though casting eyes at Moscow, and often emerging cross-eyed (one can imagine the effect the Nazi-Soviet pact must have had on leftist Zionists of Eastern European extraction), the Mapam members had established an unquestionable record in realizing Labor-Zionist ideals in their kibbutzim, and national ideals in the underground Haganah, Palmaḥ, and the illegal immigration movement prior to the state. Nor could their constructive work after the establishment of the state be doubted. Ben Gurion recognized all he shared in common with left Zionist labor, but consistently attacked, and attacked sharply, what he considered to be their heresies.

He did this on both theoretical and tactical grounds. "The Palestinian workers movement," he said in 1956, in a retrospective theoretical analysis covering an earlier period,

> . . . did not accept the Marxist theory, which Borochov
> also preached, that the aim of the bourgeois class is to
> create, and that of the proletarian class is to
> liberate . . . . The halutzim in the early decades of this
> century reached the conclusion that the worker in this
> land must be not merely a wage earner fighting to improve
> his labor conditions and the abolition of classes, but he
> must himself be a settler and builder of enterprises in the
> village and the town.[20]

On a tactical level, the closer Mapam followed the

Communist lead, the easier it was to attack. Thus, in 1951, in the election campaign for the Second Knesset, Ben Gurion unleashed a scathing attack on "the majority in Mapam which decided to join the 'forces of tomorrow' . . . 'the forces of progress.'" With the special acrimony he reserved for his favorite targets, the far right and far left, he ripped into Stalinism ("the ruler in the fortress of human salvation") which determines what is science, art, justice, freedom, democracy and socialism.[21] The peroration is as demagogic as Ben Gurion ever permitted: "And the workers of the Land of Israel must decide: Kremlin — or Jerusalem."[22]

Following the wave of anti-Zionism and anti-Semitism which swept Soviet-controlled Europe with the last gasps of Stalin, particularly after the trial of the Jewish secretary-general of the Czech Communist Party, Rudolf Slansky, in which a Mapam member was implicated, Ben Gurion went for the left Zionist party with a vengeance. In early 1953, he published a series of articles in the Histadrut daily, *Davar,* which were later collected in a pamphlet called *On the Communism and Socialism of ha-Shomer ha-Tza'ir,* under the *nom de plum* of S.S. *(Sabba Shel)* Yariv (i.e., Grandfather of Yariv).[23] In them, Ben Gurion charged that ha-Shomer ha-Tza'ir engaged in "double bookkeeping . . . acting in a Tito-like fashion and demanding payment like Stalin."[24]

At this time he demonstrated his distaste for the word socialist and equated the three totalitarian systems. He spoke of:

> . . . the corruption and danger of totalitarianism
> . . . whether it calls itself "National-Socialist" as
> in the regime of Hitler, or wears the trappings of
> "Communist," as in the regime of Stalin, or whether it
> proudly bears the Fascist name, as in the regime of
> Mussolini.[25]

In reminiscing, he stated that he had in fact left the title "socialist" behind during World War II.[26]

Ben Gurion's increasing concern with Israel's national problems was in direct proportion to his growing distance from imported ideologies. These had led, for example, to Mapam's talk of the "tragic contradiction between socialism and Zionism, in the attachment to 'the second homeland.' "[27] In 1956, he said: "The economic and social fabric of the Land is unique, and it should not be made to fit sociological definitions which evolved in a totally different reality."[28]

Ben Gurion also recognized the danger of institutional loyalties and interests blocking the path he was laying down for the nation. This was true both of the left-wing, the more doctrinaire and hence conservative, socialists, as well as his own party's pragmatic socialists. Like every true revolutionary who attains power, he feared post-revolutionary conservatism, and routine, which would hamstring and stifle the charismatic purpose. He did not call for cultural revolutions, but insisted that "routine" not become "an impairing, blocking . . . force." The twin criteria of doing-execution-pragmatism (all imbedded in the key word, bitzu'a) and of direction were what counted. What was once "revolutionary" may today be "conservative."[29]

Though the road to Ben Gurion's final stance, that of a nonsocialist socialist, began with rudimentary Po'alei Tziyyon proletarianism, the national element came to the fore early, and became the bedrock of his thought. Labor as an ideal was reinforced by the need for Jews to become workers and for labor to be done in order to build, reclaim and stake out frontiers. The kibbutz held a high place, but the pragmatist would not accord it the central place in the grand scheme for the entire people, for the entire state. And with statehood, the stress on instruments changes. The authority and the purse of the state must serve the national ideal, a people of workers, a union of intellectuals and laborers for the common good, but with a market economy, and financial gains and profits definitely not taboo.

ATTITUDE TO PRIVATE CAPITAL

In his capacity as labor leader, Ben Gurion evolved a pragmatic approach to cooperation between capital and labor. As early as 1932, he had bluntly told the elected body of the Palestine Jewish community: "We now live under a regime of property, and under the existing regime we must build the Land."[30] Obviously, as prime minister, meeting the challenge of absorbing a mass movement of immigration to settle the land for political, military and economic ends, the pragmatist would not become less pragmatic.

Following the first elections to the Knesset, and the subsequent negotiations to form a government to replace the provisional bodies which had been conducting Israel's affairs, Ben Gurion presented the Basic Principles of his new cabinet to the legislature in March 1949. The Basic Principles were those statements of joint purpose around which the coalition partners agreed to unite: these and the functional distribution of portfolios and related patronage are the keystone of coalition politics in Israel. The government program called for:

> The encouragement of private and cooperative
> capital . . . special benefits to productive capital
> investments which aid the speedy and efficient
> development of the country's resources and economic
> potential, benefits for transfer of capital from Jews
> of the Diaspora.[31]

Considering the ideological framework of the labor (senior) partners in the cabinet, it is noteworthy that this paragraph comes after such basics as land and water development, and *before* development of workers' economies in agriculture and in the towns. A few months later, addressing the Jerusalem chamber of commerce, Ben Gurion explained that large-scale and speedy absorption of immigrants could not be achieved without both state planning and private initiative.[32] But by February 1951, Ben Gurion was taking the Israel Manufacturers'

Association to task, much as he did the kibbutz movements, "for not responding to the national need," in this case, "to . . . increase productivity of labor and raise the productive capacity of our economy."[33]   He called upon all elements in the population to "display the wisdom of compromise" in all matters of principle, for the sake of two greater needs: security and immigration.[34]

The accession of Levi Eshkol, Ben Gurion's devoted and loyal lieutenant, to the ministry of finance in 1952 further lessened Ben Gurion's involvement in the details of economic matters. Thus it is only in a general way that he bears responsibility for later economic policy, which doubtless had his full blessing and support. There are varying evaluations of this policy, particularly in the debate between right-wing economic critics and official spokesmen over the extent of encouragement of private investment and initiative. However, the governments which Ben Gurion headed did pass a number of laws for the encouragement of private capital investment, and established an Investment Authority to provide tax benefits and arrangements for repatriation of capital earned on investments.[35]

Ben Gurion's attitude to private capital was far less ambivalent than that of many of his more ideological comrades in the labor movement. He did not attempt to stifle the profit motive. With his uncanny knack for finding sources in the ancient literature to support his views, he would quote the midrash (homiletical text) which makes the "evil inclination" produce good, for without it, families would not exist, nor would houses be built or fields tilled. "For the building of the land, the 'evil inclination' of love of profit is also needed."[36] He told visiting capitalists not to let their love for Israel stand in the way of their investing money for profit ("making money") in Israel, for without this incentive, "the country will not be built."[37]

On the principle-pragmatism continuum, the pragmatic urge to build, to settle immigrants on the land, far outweighed sectoral loyalties. Cooperation with and encouragement of capital investment was far more important than safeguarding the workers' control of the economy through the Histadrut. The state exercised its primacy, even though this left Israel with an ideological void.

STATE VS HISTADRUT: THE ABORTIVE DEBATE

On the whole, Ben Gurion's primacy theory was not challenged by the Mapai leadership of the Histadrut in the first dozen years of statehood. The open confrontation between what came to be known as *étatism* and voluntarism emerged against the background of the struggle for leadership and eventual succession in the party hierarchy. The Histadrut's role in the debate was overshadowed by the national issues at stake, particularly the succession issue. Nonetheless, the criticism is instructive, if not always to the point, since it affected both national consensus as well as Ben Gurion's position. The simmering resentment toward Ben Gurion for introducing "younger men" into the Knesset and government by lateral recruitment from rival *élites* (the army or the civil service) did not find expression in attacks on Ben Gurion himself. The rivalry sensed by those who had risen through the party ranks to positions of power in the party or the Histadrut was given voice once the newcomers dared criticize the Histadrut's tardiness in adapting to the new economic reality in the modernizing Israeli society.

The rivalry, already exacerbated by the generation gap, was further pointed up by differences of style. Particularly sharp was the contrast between the ideologically-rooted semantics of the Eastern Europe veteran leadership and the inelegant and pragmatic language of the *sabras,* or native-born Israelis. Moshe Dayan, the leading "young" follower of Ben Gurion, criticized the Histadrut's leadership in a speech known as the "fifth floor" — executive-suite — speech. Pinḥas Lavon, the Histadrut secretary-general, hit back hard at the "young group," the so-called *tze'irim,* in January 1959.[38] However, there was no overt clash between Ben Gurion and the Histadrut leadership until other intra-party issues intruded.

Relations between Ben Gurion and Lavon became more estranged in the fall of 1960, when Lavon demanded exoneration from the charge that he had been responsible for a serious failure of Israeli military intelligence in 1954, when he had been minister of defense (see Chapter 7). In December 1960, Lavon broadened his conflict with Ben Gurion by introducing the element of ideological difference and conflict between the Histadrut and the state. In his earlier years as Histadrut secretary-general, an office he occupied from 1956, Lavon had followed a line of cooperation with the government.[39] However, as the issues of succession and the 1954 Lavon Affair impinged on the political scene, lines were drawn, and eventually the conflict came to be seen as one between the pro-Histadrut and pro-state forces.

Ben Gurion was understood to have said at a Mapai convention in spring 1960 that the Histadrut "must bow to the needs of the state."[40] Lavon deferred his public response until December 1960, when he took up cudgels against *étatism*. Significantly this was *after* his demand for rehabilitation. Newspaper reports cited him as warning against "the spread of the dangerous philosophy of *'étatism'* among certain circles in the state." Lavon accused the *étatists* of believing that "the state could replace the free efforts of various bodies." This "was today aimed at crippling the Histadrut, but it would be used against other public bodies in the future."[41]

It was quite a battle cry, but the beleaguered Mapai leadership, torn between loyalty to Ben Gurion (either for personal or vote-drawing reasons) and the desire to keep the machine intact, finally had to reject it. Lavon was forced to resign from his post as secretary-general. The rumblings continued. In February 1961, Lavon took his leave of the Histadrut executive. In his apologia, he backtracked from the word *'étatism'* but adhered to and even sharpened his criticism of its content. Circles in the labor movement, he said, were entrapped in the snare of belief in "the omnipotent state, and they are beginning to develop an attitude of suspicion or envy of . . . the Histadrut." He complained that "there are members who believe that the state itself can assume most of the functions (of the Histadrut)."[42] Lavon received backing from a number of labor leaders and intellectual figures.[43]

Lavon's earlier formulation of the state-labor partnership, with the state as the senior partner, certainly coincided with Ben Gurion's views. Restated, these were that:

> The Histadrut must serve in the future as well as the force which will forge new social forms, though this is also a responsibility of the government . . . there can and must be full coordination between the activities of the Histadrut and the activities and policy of the government.[44]

The malaise surrounding the state-Histadrut issue, stripped of its personal elements, was a reflection of the death of ideology in the face of new situations: industrialization and a defense-centered national policy. In this context, Ben Gurion's approach, advanced so eagerly by his younger lieutenants, was to solve these problems by enhancing state primacy. At the same time, however, neither Ben Gurion nor any other Israeli leader proposed a social blueprint or platform which would give form and detail to the general aims accepted by the vast majority in the labor movement. This hiatus in Ben Gurion's national policy was perhaps his greatest weakness as a leader.

The ideological malaise, keenly felt by a limited circle of pro-labor ideologists and ideologically motivated labor leaders, coincided with an attempt by a dissident, Lavon, to raise the issue of Histadrut subordination to the state to the level of a grand debate. Ben Gurion was much more concerned with other aspects of the political struggle with Lavon, and therefore the debate never really got off the ground. Its importance lies in that it was almost an exercise in futility. The state had established its primacy over the Histadrut. The compromise for the sake of "ingathering," of enhancing Israel's strength, was a pluralistic society. "Our state is neither capitalist nor socialist," Ben Gurion told Mapai's Council in April 1951.[45] The state's need for private capital would be offset by the political strength of the workers and the economic activity of the Histadrut and state-owned economic sectors.[46] The pragmatism of building took primacy over class interests. Even the word socialism fell into disrepute as the labor leader found himself a state-builder.

CHAPTER SIX

The Religious-Secular Axis: Conflict and Consensus

In this chapter, the delineation of the spheres of influence and the setting of public policy in some realms of religious life will be analyzed. It will be seen that for reasons of expediency, Ben Gurion pragmatically continued to abet religious hegemony in some areas, and attempted in others to limit the power of the resilient religious establishment. One major motivation for refraining from interference in the preserves of orthodoxy was a tacit agreement between Ben Gurion and the Mizrachi leadership, which gave him free rein to formulate political and defense policy, and, in exchange, limited the clash between religious and secularists on religious matters.

Two issues will be dealt with, each having a different outcome: unifying the educational system, a qualified success for Ben Gurion; and the definition of "Jew," where he came a cropper. These issues will be discussed from the point of view of the primacy of state policy in defense and foreign affairs over the religious conflict, the pragmatic adjustment to the social strength of the religious groups and their establishments, and the definition of consensus through conflict.

Before beginning this discussion, it is necessary to review the general historical and religious background, to ascertain Ben Gurion's exact stand on religious issues, at the outset of statehood, and to examine briefly the lack of a constitutional solution to the overall problem of the role of religion in the state.

The Histadrut was founded in 1920; the Zionist movement in 1897. The Jewish religion dates back to distant antiquity: its years are not numbered in decades, but in millennia. Over the centuries, the rabbinate became the group which maintained leadership both in spiritual and legal matters. One of its functions was the preservation of socio-religious patterns. In Mandatory Palestine the orthodox rabbinate had been accorded recognition and status as the government's surrogate with regard to the personal status of Jews. The rabbinical courts had exclusive jurisdiction in matters of marriage and divorce, alimony, and confirmation of wills of members of their community.[1]

With the growth of the religious groups in Zionism — the Mizrachi, and particularly its youth and labor wings (ha-Po'el ha-Mizrachi) — especially from the 1930s, there arose a political establishment which saw as its major functions: the defense of the rabbinate's prerogatives, the preservation of Jewish religious patterns in society, and the setting up of a religious educational system. The political and clerical establishments were not one and the same; there were often differences between them. So, too, were there varying shades within Mizrachi itself.

To the right of the Mizrachi stood the non-Zionist Agudat Yisra'el and its younger, labor element (Po'alei Agudah). Further to the right were the rigid *yeshivot* (Jewish religious or talmudic academies) and a small fanatic element which opposed Zionism and later the state since these were motivated by secular forces rather than by the hand of the Deity. The Agudah groups cooperated with organized Zionism in the stormy pre-state period and entered the provisional government with statehood. Though the political following of the combined religious parties never reached 15 percent of the voting public, the broader religious or "observant" category would cover many who voted for other parties but followed religious tenets in their personal life.

Ben Gurion may be termed a secularist in the sense that he did not wish to conduct Israel's affairs or have life in Israel evolve in accordance with religious or clerical laws and directives. Yet, as leader of the nation, he had to take into account the desires of the sizable observant Jewish minority. Ideologically, his sense of Jewishness, freed from formal and ritualistic proscription, embraced the centrality of the Bible as the Jews' unique document and claim to separate existence, observance of national holidays, a kind of theism, and a belief in the singularity of the prophetic heritage and Jewish historical experience. These, as well as the need for national and coalition compromise, led to a distinct enshrining of Jewish ritual and orthodox practice in the law and life of Israel.

The ever-shifting, but nonetheless constantly invoked *status quo*, which determines the role of Jewish ritual in the daily life of Israel, is based on various procedures, laws and customs evolved prior to and during the Mandatory period. More particularly, in a letter sent to Rabbi Yitzḥak Meir Levine of the ultra-orthodox World Agudat Yisra'el in June 1947, signed by Ben Gurion and two Jewish Agency colleagues, "the Jewish State when it shall be established" undertook to keep Saturday (Shabbat) as the official day of rest, to observe kashrut in official (state-operated) dining halls, to maintain orthodox control over the personal status (essentially marriage and divorce procedure) of Jews, and to continue to operate four ideological "trends" in Jewish schools.[2] The trends were ultra-orthodox, orthodox, general, and labor.

The coalition's trials and tribulations in delineating the *status quo*, which had the effect of setting outer boundaries beyond which Ben Gurion and Mapai were unwilling to step in placating their religious partners in government, are partially dealt with further on in this chapter. They represent resolution through conflict. At this point, the discussion will center on the place of religious practice in the day-to-day life of Israeli Jews as a reflection of Ben Gurion's national policy of compromise, of deferring clashes of "principle" and a potential *Kulturkampf* between orthodox and secular for later generations. In other words, this process represents resolution by consensus, within the boundaries set by conflict.

Ben Gurion believed that there was a basic difference between the issue of "religion and state" in Israel and that of "Church and state" in Christian countries. Judaism was not a matter of faith or belief alone. "The Jewish religion is a *national* religion . . . it is not easy to separate the national from the religious aspect." Thus, for example, Israel's holy days or holidays have a dual meaning: "religio-cosmic" and "historico-national."[3] In this sense, Ben Gurion accepted the observance of religious holidays as days of rest for the entire nation, with the various ideological segments of the population giving them the content which suited their various dispositions.

Referring to the continuation, in the newly established State of Israel, of the jurisdiction of the rabbinate over matters of personal status, Ben Gurion wrote: "The existing arrangement is the fruit of compromise which naturally cannot satisfy all opinions, as is the way of compromise; (it) was adopted to prevent a war over religion . . . which might drastically impede the 'merging of exiles,' [a goal] which occupies a crucial place in the state." He called for the establishment of a "national minimum . . . which would guarantee that observant, traditional, and secular may live as they desire, without coercion or violation of conscience, while maintaining the Jewish character of the state and of the Jewish people in it." [4]

In the realm of personal status and the powers of the rabbinate, a number of laws were adopted which gave further legal sanction to the situation prevailing when the State of Israel, on its foundation, retained the Mandatory procedures.[5] These laws made "matters of marriage, divorce and maintenance between Jews the exclusive jurisdiction of rabbinical courts," and the religious court justices *(dayanim)* became state employees, with appointment procedures and status roughly comparable, *mutatis mutandis,* with those of judges in secular state courts.

Days of rest for Jews were fixed as the Sabbath (Saturday) and other Jewish holidays. A special ministerial committee, comprised almost automatically of two non-religious and one religious member (by virtue of the distribution of offices in the coalition), was empowered to authorize work in certain services or activities essential to the security or economy of Israel. This did not include public transportation from Friday sundown to Saturday night, with certain limited exceptions.

The serving of kosher food in the army was enjoined early in statehood, and actually most dining facilities operated by public institutions follow the same practice. Ben Gurion did not permit the establishment of separate "orthodox" units in the armed forces, but did agree to exempt talmudic students from the draft. The military made special arrangements, combining studies and military training, for those talmudic institutions which were prepared to cooperate with the state regarding the recruitment of their students. Religious women, originally exempted from military service, were made liable for "national service" — this in spite of strong opposition in Israel and abroad by the rabbinate and ultra-orthodox elements. However, this watered-down provision is a dead letter, and from time to time the question of military service for talmudic scholars and national service for orthodox women becomes grounds for public controversy.

While it may be true that within the limits set by the conflict there were elements of political extortion and opportunism, and that some or even many parts of the above-described compromise were against the will of the majority, this approach ignores the broad area of consensus. Ben Gurion and the non-religious parties took three basic factors into consideration: the sizable religiously-observant minority, the existing *status quo ante* 1948, and the inextricably interwoven patterns of religious and national life. Thus, though Ben Gurion certainly was not satisfied with details of the compromise he himself had helped to mold, there was an area of agreement and toleration which did to a great extent recognize historical customs and sociological facts, and was in consonance with his general approach to Jewish statehood. Since the views of the "interested majority" would shift from issue to issue, and no academic study has been made to indicate the extent of the floating opinion on these issues, it is difficult to go beyond the general assertion that within the boundaries set by conflict and political bargaining, a great deal of the national life-style relating to religious issues was consensually adopted.[6]

Not too long after leaving office, Ben Gurion tended to explain the compromise as a question of priorities. Personal status or kosher food was secondary to more urgent matters. He felt that, in the national interest, it was wise to retain the support of the religious parties for measures of vital concern to the state and to pay the comparatively small price of religious *status quo*.[7] Ben Gurion added that he had driven a hard bargain, and that although he had been unable to "keep religion completely out of politics, for religious parties existed," he had seen to it that Israel remained a secular state. He interpreted this as one "ruled by a secular government and not by a religious authority . . . ." He hoped that the religious would exercise their influence as pressure groups and public movements, rather than as parties.[8]

As is evident from Ben Gurion's statement above, the arrangement with the orthodox was cause for some apology. Certainly, the partnership with the orthodox seems *prima facie* a strange one: Mapai had a secular, socialist, and at times anti-religious coloration. However, over the years of partnership in the Zionist coalitions, the labor groups and the religious Zionists, particularly their labor element, had found a *modus vivendi.* For long-range strategic purposes, the religious were the easiest group with which to form a partnership, as they were least interested in pressing for independent policies relating to international and defense problems. That is to say, they were mostly inclined to go along with Ben Gurion on these issues, leaving him considerably more latitude than the left would. Furthermore, Ben Gurion's pragmatism found an excellent rationale: both the state and the people were in the making; wisdom therefore dictated putting off the decisions on basic state-religion relations to a later stage.

The clearest enunciation of these Fabian policies may be

found in the debate on a constitution for the new state. This subject is treated at greater length in Chapter 12. To summarize, in February 1950, the First Knesset began to debate the issue of adoption of a written constitution. The orthodox opposed this move, claiming that the Mosaic law was already Israel's constitution. One Agudah speaker said: "In a secular constitution we see an attempt at a divorce from our holy *Torah.*"[9] The left (Mapam) and right (Ḥerut) found themselves in uneasy alliance over the necessity for a constitution or bill of rights: the former in order to preserve and enshrine its labor ideology as a national heritage; the latter in order to defend itself and other minorities from deviation from constitutional freedoms through what they called a parliamentary "mechanical majority."[10] The gradualist line won. Left and right voted against and the orthodox abstained. Nonetheless, a "compromise" proposal, adopted in June 1950, directed the Knesset's "Constitution and Law Committee to prepare a draft constitution for the state . . . (which) shall be constructed section by section in such a manner that each shall in itself constitute a fundamental law . . . all the sections together shall comprise the State Constitution."[11] This of course meant that the dreaded *Kulturkampf* had been postponed, and that piecemeal legislation of specific, basic or "constitutional" issues would be enacted.

Ben Gurion briefly summarized his views on this gradualist strategy in early 1951. Characteristically, the rationale is *raisons d'état.*

> Whoever now wishes to stir up a war of religion . . . strikes at the soul of immigration and sabotages the security of the state . . . saving the nation and preserving its independence and security in this conflict-ridden and storm-tossed world have priority over any religious or anti-religious ideal.
> Necessarily, in this period of laying foundations, people of differing principles and varying interests must work together . . . in an effort to concentrate the people in its

land . . . and when the great hour comes the ingathered
nation will decide the great questions.[12]

STATE EDUCATION

The problem of unifying Israel's educational patterns was much
more complicated. The masses of new immigrants streaming
into an Israel which was to double its Jewish population within
four years came from two major sources: Eastern Europe and
Arab lands. In both cases, there were considerable numbers of
orthodox or traditional, observant immigrants. The question
arose as to the type of education which would be provided in the
camps and new villages set up for the immigrants. At that time,
political "trends" dominated separate school systems: labor,
"general" (non-labor), and two orthodox (the more moderate,
Zionist Mizrachi and the more rigid and non-Zionist Agudah).

  The conflict in the cabinet reached crisis proportions in early
February 1951. Labor proposed a compromise, whereby the
children of *all* Yemenite immigrants would join orthodox
schools and children of other orthodox parents would be
registered in the school of their choice. The orthodox were
apprehensive about the application of this proposal, and were
especially disquieted by the fact that the labor movement was
sponsoring religious schools within the labor trend. Ben Gurion,
at a meeting of the Knesset members of all coalition parties,
admitted that "education raises storms. Indeed the issue
extends down into the depths [of Jewish existence and future]
and there are also party interests involved."[13] The orthodox
wished to have four inspectors appointed in each school district,
one from each trend (labor, general, Mizrachi and Agudah), to
oversee all the religious-education schools. Ben Gurion opposed
the proposal on the grounds that this would accord the
orthodox a monopoly over religious education, in that their two
representatives would also be supervising religious schools of the
labor trend.

  The debate gave Ben Gurion an opportunity to trade biblical
citations with his opponents, an opportunity he never let pass.

At the root was his view that his (or his group's) secular interpretation of Judaism was as valid as that of the orthodox. Politically, though, the tactical consideration for bringing the crisis to a head was to demarcate a line behind which his party would not retreat, a line which would indicate to the orthodox the outer limits of realistic bargaining, beyond which their demands would become counter-productive. On the strategic level, Ben Gurion was laying the groundwork for a national education system which would abolish the trends. Allowing the trends to dig in deeper would make it costlier to diminish their influence or uproot them totally when the time came.

In the Knesset, Ben Gurion threw down the gauntlet. The government's proposals were final; take them or leave them. The vote would be one of confidence in the cabinet.[14] The right wing and the left jumped on the orthodox bandwagon, forcing Ben Gurion's resignation. By law, the resignation of the prime minister obliged the resignation of the government (cabinet), which would carry on as a caretaker until new elections. That summer (1951) the elections produced no basic changes, in the sense of providing a majority for any single party. The right wing made considerable gains, but not at the expense of either Mapai or the orthodox. The General Zionists improved their position at the expense of Ḥerut, and the left-wing Mapam declined. Perhaps the most significant change in terms of future coalitions was the breach in the short-lived United Religious Front, with the Zionist Mizrachi—ha-Po'el ha-Mizrachi separating from the Agudah factions.

Seven weeks passed from the date Ben Gurion received his mandate from the president until he carried it out and presented his cabinet to the Knesset. The elections had provided a breather, and the new government decided to lengthen the caesura by deferring the state education issue for a year. It was a somewhat narrower coalition: the Progressives did not enter at that time, and only the four religious parties joined with Mapai. According to Ben Gurion's own testimony to the Knesset, 55 separate negotiating sessions were held with the various parties.[15] The newly-strengthened General Zionists apparently had tried to overplay their advantage; their demands, particularly for cabinet representation and control of key portfolios, boomeranged. Mapam, under its ha-Shomer ha-Tza'ir majority, displayed ideological rigidity, particularly in foreign policy (big-power orientation), and its participation had to wait for the next elections, following the split in its ranks.

Though in the ensuing Knesset debate Ben Gurion stressed his desire for a broad coalition, he was not ready to broaden his basic policy, or water down his principles sufficiently for either left or right. These principles as well as Mapai control of key ministries were more important than superficial "national unity" cabinets which would interfere with his grand designs. [16]

To return to his coalition difficulties with the religious parties, and the limits of negotiability he displayed, the new government was barely a year old when a new crisis arose. The coalition agreement of October 1951 had determined a year's moratorium on the major issues in question, and particularly the State Education Law (the word *mamlakhti* — national or state — appears here) which was designed to abolish the four-trend system in elementary schools. [17] The crisis was again one on which Ben Gurion was unwilling to compromise, though the issue was explosive at home and abroad. The ultra-orthodox coalition members organized demonstrations in Israel and overseas, particularly in New York, enlisting their sympathizers to paint Israel as a Godless state. It was resolved by the withdrawal of the Agudah from the coalition and the entry of the General Zionists and Progressives in December 1952.

At this point the State Education Law deserves some analysis, embodying as it does, both in its name and concept, the idea of state primacy, one of Ben Gurion's central aims. During the earlier coalition crisis over religious education, Ben Gurion had inveighed not only against "this miserable regime of [educational] trends" but against the inheritance of "sick, despicable and hindersome fragmentation . . . which bears within it not only the poison of *cabinet crises,* but also the venom of the *crisis of national-state purpose* (mamlakhtiyut)." [18] The four-trend system was an improvement, when viewed against the background of the fragmented political scene. Though the number of parties contesting the 1951 elections was smaller than that in 1949 (17 in place of 21), those actually returned to the Knesset showed an increase from 12 to 15. Nonetheless, the four trends would guarantee continued politicization of education. Ben Gurion saw this as being as undesirable as a politicized army, against which he had acted almost immediately after statehood.

The Law provided for two "state-national" trends: state and state-religious. The obvious desiratum of outright unification of all schools into a single national system was unattainable. Two systems, though less desirable than one, were preferable to four. The state (non-religious) system would cover all but the obviously orthodox schools, and implement a single pattern of education, a system obtaining in all countries deemed worthy of emulation by the proponents of the Law. There was the additional danger of the labor-trend schools becoming more and more fragmented as the left-right, pro-Soviet—anti-Stalinist dichotomy grew. The orthodox or religious trend would guarantee a greater measure of homogeneity in the camp of the observant.

There was a loophole, however, for those orthodox groups which would not accept state control of education. "Recognized educational institutions" could receive financial support from the ministry of education, which would exercise minimal control and supervision of a "basic curriculum."[19] This eventually led to a ramified "independent school system" maintained by the Agudah, whose subsidization from the state rose in proportion to cabinet crises. Labor also sacrificed its control over the religious-trend schools operated by its religious satellites, since authority to supervise the state-religious system was vested in a council which had a preponderance of Mizrachi members. (It is also worth noting that usually an official of that party has held the key position in the ministry of education's administration of state-religious education.) Nonetheless, the adoption of state education did create a greater sense of unity and in theory provided a platform not overtly under party control, and thus could eventually bring about reform in practice as well. Ben Gurion saw the two-trend system as a major achievement.

> There are not many days in Jewish history which can compete in importance and grandeur with May 14, 1948, the day of the Declaration of the State of Israel; but the day upon which State Education was proclaimed by the Government of Israel [November 8, 1951] is also worthy of being recorded in our history. The removal of education from the sphere of parties and its establishment under the authority of the government are a decisive step toward the strengthening of the state and the unification of the nation.[20]

WHO IS A JEW?

However, the most important — and perhaps the most persistent — religious crisis was the controversy about "Who is a Jew?" The Law of Return, passed in 1950, had recognized that "every Jew has the right to come to [Israel] as an *'oleh*," this being a term more laden with historic overtones than the neutral word "immigrant."[21] From time to time, the minister of the interior, usually a member of the Mizrachi (National Religious Party — NRP), issued administrative orders defining the terms of the Law. The ministry was also charged with registering citizens and issuing them identity cards in which both "religion" and "nationality" *(le'om)* are recorded. In 1958, the incumbent minister of the interior (rather unusually, he was a member of Aḥdut ha-'Avodah) issued instructions regarding registration, according to which "any person declaring in good faith that he is a Jew, shall be registered as a Jew and no additional proof shall be required." The government added the qualification that the registrant not be of another religion. The instructions also permitted parents of a child to register him as a Jew, even if his mother was not Jewish.[22] This flouted the orthodox position, which obliges the formal conversion of a child of a non-Jewish mother, and forced the resignation of the National Religious Party representatives in the cabinet.

On July 11, 1958, Ben Gurion informed the Knesset of the resignations and stated that he would not nominate replacements in the hope that the National Religious Party would reconsider.[23] NRP spokesmen in the Knesset defended their position: the new regulations were "in outright opposition to the way-of-life of the people," and destroyed "the wall which preserved the Jewish people for thousands of years." They admitted that the problems occasioned by the arrival of non-Jews married to Jewish spouses had in some cases been resolved in line with orthodox practice. There were other cases (among the recently arrived immigrants from Poland and Rumania, which again permitted Jews to leave) in which the non-Jewish partner had not abandoned his previous religion. The Jewish people should not change its national and religious character for the sake of these few cases. They accused Ben Gurion of upsetting the *status quo*, "not only of the inter-party coalition agreement, but that ... which existed in the Jewish people since its beginnings as a nation."[24]

Ben Gurion did not debate the issues of principle at that time, nor did he insist on carrying out the government's decision. He found a way that obliged him neither to gainsay his left-wing partners, with whose point of view in this case he agreed, nor to force a principle decision which might shatter his unwritten pact with the orthodox. He closed the debate with the following brief statement:

> There is, in my opinion, no Jewry anywhere in the world more rooted, true, rich in content and original than in Israel. And often have I stated in the name of the government that this is a state of law and not of *Halakhah* (orthodox religious law).[25]

The reference to a "state of law" rather than Halakhah is Ben Gurion's way of stressing the sovereignty of the Knesset in religious matters. If some halakhic regulations are given force of law, it is by delegation of the Knesset's power of legislation. Halakhah, according to this approach, has no autonomous validity in Israel's state or legislative life.

Ben Gurion announced that the government had appointed the minister of the interior, the minister of justice and himself to reformulate registration regulations for children of mixed marriages, "which will be adapted both to the accepted tradition of all circles in Judaism, orthodox and free-thinkers . . . as well as to the specific conditions of Israel as a sovereign Jewish state, in which freedom of conscience and religion are guaranteed and as a center for the ingathering of the dispersion." These regulations would be drafted upon receipt of the opinions of Israeli and Jewish rabbis, scholars, writers and other intellectuals.

At the end of October 1968, Ben Gurion wrote a carefully worded and lengthy letter to some 50 selected spiritual and intellectual figures, so-called "sages." In the letter he explained that for security reasons it was necessary that Israeli residents bear identity cards in which both "religion" and "nationality" are registered.

> The question has arisen as to how to register, under "religion" and "nationality," children born of mixed marriages, with a Jewish father and a non-Jewish mother who did not convert to Judaism, but both agree that their children be registered as Jews. There are those who say that since registration is a civil matter and does not serve religious purposes . . . we should not follow religious standards; there are others who say that one cannot separate "religion" and "nationality" . . . we should follow the religious standards both in registering nationality and religion.

Ben Gurion further explained that the public policy of the state was to guarantee freedom of conscience and to prevent coercion of a pro- or anti-religious nature. Israel was ingathering the dispersed Jewish communities and "efforts must be made to heighten that which is joint and unifying and remove as far as possible that which divides and sets them apart." The Jews of Israel are the majority; there was no danger of their being assimilated into a foreign culture, to the contrary.

> On the other hand, the people in Israel does not see itself separate from the Jewish people in the Diaspora, but just the opposite. There is no Jewish community in the world which lives with such a deep feeling of unity and identification with the totality of Jews in the world as does the Jewish community in [Israel]. Not by chance do the Basic Principles of the government say that[it] will see to "the deepening of Jewish consciousness among Israeli youth, rooting it in the past of the Jewish people and its historic heritage; and heightening its moral connection with world Jewry out of the recognition of the community of destiny and the historic continuity which unites the Jews of the entire world down the generations and in their lands."[26]

Replies came in over the following months. The overwhelming majority supported the orthodox position. Not surprisingly, all the orthodox rabbis rejected the new proposals; some were angered that opinions of non-orthodox Jews were polled, while others were incensed at questions being addressed to rabbinical authorities outside Israel. The Conservative rabbis backed the orthodox stand. More liberal authorities, even among the orthodox, sought to create a transitional category; Hebrew, Jewish resident, resident convert as opposed to "righteous" (or permanent) convert, and so on. A preliminary study of 46 replies shows only two definitely supporting a change from the halakhic ruling. Some of the attempts at a compromise are interesting: one proposal was to make the Halakhah palatable by entrusting its administration to the secular authorities: a kind of Rousseau-like civic religion, along the lines of Soviet marriage and divorce procedures. At any rate, if Ben Gurion sought a way out of the difficulties, the opportunity now presented itself, a face-saving line of retreat.

In the meantime, in December 1958, Ben Gurion announced to the Knesset the appointment of an elderly Sefardi rabbi, Ya'akov Moshe Toledano, to the vacant post of minister for religious affairs. The orthodox spoke of the breaking up of "Mapai's partnership of many years with national-religious Jewry."[27]

Ben Gurion took the opportunity to deliver a brief dissertation on the question of state and religion. He stressed that the religious parties had signed the Declaration of Independence, whose final editing was at his hands. Not only had the declaration not obliged observance of orthodox law, but it had actually included guarantees which were in distinct opposition to the Halakhah. There were two such examples, he said: equal civil rights regardless of sex, religion, race or national origin, and freedom of conscience and religion. The government's Basic Principles, endorsed by all coalition partners including the orthodox, had forbidden both religious and anti-religious coercion.

He added that he would accept the supremacy of orthodox law, if, as he had told a group of orthodox American rabbis, a million orthodox Jews moved to Israel and decided to base Israeli law on the orthodox codes. "I would assume this lovingly and would do all that was written [in the orthodox code of laws], for the addition of a million Jews is more important to me than even freedom of conscience and religion." The address was interrupted by an Aḥdut ha-'Avodah member who shouted, "But they must decide this by means of the Knesset! " Ben Gurion replied, "Certainly, only by elections to the Knesset, not in the office of the rabbinate."[28]

Again, the point made is that of Knesset supremacy. As for Ben Gurion's foregoing his freedom of conscience for the sake of another million Jews living in Israel, this would seem to be oratorical hyperbole, designed to stress his overall national interest in strengthening Israel. Nonetheless, stripped of exaggeration, it does indicate a scale of values. Israel's strength is more important than the content or life-style of its society.

On this occasion, Ben Gurion repeated that his committee was awaiting the replies of the "sages" to its enquiry about the registration of children of mixed marriages. In the meantime, the regulations contested by the NRP were shelved.

The denouement to this story of political misjudgment came in December 1959, when Ben Gurion presented his new cabinet, which included the NRP. He returned Toledano as minister for religious affairs: to drop him would have been too embarrassing. The following Basic Principle regarding "Religion in the State" was read out by Ben Gurion:

> In this period of ingathering the dispersions, Jewish communities, having been for hundreds of years under the influence of widely divergent cultures and environments, are divided in their points of view and opinions and differ in their customs and manners. The unification of the nation and an orderly state life demand the development of mutual tolerance and the freedom of conscience and religion. The government will prevent religious or anti-religious coercion from whatever source, will guarantee the provision of public religious needs by means of the state, will maintain freedom of religion and conscience for the non-Jewish communities . . . and will guarantee religious education for those children whose parents so desire. [29]

With slight variations in wording, this is exactly the same statement as that made by Ben Gurion in presenting his government four years earlier. [30] It is an expansion of the same idea expressed eight years earlier on a similar occasion. [31] However, there was an important addition: *"The government will maintain the* status quo *in the state with regard to matters of religion."* [32] The head of the NRP, Moshe Ḥayyim Shapiro, was appointed minister of the interior. The Mapai—NRP collaboration was restored.

The restoration indicates a return to Ben Gurion's basic pragmatism with regard to religion. He had temporarily permitted himself to deviate from it, as a result of the efforts of the left — efforts which Ben Gurion had supported and brought to the previous stage, shattering for a time the tried partnership with the religious. It seems clear that he would have preferred to impose his will on the orthodox. This was impossible. Their leaving the coalition presented two dangers: one political, the other national.

On the national scene, the tension between the orthodox and secular camps would probably have reached the breaking point, without the mitigating factor of the NRP's conciliatory influence. Politically, Ben Gurion would have been almost totally at the mercy of the left wing: Aḥdut ha-'Avodah and Mapam. His freedom of action in security and foreign affairs, and particularly his rapprochement with Germany, would have been limited by reducing his field of maneuverability. The "sages of Israel," who obviously would have opted for Halakhah, made it possible for him to retreat in dignity.

At this point, one may ask why, given Ben Gurion's experience with the orthodox and his political acumen, did he find it necessary to support the proposed change in registration procedures. One of Ben Gurion's close aides has offered the following explanation: left to his own initiative, he would not have proposed the change. Once the new regulations were placed on the cabinet table, he felt conscience-bound to support them as they were in consonance with his own beliefs. [33]

In the final analysis, the religious establishments proved to be stronger than Ben Gurion: they bent with resilience, but not beyond the point of demoting halakhic considerations in the civil registration process. Pragmatism dictated Ben Gurion's surrender. National policy interests took precedence over his personal convictions and those of his party and its other non-orthodox coalition partners.

This conflict, when added to other points of friction within the coalition, especially the succession and Lavon issues, helped dim the leader's charisma (see Chapter 13.) Ill-advised to enter the fray, Ben Gurion emerged from it battered and ailing.

CHAPTER SEVEN

Defense

In the previous chapters, we have discussed attempts to assert state primacy over institutions which predate the establishment of Israel. This chapter will deal with state-building through an instrumentality which achieved publicly recognized status only with the creation of the state. State primacy will be explored from the vantage point of the legal and institutionalized creation of Israel's armed forces and defense ministry. This led to the disbanding of rival military organizations and the depoliticization of the armed forces and their effective civilian control.

Since Ben-Gurion's first responsibility was to maintain Israel's existence, and this, in his view, could only be guaranteed by military deterrent superiority, security policy will be discussed. The essence of this policy may be described as the ensuring of state existence so that the instrument of statehood would be able to assert primacy for its purpose of gathering Jews into Israel and building a viable society. This will be analyzed both from the point of view of institution-building and of defense policy vis-à-vis the Arab states. It will be seen that the principle of Israeli survival through strength was matched by a pragmatic use of power. Principles and pragmatism were merged in a single-minded effort to raise Israel to the status of a power in the Middle East, whose future would never be in question. This, Ben Gurion believed, was the prerequisite for Arab recognition and for peace. Once the Arabs acknowledged Israel's permanence, negotiations and peace would eventually come about.

Ben Gurion's role as military leader in the War of Independence of 1948 will not be considered here. This is not a military history, nor does the author possess the qualifications of a military historian. It shall be taken as read that Ben Gurion "determined the courses of the struggle . . . singlehandedly, the advances and the retreats, the achievements and the failures."[1]

UNIFYING THE ARMY

In effect, Ben Gurion's role as minister of defense predated statehood. From the beginning of 1947, he had been charged with direct responsibility for defense and security affairs in the Jewish Agency—Zionist Organization. At the time of the establishment of the state, the Jewish forces consisted of one large framework — the Haganah — which accepted legitimate Zionist Organization political discipline and general decisions, and two "dissident" groups — Etzel and Lehi. The Haganah was under the direction of the Jewish Agency, though in practice the labor elements dominated it. Within the Haganah, the permanently mobilized *Palmah* units had their own command, and were under the influence of the left-wing ha-Kibbutz ha-Me'uhad federation. Etzel (acronym for *Irgun Tzeva'i Le'umi* — National Military Organization) had not accepted Jewish Agency discipline. It was an offshoot of the Revisionist Zionists who had left the World Zionist Organization in 1935. In 1937 Etzel formed its own units. Lehi (*Lohamei Herut Yisra'el* — Fighters for the Freedom of Israel) had broken off from Etzel over policy vis-à -vis the British after the outbreak of World War II (September 1940). In May 1948, Etzel numbered about 3,000 and Lehi about 500 men, at most. The Haganah could field close to 45,000 men, mostly reserves.[2]

With the advent of statehood, Ben Gurion's basic plan was to transform Israel's army into a regular force. He turned away from partisan tradition fostered by conditions of secrecy and by the voluntaristic and egalitarian mystique of the Palmaḥ. He saw the military forces as an arm of government, which consequently must be under civilian authority and control. In his capacity as head of government and minister of defense, both before the establishment of the state and afterward, his aim was to exercise personal, civilian control over the armed forces. Depoliticization in this sense meant stripping political parties of influence on or control of armed groups; conversely it meant a chain of command headed by Ben Gurion. He had to wage a constant battle at the top level of government to win support for his point of view. On May 12, 1948, two days prior to the proclamation of Israel's independence, in the proto-cabinet (Minhelet ha-'Am: the People's Administration), Ben Gurion threatened not to head the ministry of defense unless his policy of civilian control of a unified force was adopted.

> If the system now existing in defense matters
> continues . . . I shall not accept the defense portfolio; the
> multiplicity of authorities is very dangerous. Without a
> decision to adopt two principles:
> 1. That the army and all parts of the army be subject to
> the rule of the people and only the rule of the people —
> now the People's Administration, and hopefully in a few
> months an elected government;
> 2. That all who act in the Haganah or the army act only in
> those areas of authority delegated them by the elected
> government, and this applies to a platoon or division
> commander and to the chief of staff:
> Without these two principles being guaranteed I shall not
> accept the defense portfolio . . . . Anarchy and state are two
> opposing concepts, especially in wartime and especially in
> a war for life and death.[3]

Given the apparatus of statehood, Ben Gurion determined to exercise close control over the former Haganah, and to unify and depoliticize Israel's armed forces emerging from the underground.

On May 20, 1948, less than a week after the proclamation of statehood, the Mizrachi leadership claimed that its party "had been discriminated against in appointments to the defense establishment" *inter alia.* Ben Gurion proposed that the provisional government appoint a committee to investigate the politics of his appointees since 1947, when he assumed the defense portfolio. According to Ben Gurion, of 15 appointees, chosen on the recommendation of Yisra'el Galili of Mapam (the Aḥdut ha-'Avodah wing), who had been serving as chief of the National Command of the Haganah, only one was from his own party, another had been non-party, while all the rest came from other parties, mainly Mapam. Ben Gurion told the cabinet that:

> . . . never did I ask about the political affiliation of a man whom I appointed, and I will not continue with the defense portfolio if it will not be guaranteed that the *entire army be subject to the government . . . and only to it,* and that all the soldiers and units of the army be equal in rights and that each commander operate solely according to the defined authority given him by the government.[4]

The cabinet accepted Ben Gurion's approach on May 23, and three days later it published the Ordinance for the Establishment of the Israel Defense Forces (IDF). The key provision of the Ordinance of May 26, 1948, prohibited the "establishment or maintenance of any other armed force." As a matter of course, the minister of defense was made responsible for executing the order. A short while later, Ben Gurion said that with the promulgation of the ordinance, "the Haganah shed its character as an underground organization and has become a regular army."[5]

Ben Gurion was still referring solely to the Haganah. It was only on June 3, 1948, that the commander of Etzel signed an agreement according to which his forces were to be bound by Israel government conscription and mobilization orders. The arrangement provided for a transfer of arms and an end to separate arms procurement and manufacture. Ben Gurion later complained that Etzel's arms were not turned over in full to the IDF. In the initial period of the absorption of Etzel into the army, about 1,000 men joined the IDF, under terms which permitted their continued existence as separate formations within the various regular brigades, "for the sake of [family] peace."[6]

Toward the end of June, the Etzel brought a ship called the *Altalena* (*nom de plume* of Vladimir Zeev Jabotinsky, the late Revisionist leader) from France to Israel, laden with 900 men, 5,000 rifles, hundreds of light machine guns, five armored half-tracks and quantities of bombs and other ammunition. It arrived during the first Arab-Israel truce, a period in which the UN mediator had ruled against the import of arms. Negotiations had taken place between the Israel government and Etzel regarding the use of the weapons and their destination. Although there are charges of breach of faith from both sides, it is a fact that fire was exchanged when the *Altalena* first berthed at Kfar Vitkin, north of Tel Aviv, and later at Tel Aviv itself, where the Etzel wished to land the arms and men. First, regular Haganah units engaged Etzel members who had previously joined the IDF, but had been mobilized by their former commanders to help with the unloading. In 48 hours at Kfar Vitkin both sides suffered losses: IDF — two killed, six wounded; Etzel — six killed, 18 wounded. Then, at Tel Aviv, units mainly of Palmaḥ prevented the unloading by force, in accordance with Ben Gurion's orders. By accident or, more likely, by design, artillery fire hit the ship which exploded. The Etzel men aboard again suffered a number of losses, and those who jumped overboard were, according to Haganah sources, helped ashore by their former adversaries.[7] The incident left a deep scar.

Although by the time of the *Altalena* incident Israel's arms supply had increased significantly, as compared to the pitiful amount in its hands a year or so earlier, the quantity of arms destroyed on the *Altalena* was far from negligible. Beyond this, moral damage was incurred; the facade of Jewish unity was broken.

At a cabinet meeting on June 22, the day the *Altalena* moved berth from Kfar Vitkin to Tel Aviv, Ben Gurion had blocked last-minute partisan attempts at mediation for the following reasons:

> What happened endangers our war effort, and in addition it endangers the state. For the state cannot exist as long as it has no army and *no control over the army.* This is an attempt to destroy the army, an attempt to murder the state. These are the two questions, and on these questions there can, in my opinion, be no compromise. If tragically it will be necessary to fight over this — fight we must. The moment the army and the state give in to another armed force, there will be nothing left for us to do.[8]

Ben Gurion later justified his action by warning that Etzel would have used the arms for a political take-over of the state. Naturally Etzel denied this; it is of course difficult to predict what might have happened if the internal arms balance had shifted so drastically. Wittingly or unwittingly, Ben Gurion had acted out Weber's definition "that a state is a human community that (successfully) claims the *monopoly of the legitimate use of physical force* within a given territory."[9]

The matter of the threat from the right as seen by Ben Gurion and his followers was not settled. Only in September did Etzel disband its separate command and units in Jerusalem, following a stiff ultimatum issued on September 20, 1948. The timing was important. On September 17, Count Folke Bernadotte, the UN mediator, had been assassinated by members of the so-called "Fatherland Front" (actually a cover for Lehi). The international reaction and the shock which ensued in the Yishuv set the stage for the crackdown. The language of the ultimatum proposed by Ben Gurion and approved by a special committee of the provisional government headed by him, was unequivocal. Etzel members were:

. . . to accept in practice as well as in theory the law of the state regarding the army, mobilization and arms, to hand over all arms in their possession to the IDF, to disband the special units of Etzel, to transfer all those liable for military call-up in Etzel to the IDF, and the status of members of Etzel is to be like the status of every other Jew. If the demands of the government are not met, the army will move, using all means at its disposal. [10]

The last phrase was no empty threat. In spite of the invasion and war waged by forces from five Arab countries augmented by irregulars, the IDF had reorganized, expanded, and absorbed locally mobilized recruits, as well as recent arrivals from the displaced-persons camps of Europe. By October of that year, the IDF had about 90,000 men and women on its roster. [11] Etzel accepted the ultimatum and its separate units were disbanded and absorbed into the IDF. At the same time, about 200 Lehi soldiers were detained in Jerusalem in connection with the Bernadotte assassination, and later released. This ended the separate existence of Lehi as well, since its members outside of Jerusalem had joined the IDF even before the first agreement with Etzel.

Having settled the problem on the right, Ben Gurion then turned to the left. The personal and ideological differences in Mapai had by 1944 led to a split in its ranks. A more doctrinaire socialist group, which also had opposed the various partition proposals of 1937 and 1946-7, centered on one of the federations of collectives called ha-Kibbutz ha-Me'uhad. It had played an active role in the Haganah and provided leadership and training facilities in its affiliated kibbutzim. In 1941, the Haganah formed its shock troop detachments, the Palmah, which was a permanent force of volunteers who did national service on kibbutzim, usually spending half of each month working and half of each month engaged in military training. Members of ha-Kibbutz ha-Me'uhad dominated the Palmah. [12] In January 1948, the Ahdut ha-'Avodah splinter from Mapai, based on its ha-Kibbutz ha-Me'uhad membership, formed a joint political party with the even more doctrinaire socialist *ha-Kibbutz ha-Artzi* federation of ha-Shomer ha-Tza'ir. The party, Mapam, had a pro-Soviet orientation.

Ben Gurion therefore saw the Palmah as presenting a threat to his doctrine of a unified command and a single army and, because of its specific political loyalty, a potential political challenge to his party's power and his own leadership. This was particularly true in view of the fact that the Palmah had developed a mystique of its own and had won growing popularity by dint of its actions before and during the war. Ben Gurion moved against the Palmah a few days after settling with the right. On September 29, 1948, he instructed the then chief of staff, General Ya'akov Dori, to disband the separate staff HQ of the Palmah and to place its units under the direct control of the IDF High Command. Ben Gurion laconically wrote some ten years later, that "the Palmah brigades obeyed this order."[13]

Actually, though, things were certainly not that simple. In mid-September 1948 he had tried to convince a meeting of Palmah commanders, almost all of them members of Mapam, that the Palmah did not require its own separate staff. Later, at a meeting of the IDF General Staff, Ben Gurion explained that the army was to be a single, united force, organized on the professional lines of a regular army: ". . . with the creation of the state, the entire army is subordinate only and solely to one authority, the government of Israel, and its organization has been adapted to the war needs of regular armies and not to the tradition of the Haganah." The government was, in this sense, the minister of defense.

The Palmah, with its separate command and its own recruitment and quartermaster support, was an anomaly. With his usual acumen, Ben Gurion touched *en passant* on the main issue, which was the major reason for disbanding the Palmah staff. Referring to his meeting with the Palmah officers, he said, "Only a few claimed that the Palmah has its own special ideology, and *no one argued (at any rate, not openly) that the Palmah had special political or party tendencies . . . .*"[14] This was the background for Dori's orders.

It took General Dori over a week just to frame the order and send it to the Palmaḥ HQ. Its phrasing is rather apologetic, explaining that the three Palmaḥ brigades would be deployed more efficiently if they were under the direct command of the General Staff; their separate chain of command created over-lapping authority among the three command elements (General Staff, front or area commands, and Palmaḥ HQ); and that this wasted manpower and lowered efficiency. The timetable of transfer of functions, including conscription, training and education, were to be worked out with the acting commander of Palmaḥ and the relevant IDF General Staff departments. It was hardly a laconic order.[15]

A month was required for its implementation, following an appeal to the Supreme Command by Palmaḥ HQ, for the continuation of its separate identity. The appeal was based on three points: the commando and attack nature of the Palmaḥ, its unique *esprit de corps,* and the merging of the "pioneering" agricultural and military aspects which embraced all the pioneer youth movements.

Ben Gurion replied to the argument by hoisting the Palmaḥ with its own petard:

> I believe that pioneering values must be shared by all
> military formations . . . . I do not believe that pioneering is
> the monopoly of the select few . . . . Whoever is qualified to
> convey pioneering values to the army should do so on
> behalf of the entire army . . . and has no need to
> emphasize that activity only within certain brigades. There
> is no need for a separate national HQ of the Palmaḥ for
> that purpose.[16]

The deeper justification, which Ben Gurion did not stress at the time, was framed by his long-time friend, Shlomo Lavie, who wrote in a newspaper article a few months prior to the disbandment: "If one party maintains a private army, all the parties will organize private armies of their own . . . ."[17] Ben Gurion saw fit to include this and the lengthy surrounding citation in his *The Restored State of Israel*. Lavie had expressed what Ben Gurion thought: state primacy would not abide armed particularist rivals.

The removal of the challenge from the right and left saw Ben Gurion in charge of a largely united army, still in the process of formation as it fought, but whose basic principles of organization and control were established. It was in this formative period that Ben Gurion also decided not to maintain separate units for orthodox soldiers. Such orthodox units would of course ease the question of these soldiers' religious observance, but he felt that the danger of an entire unit of one special type being decimated in battle was an overwhelming negative consideration. He may also have had other reasons at the back of his mind: the prohibition of politically or ideologically separate forces.[18]

In brief, in addition to playing a leading role in the creation of an army under conditions of war and mass immigration, and taking basic strategic decisions on the conduct of the battles, Ben Gurion at the same time was able to create a unified high command over all branches and forces, under a single chief of staff, and a depoliticized army, loyal to himself and to the government, free from political intervention in the choice of officers and in their advancement. Recent information indicates that Ben Gurion hesitated to appoint area commanders from the Palmaḥ ranks in the newly organized or reorganizing forces in the fall of 1948, though the acting chief of staff, General Yigael Yadin, recommended these postings. This raises the question of depoliticization and meritocracy. One can assume that Yadin's choice was based on merit; Ben Gurion's objections stemmed from political distrust. Depoliticization, as defined by Ben Gurion, called for prohibition of extra-governmental control or influence. Presumably this is the reason why he deferred taking the decision to make the appointments, though Yadin claims that the absence of area commanders seriously hampered the conduct of war. One must then conclude that even Ben Gurion was not able to distinguish between loyalty to the government, i.e., the cabinet, and loyalty to the minister of defense, i.e., himself.[19] As the war abated and the institutions crystallized, it became necessary to give these frameworks and practices a legal basis in the new Knesset, Israel's first elected parliament, which replaced the previous temporarily appointed emergency administration.

CIVILIAN CONTROL

Within the first two years of statehood, a dozen laws and ordinances governing the minister of defense's powers and the organization and regulation of the IDF were enacted. The key piece of legislation was the Defense Law of September 1949, which established the basic organization of the IDF.[20] The law should be seen in the context of one of Ben Gurion's fundamental strategy approaches. Because of its importance, the speeches and debates relating to this law will be given at some length. In introducing the law, Ben Gurion voiced the Israeli version of the encirclement theory.

> Our country is but a small section in the midst of a
> gigantic . . . territory, completely inhabited by Arabic-
> speaking peoples . . . . We are few, and even if our numbers
> should increase, we shall remain a tiny minority in the
> midst of an Arab sea.[21]

There were, he said, a number of factors which would build up Israel's security, aside from the army itself. There was mass immigration; land settlement and dispersion of the population as a first line of defense; autarky in food production and in arms manufacture; improving land and sea communications; improving the health of young people and of the nation; and finally "a most important factor in the area of defense" — an active foreign policy aimed at reaching peace. It is significant that preparedness for war preceded peace as a policy.

Ben Gurion described in his speech the future format of the IDF: a small professional cadre, and large reserves, which would cluster around this cadre. The reserves would come from a general conscription of men and women who would begin their military training and service at the age of 18. A fourth element would be the border villages.

This law provided for the universal conscription of men and women for military training and service. Married women and mothers were automatically exempted, while orthodox women could be exempted upon request. The reserves (men up to the age of 49 and women up to the age of 34) were liable for service up to 14 days a year on active duty. Before joining the reserves, men were to serve for a two-year period and women for one year from the age of 18.[22] The law made provision for the establishment of a mobilization office in the ministry of defense to deal with this. Conscripts, with the exception of those enlisted into the air force and navy, were required to serve up to a year on agricultural duty, upon completion of their basic training. The law, Ben Gurion said, was thus based on two fundamental requirements of Israel's defense: "military ability and pioneering ability."[23]

The defense minister, who was made responsible to the Knesset for the execution of the law, was given authority which made him for all intents and purposes commander-in-chief.[24] He was empowered to mobilize the entire reserves, or part of them, without previous consultation with the Knesset, at any time that "the security of Israel is at stake." He was required to bring the mobilization order before the Knesset Foreign Affairs and Security Committee "at the earliest possible opportunity." There was a built-in veto, in that the order was to be approved by the committee within 14 days; otherwise, it would be void. The committee was free to approve the order with or without alterations, or it could void the order or decide to bring it before the plenum of the Knesset.

Two factors enhancing the minister's power in this regard merit mention here. First, the time-limit clause is of little effect. In the Sinai Campaign of 1956, the period from full mobilization to the end of the campaign was less than two weeks. Second, the committee would provide an accurate reflection of the majority strength within the Knesset, and since labor always had a plurality in the Knesset and a majority in the coalition, it was almost a foregone conclusion that the head of government, who was also minister of defense during most of the Ben Gurion period, would invariably gain the committee's backing.[25]

The creation of easily mobilized reserves, which was the major organizational provision of the law, was necessary, Ben Gurion said, since the structure of the Haganah was insufficient to ensure Israel's future security. Again, it was his penchant for a large state-controlled organization, better exemplified by the British army tradition than the underground Haganah-Palmaḥ experience, which was being expressed. "The ability of an army today is measured mainly by its capability to carry out combined operations involving large military units: battalions, brigades and divisions; and in the combined operations of land, air and sea forces."[26]

Furthermore, Ben Gurion, while wishing to create a regular army organization, at the same time wanted to preserve and routinize the charisma of the kibbutz return-to-the-land, and the "pioneer" philosophy which had motivated him personally as well as the Haganah in general and the Palmaḥ in particular. Thus, universal military training was to include service on the land. This would help inculcate in the recently arrived immigrants a new identification with Israel, erasing their previous Diaspora experience and building their self-pride.[27]

There is of course an implicit conflict between the informality and voluntarism of the kibbutz-based underground, and a serried and ordered army. Ben Gurion tried to resolve this by providing within the army both the "pioneering" framework and the educational element which was to preserve the essence while the form changed. The depoliticized army would help overcome sectoral and ideological cleavages. "Only the army can and must serve as the unifying factor . . . shaping the new form of the nation . . . ."[28]

As usual, Ben Gurion was the butt of attacks from both right and left in the ensuing debate. The left claimed that he was an *étatist*, demolishing pioneer values. Its Mapam spokesman insisted that the soldier must be political and ideological, the armed exponent of the idea. The law making the IDF one of the nation's principal educators, he claimed, bypassed the political parties and thus tended to foster ideological uniformity. It jeopardized voluntarism and fostered centralism, rather than the "people's army" which Palmaḥ had been. The latter remark was perhaps a romantic recollection of the early volunteer and egalitarian Red Army of 1917. The permanent army cadre would lead, he thought, to the creation of a military *élite*.[29] The moderate right (General Zionist) spokesman wanted to restore the public committees which had functioned alongside the Haganah, and to charge them with a status similar to that of a draft board, both for conscription and for reserves duty. Both the General Zionist and the nationalist right (Ḥerut) feared that the educational activities of the IDF, and particularly the one-year agricultural service, would detract from the army's professionalism and fighting capability.

The proposed table of organization of the army, and particularly the reserves system, was criticized for downgrading "territorial" defense, that is static defense of settlements based on units of settlers. Furthermore, the British organizational pattern was attacked. These two points were, of course, central to Ben Gurion's concepts of reorganization. As was to be expected, the non-religious groups, including some members of Mapai, were critical of the exemption from military service granted to orthodox women. They claimed this was discriminatory and gave the religious a monopoly on morality, alluding to the orthodox presumption that girls in military service might misbehave. Ben Gurion admitted that political considerations had obliged the exemption of these women.

Most trenchant was the criticism of the vast authority vested in the minister of defense. The Mapam statement sums this up:

> The law advises us to transfer authority to the minister of defense virtually in all matters. The minister of defense is able to declare any activity in the country as being under the rule of the army (by ordering mobilization) without

consulting the Knesset . . . . Power for the minister of
defense, that is actually the basic and main idea of the
law.[30]

Ben Gurion made his position clear, especially in his reply to
Mapam. First, on the question of the powers of the minister, he
said:

> The army is being built in an unstable period and in a land
> of immigration. Great elasticity is required in means of
> operation. It is impossible to predetermine all the details
> of the law and therefore the power to issue ordinances was
> reserved for the government; with regard to this law, for
> the minister of defense. But the overall supervision always
> remains in the hands of the Knesset.[31]

In effect, the power of the minister and depoliticization were
two sides of the same coin. Ben Gurion did not miss the
opportunity to restate his basic opposition to the fostering of
political or sectoral loyalties in the army.

> If [the Mapam spokesman] had in mind the creation of a
> special pioneering force within the army, I must state most
> clearly that as long as I am the state emissary for defense
> affairs, there will not be two kinds of army: one "pioneer"
> and the other "non-pioneer"; there will be but one unified
> army.[32]

With the passage of the law, the concept of one unified army
based on the British organizational pattern, the Swiss reserve
system, and the compromise with the religious parties — all Ben
Gurion initiatives or principles — received legal standing. The
minister of defense was granted great power, and the basis for
the civil-military relationship was established.

This then is the principle: state (civilian) control of the
military. But there is the personal factor to contend with, the
chemical interaction of the individual representing the state and

the military instrument he created. One of Ben Gurion's critics is reported to have told the Knesset Foreign Affairs and Security Committee in 1960 that only Ben Gurion could rule the army. Ben Gurion said in his defense that at least 10 others were capable of doing so.[33] This retort does indeed show that Ben Gurion was well aware of the personal factor. In 1960, others could "rule" the army. However, in the earlier period, it seems that the civilian authority had to be a man who could elicit deep personal loyalty. The point to be borne in mind is that Ben Gurion *was* in the early stages *the* civil authority. The army was loyal to him, and he weeded out (or was willing to release) people near the top who might challenge his unique position. On the other hand, Ben Gurion did obtain cabinet approval for major defense actions, but during most of his service, he did not consult with it until he was quite sure his policy would be accepted.

On two noted occasions the cabinet overruled Ben Gurion on military issues: 1) the proposed capture of the West Bank after the Jordanians blew up the water pipeline to Jerusalem in 1948; 2) the plan proposed by Ben Gurion in late 1955, when serving in Moshe Sharett's cabinet, for the seizure of Sharm-al-Shaykh and the opening of the Straits of Tiran to Israeli and Israel-bound shipping.[34] The latter will be discussed elsewhere. Regarding the former, in a conversation with the writer, Ben Gurion said that he had never seen defense matters as relevant to party politics, and had refrained from intra-party consultations on military decision.[35] However, when the Jordanians sabotaged the water pipeline between the coast and Jerusalem, Ben Gurion proposed to his cabinet that they take advantage of the opportunity to launch a general offensive which would bring all of Palestine under Israel's control.[36] To his surprise, the cabinet, including members of his own party, with whom he had not conferred in advance, voted him down. Until then, he said, he had regarded such decisions as supra-party or mamlakhti. At any rate, following this setback, later described by him as "a weeping unto the generations," he decided to consult regularly with his colleagues in Mapai, even on defense matters, prior to cabinet meetings.

Although the general opinion is that Ben Gurion had firm control over the military, this control was not absolute from the outset. There is at least one case in which he claims that an important military action was taken without his approval. At a meeting with university students in spring 1970, Ben Gurion was asked whether he had been responsible for the withdrawal from Sinai early in January 1949. "There was no withdrawal," he was quoted as saying,

> There was a penetration into part of Sinai without permission and the man who did this did so on his own responsibility; he [referring to Yigal Allon] received an order to return and followed the order. This man did something no commander may do of his own accord . . . giving the recipient of the order his due, let it be said that he obeyed it. [37]

There had been sound tactical grounds for this penetration, and the official histories had never referred to any breach of procedure in connection with the operation.

STRATEGY CONSIDERATIONS AND RETALIATION RAIDS

During the late 1940s and early 1950s, Ben Gurion's outlook and emphases changed. From viewing the Jewish state as a means for immigration and development, he began to regard the state's existence as basic to all else. Defense became an end in itself, for the state's existence was still very much in question. Thus, immigration was seen both as an abstract principle for which Jewish statehood was attained, and also as a means of strengthening the military (i.e., survival) power of Israel. The overwhelming numerical superiority of the Arabs made immigration not only a central national aim, but "first of all, a necessity for security."[38] Similarly, immigrant absorption and, particularly, the successful integration of Jewish immigrants from Arab countries were seen as a part of the total strengthening of Israel.

In his overall strategy and outlook on security, Ben Gurion was greatly influenced by the impelling need for close land settlement. This policy might be formulated as follows: if we do not go to the borders, the borders will come to us.

> If the state does not get rid of the desert, the desert will get rid of the state . . . . Wilderness is the natural ally of our enemies, and the greater the wilderness, the greater the danger.[39]

Immigration, settlement and morale were the basis for Ben Gurion's grasp of strategy. Though he believed the army should have sufficient striking power to operate outside Israel's borders if necessary, Israel's limited manpower necessitated the use of the natural framework of settlements as at least a holding operation to enable the IDF to move freely and effectively against the major threat, which over the 1950s came to be seen as Egypt.

Israel's geopolitical situation, a small island in the midst of a vast Arab sea, was, in Ben Gurion's eyes, the physical hallmark of Israel's encirclement. Israel therefore could ensure its survival only by its visible deterrent strength. "The security of Israel is dependent first and foremost upon its ability to defend itself by its own power and to deter its enemies until these enemies cease being its enemies."[40] Peace and security needs become intertwined, because peace, or at least absence of war and hostility, was guaranteed only by this strength. This stance led to the "retaliation" or deterrent raids of the early 1950s. These should be seen as the pragmatic application of his principle of the use of military power to ensure Israel's survival, as opposed to Sharett's policy of reliance to a greater extent on diplomacy and international guarantees.

Lacking a peace treaty with the neighboring Arab states and besieged by threats and acts originating from their territories, Ben Gurion sought to communicate with the Arabs both through diplomatic contacts and by military means which were designed to make the Arabs stop infiltration or incursions.

There were certain limitations on the use of armed responses to Arab provocation. Despite the growing number of Israeli casualties inflicted by Arab infiltrators — the number for 1951 alone was 137 — and despite the fact that such incidents were in violation of the 1949 armistice agreements, each individual act did not constitute a *casus belli*, in the accepted sense.[41] Furthermore, Ben Gurion, notwithstanding his concern for the security of the population, was understandably reluctant to engage in a war that might jeopardize the existence of the state.[42] Yet some armed reprisal was necessary for tactical, strategic and ideological reasons.

> In every case of injury to . . . our citizens or violation of the peace of our borders, we turn first to the UN [Truce Supervision] observers . . . . If they do not succeed . . . we feel it our duty to take effective steps to protect the lives of our citizens and the security of our borders . . . . If our rights are infringed by acts of violence on land or sea, we shall retain freedom of action to protect these rights in the most effective manner.[43]

The pattern was hard to break. First, diplomatic protests to the governments responsible for the infiltrators and to the UN had in themselves no deterrent force, since they always related to incidents which had already occurred. Even protests over extended violations of the armistice agreements, for example the Syrian seizure of the demilitarized Al Ḥamah zone in 1951, had no effect. Second, the State of Israel was the product of an ideology which had in part protested the Jews' lack of security, and had demanded a state as the only means of assuring this security.[44] This was poignantly stated in November 1955, in an address to the Knesset.

> It is our duty to tell the powers of the world, without any exception, with all the political modesty of a small people and all the moral strength of a son of the Jewish people; *the Jewish people in its land will not be like sheep led unto*

> *the slaughter* . . . what Hitler did to six million helpless
> Jews in the ghettos of Europe, no persecutor of Jews will
> do to free Jews in their own motherland. [45]

Third, the pre-state activist tradition, represented initially by
the early leaders of the Haganah and later by Ben Gurion, was
geared to answer Arab raids in kind; the creation of the state
facilitated and legalized the acting out of this tradition. Finally,
lack of response would have undermined Ben Gurions's claim of
the equality of Israel and the Arab states; he expressed one
aspect of this claim at the end of 1951: "If the Arab states do
not in principle accept the existence of Israel, we in turn are
under no obligation to accept the present situation in the
Middle East." [46] This may be seen as an attempt to introduce
mutuality into a basically asymmetric situation: considering
both the Arab size and the eventual Arab aim of politicide.

The resulting policy of limited conflict ("retaliatory raids"),
initiated by Ben Gurion in his capacity as minister of defense,
was ultimately based on the right of self-defense and the desire
to maintain the *status quo*. The latter was understood by Israel
as meaning that, in the absence of further action, the 1949
armistice agreements were to constitute the factual and legal
basis for the territorial limits of Israel and for its neighbors'
relations with it.

A corollary to this doctrine was implicit in the "retaliatory
raids" policy; violations of the armistice agreements, such as
armed infiltration, constituted acts of aggression, for which the
states from whose territories the acts had originated were held
accountable, whether or not the governments in question had
sanctioned the acts. Hence Israel reserved for itself the right to
reply militarily, in a manner or scale not always related to the
magnitude of the provoking acts and against objectives not
necessarily organically related to the origin of the acts themselves. The raids were therefore not intended as punishment,
but as statements that Israel would not tolerate violations of its
security and as inducements to the Arab countries to prevent
their recurrence or to cease fostering them. [47]

However, for the first two years such raids attracted little world attention, because they were on the whole small affairs, concerned more with demonstrating strength than actually employing it. The rule of caution and control was broken at the Jordanian village of Qibiyah on October 14, 1953, where operations exceeded the intentions of the planners and caused a large number of civilian casualties.[48] International condemnation quickly followed. While on leave from the government in 1954, Ben Gurion responded to this element with the following bitter observation:

> . . . only political infants will imagine that the major
> powers will damage their relations with the countries of
> the Arab League in order to preserve the lives of citizens of
> Israel. This task is incumbent on the State of Israel itself
> and only on it.[49]

The raids following his return to office at the beginning of 1955 and until the Sinai Campaign were on the whole larger, apparently with a view to inflicting damage as an objective of equal rank with showing strength.

A recent study by two Israeli scholars on "The Strategy of Controlled Retaliation," affirms that the policies were conducted originally under Ben Gurion as a reaction in order to achieve military and political gains, for deterrent purposes rather than as a punishment.[50] "The operational planning and performance are subjected to the control of the political level," they write. As responses to Arab initiatives, the retaliation raids were attempts to restore "current security" rather than "basic security at a strategic level." In addition to these stated aims, the controlled military action served latent purposes: to sharpen the conflict, to achieve diplomatic gains or to improve possibilities of arms' purchases; to lead to actual warfare; to improve the morale and fighting ability of the IDF and to raise civilian morale.

The controlled retaliation policy acted as a substitute for war. It allowed Israel to respond to Arab provocation without having to fight daily battles. In addition, its contribution to keeping the Middle East hot (but just below the boiling point), and its demonstration of Israel's determination to maintain the *status quo* eventually led the United States and other Western powers to drop their demands for border adjustments and the repatriation of refugees. However, in the long run, the policy did not achieve its purpose of providing a deterrent.

It became clear that "the Israeli counter raids, though costly to the enemy, no longer had the power to deter them."[51] The strategy for a preventive war was worked out by Ben Gurion; with his return to the premiership, the stage was set for the Sinai Campaign of October 1956. The 1955-6 pattern of attack and counterattack contributed to escalation. In any case, Egypt's gearing up to strategic weaponry through the Soviet arms deal of 1955 meant that the days of the policy's effectiveness were numbered.

The policy may also have been counterproductive in preventing the threat of encirclement from being realized. While the retaliation raids projected the picture of a strong and capable Israel, they also caused the Arab states to see themselves as under attack. In some cases, this may have contributed to a move toward Arab unity. After the Naḥallin raid on Jordan of March 28, 1954, relations between that country and Egypt improved considerably. The first Gaza raid in early 1955, which Nasser claimed "caught him with his pants down," intensified the Egyptian's search for arms.[52] The resulting Soviet arms supplies considerably supported his claims to the leadership of the Arab world. The attacks on *fidaiyun* bases gave publicity to these terrorist groups and in Arab eyes augmented Nasser's prestige. Counterbalancing this tendency, however, was Ben Gurion's own rhetoric supported as it was by the few but salient facts of the reprisals. A short sketch on his leadership characterizes these traits: "Great caution and refraining from big adventures in terms of content, shrouded in a thick layer of sharp and daring rhetoric."[53] It seems probable that he gave pause to the Arabs with words like: "To keep the peace does not mean to submit to invasion of our country. Every invader who does not leave when asked, will meet with a bullet or a shell."[54]

PRELUDE TO SINAI

By the middle of 1955 Ben Gurion was aware of the limitations inherent in the reprisal policy. He sought to overcome this difficulty by pressing for Arab acceptance of the *status quo*, the principle upon which that policy rested. In July he outlined a three-step program for reaching peace with the Arabs. The first step called for adherence to the terms of the armistice agreements.[55] The following month he wrote that Israel pledged itself to scrupulous observance of the ceasefire with Egypt, Jordan and Syria on the basis of reciprocity. He added that his country would take all steps possible to reduce tensions on the borders.[56] After the September announcement of the arms deal, he continued pressing for Egyptian fulfillment of the armistice agreement and made this the condition for further talks during the January 1956 attempts at secret negotiations with Nasser. He realized, however, that the arms shipments had altered the situation and told a secret American emissary, Robert Anderson, then assistant secretary of defense, that Israel would need compensating arms in order to negotiate as an equal with Nasser.

The arms did make a difference, as even the American emissary admitted.[57] Ben Gurion allowed himself no illusions: "The rulers of Egypt are buying weapons for one single purpose: to uproot the State of Israel and its people", once assured of technical superiority, the Egyptians would not hesitate to attack.[58] Yet he did not proclaim that war was unavoidable. On the contrary, he said:

> It is not permissible to say that the war is inevitable. It is possible to prevent it, if we receive arms which are of the same quality as those the Soviets are shipping to Egypt. It is possible to posit with near certainty that a war will then

not break out because Nasser will not dare to attack us,
and we will never think of attacking him. [59]

Moreover, as he had told the Knesset a few days earlier on
January 2, 1956, in reference to the impending Israel-France
deal (see Chapter 10), there was a chance of acquiring such
arms. [60] In other words, by swinging from talk of preventing
war to the practical measures of arming Israel, he attempted to
achieve maximum diplomatic and military maneuverability.
This is a principle still followed in Israel's foreign-defense
policy.

The factor of a projected arms imbalance, however,
aggravated the encirclement problem. Over the years, the
Egyptian regime consistently tightened its control on the Gulf of
'Aqabah. In September 1955, Nasser, probably made confident
by the soon-to-be delivered weapons, interdicted this waterway
to all Israeli traffic. Ben Gurion typically sought a response which
would stop just short of war (or on the brink) and present Egypt
with a *fait accompli* before its army had assimilated the new
weaponry. At the end of October he ordered Chief of Staff Moshe
Dayan to prepare a plan for capturing the Straits of Tiran, which
control the narrow ingress to the Gulf. In the presentation of his
cabinet on November 2, 1955, Ben Gurion alluded to the war
option.

> Egypt now seeks to seal the Red Sea route to Israeli
> vessels, contrary to the international principle of freedom
> of the seas. This one-sided war will have to stop, for it
> cannot remain one-sided forever. If our rights are assailed
> by acts of violence on land or sea, we shall reserve freedom
> of action to defend those rights in the most effective
> manner. We seek peace — but not suicide. [61]

The cabinet deferred implementation, and Dayan appealed the
decision in a letter to his minister on December 5, 1955. The
appeal, he wrote, was really aimed at the cabinet, though
formally it was channelled through his superior, who "after all

was the one anxious to instruct the army to break the blockade." It thus reflects a line of thought which is essentially Ben Gurion's: the concern with rights, the interpretation of encirclement. In brief, the memorandum stressed that Egypt's threatened closure of the airspace over the Straits to Israeli commercial flights could lead "to the loss of our naval and aerial freedom of passage through the Straits. Eilat will thereby become for us a coastal strip along a closed lake." This, Dayan believed, was part of "an overall plan to seize the Negev."[62]

Shortly thereafter, the border situation not having improved, despite UN Secretary-General Dag Hammarskjöld's mediations at the end of 1955 and the beginning of 1956, it became clearer that a large-scale general action, war in other words, would be necessary some time in the near future. But while preparing the nation for any eventuality, Ben Gurion was reluctant to use the "other words." He strenuously cautioned Israel against considering itself at war and demanded that the concepts of "no-peace" and "war" be differentiated. He admitted on January 5, 1956, that the existing situation of Israel — no peace treaty and daily violations of the armistice agreements — could not be called one of peace, but he refused to stipulate what made for war.[63] For pragmatic reasons, he publicly rejected the idea of a "preventive war. " He argued that a "second round," particularly if initiated by Israel, would only lead to a "third."[64] Israel, he tirelessly repeated, would only fight a war if war were forced on it.

However, two other Ben Gurion statements, one a year before and the other on the eve of the Sinai Campaign, indicate that only a semantic point was involved. Upon officially assuming office as prime minister, he remarked that it was ridiculous to speak of "preventive war," because for Israel any war would be defensive in character as the country had been under attack for seven years.[65] In a Knesset debate on October 17, 1956, two days after he had informed that body that the international search for arms had been successful, in a remarkable speech that quoted a 52-line poem celebrating the secret night-time weapons delivery, he replied to opposition leader Peretz Bernstein's demand for a more offensive policy:

> I wish to tell Member of Knesset Bernstein, who, I think, was an officer in the Prussian army or the Dutch army and is experienced in these matters, that even in defensive operations there is the need to take aggressive action. In most cases, the best way of defense is through offensive action. And if we have to defend ourselves, we will not sit at home and defend ourselves. We intend to carry the war to the other side and to defend ourselves with sharp attacks, because defense also requires offensive operation.[66]

A decision had been made in principle. The final decision which determined the timing of the "defensive actions" came on October 24, after secret negotiations with the French had assured Ben Gurion that the risks could be minimalized.[67] The previous summer's Suez Canal crisis had brought Israel some relief from its feeling of total isolation, but the attachment of Jordan to the Joint Egypt-Syria Military Command put the capstone on the pattern of encirclement. The 1956 Sinai-Suez war began on October 29, 1956, and ended with the IDF in full control of the Sinai Peninsula, five days later.

THE SINAI CAMPAIGN IN RETROSPECT

Could the decision have been otherwise? Could Israel have improved its position, which Ben Gurion understood as one verging on full-scale and costly war, by other means? "Continued mutual distrust contributed to interlocking arms races in the Israel-Arab zone," J.C. Hurewitz has written.[68] Egyptian access to great quantities of Soviet arms, on the one hand, and the mounting infiltration acting as a further irritant to boycott and blockade, on the other, led to the decision that a preemptive war must be fought with Egypt. That war, Ben Gurion's decision, and the IDF's swift victory accomplished Israel's basic aims of opening the Gulf of 'Aqabah, halting infiltration from Sinai and Gaza, making a shambles out of Nasser's encirclement attempts, and "restoring a qualitative weapons lead by the destruction or capture of much of Egypt's Soviet bloc equipment, which was conveniently, if threateningly, stockpiled along Israel's southwest frontier."[69]

The general geopolitical situation — Arab encirclement, growing Arab strength, and Israel's increasing isolation — was the key factor in Ben Gurion's strategic evaluation which led to the Sinai Campaign. By early 1956, he recognized the race between the two superpowers for influence in the Arab world as being detrimental and dangerous to Israel. In addition, Britain was trying desperately to cling to its shrinking bases of power. All these factors worked against Israel. France, whose influence in the Middle East had been severely curtailed by the British during and immediately after World War II, was a ray of light in the sharpening regional situation, largely because of its position in Algeria.

Ben Gurion used the French-British intervention in Egypt to ensure air cover over Israel and free his army and air force to sweep Sinai, destroy the Egyptian military capability, and open the Straits of Tiran. His verbal efforts to disassociate the Sinai and Suez actions from each other reflect both an attempt to explain Israel's immediate aims and to prevent it from appearing as riding on the coattails of the two European ex-imperial powers. The Israel-French liaison of the time illustrates another aspect of Ben Gurion, his great caution. The IDF had not been tested in a major action since 1948-49. The Egyptian army, with much greater firepower and new equipment, was not the defeated Egyptian force of eight years earlier. Thus prudence dictated the association with the French and their British partners. Another of Ben Gurion's traits — that of honoring his personal commitments to foreign statesmen — is illustrated by the fact that he has *never* admitted to his secret trip to France in October 1956, at which Anglo-French-Israeli collaboration was worked out in detail.

Survival above all, this was the thrust behind policy decisions. Yet as an educator — for to a great extent that is the role of every state leader and one which Ben Gurion recognized and relished — he was anxious to keep alive the basic Jewish antiwar sentiment, which his labor movement had honed over the years of conflict with the Revisionists. Thus, in early 1956 he said:

> War is the most bitter and serious matter in the life of a people . . . . There is a difference between lack of peace and war. There are movements which see war as an ideal, national or social, that in war man becomes elevated as it were and the heroism of a people reveals itself. This approach is an abomination to us, it contradicts everything dear and holy in our movement and our people . . . . We shall make war only out of bitter and inescapable necessity . . . we do not rejoice at the prospect of battle.[70]

Ben Gurion had to weigh the immediate advantage of war against the long-term dangers of big-power intervention or involvement. He was well aware that Israel's ability to win a regional victory would not guarantee a solution in the second realm of his reality — the world scene. To be justified morally and politically, war must be "inevitable," and on balance defensive. To protect the territorial base of Jewish existence, anything, even war, is permissible. It must be a last resort, and not a technique, and is not to be fought for aggrandizement.

After the Sinai Campaign, Ben Gurion was overwhelmed by the wine of victory. Setting caution aside, he made a speech which staked out a claim on Sinai and particularly the two islands in the Straits of Tiran. Sobriety, restored by external political pressures, expressed itself in the withdrawal from Sinai. Ben Gurion has said that this was the one speech he regretted having made.[71]

AVOIDING CONFLICT WITH THE POWERS

For all his negation of conquest and aggrandizement, Ben Gurion was well aware of the role of force. In April 1950, he tried to clarify relations between the state and Zionism by explaining that it was not the Zionist movement that was the state in the making, the state *en route,* but rather, citing "a great political and military sage, Napoleon, who said correctly, 'the army — that is the state *en route.* Wherever the army goes — the state goes with it.' "[72] In the period of political maneuvering prior to the 1948 war, and during the war itself, Ben Gurion combined the use of force with shrewd diplomatic moves in order to achieve what Israel Beer, a left-wing critic, has called "his grand design." Beer — a former army officer and military historian — believed this was aimed at acceptance of the ongoing British role in the Middle East, and collaboration with Britain's client and closest ally, 'Abdallah of Jordan. [73]

It is clear that Ben Gurion prudently tried to avoid head-on conflict with the British during Israel's War of Independence. He said so in retrospect, in 1956: "Our careful avoidance of fighting the British army helped us greatly." He actually forswore, "as prime minister, minister of defense, Knesset member and citizen . . . " allowing the IDF "of its own initiative" to clash with "any European, American or Asian army not from this region."[74] This echoed a similar earlier statement of 1949.[75] It explains the order to Allon to retire from Sinai in early 1949, for the danger of British intervention was then real.[76] The future of Israel in 1949-50 was not as secure as it appears to be today. Ben Gurion's prudence sought to guarantee control over a land base in Palestine, even if it did not include all of the country up to the Jordan. This meant less activity against Jordan, the prime goal being the maintenance of control over Jewish settled areas and wresting a contiguous land area from the Galilee to Eilat.

Ben Gurion's inability to carry the cabinet vote on his plan to capture the Hebron hills, the Old City of Jerusalem and the area up to Ramallah in the center of the country, down to the Jordan and the Dead Sea, in September 1948 has already been mentioned. Yigal Allon remarked on this and claims that a "lack of initiative" was shown in the Jerusalem area. [77]

Beer, like all conspiracy theorists and most Marxists, tried to fit policy into a grand strategy; to make of Ben Gurion's caution and prudence an integrated design, prearranged with 'Abdallah for the partitioning of Palestine. Until more documents are available and the intentions of the principals made known, it would seem advisable to assume a tacit rather than an explicit approach. Ben Gurion did not want to weaken 'Abdallah too much, nor did he seek a direct confrontation with Britain, Jordan's protector and patron. The Bedouin amir and later king appeared to be the best possible partner with whom to live peacefully and eventually conclude a contractual peace, sharing Palestine. This could also have served as a bridge to a reconstituted relationship with the British.

The 1957 withdrawal from Sinai was another exercise in avoiding confrontation with big powers. The Israeli-French-British collusion inflamed US Secretary of State John Foster Dulles and disturbed President Eisenhower. The American position again paralleled that of the USSR, as it had in 1948, but against Israel this time. Under the combined pressure of the superpowers and the insistence of "friendly" powers, Israel fought a losing battle to retain some of the fruits of the 1956 victory. The international pressure was too great. Ben Gurion, in one of his less buoyant addresses, faced the Knesset in early March 1957 to announce what he had been able to salvage from the Sinai victory. The speech, interrupted by the opposition in concert, is an apologia, attempting on the one hand to prove that the Sinai effort won some important gains; on the other to review the international negotiations and particularly the US-Israel diplomatic exchanges which made withdrawal a necessity. It is an outstanding example of pragmatic adjustment to what Ben Gurion perceived as the stern international reality, which took precedence over the principle of Israeli occupation of the Straits of Tiran and the Gaza Strip. For that reason, it will be quoted at some length. [78]

Ben Gurion reminded the Knesset that in proposing the Sinai Campaign to the cabinet on October 28, 1956, he had advocated "not a campaign of conquest, but a campaign of salvation." The danger had been Egypt's preeminence in arms,

linked with its tripartite military pact with Jordan and Syria. He
noted that

> . . . it would have been easy to cut the country in two
> through the tiny strip around Netanyah, bomb our air bases
> and . . . Haifa and Tel Aviv . . . thus preventing mobilization
> of the reserves . . . .

The main purpose of the campaign, to shatter the Arab
military capacity, was tied to the interest in the Eilat coastline
and the Straits of Tiran: "the most important thing is freedom
of shipping." He had realized, even on October 28, 1956, that
the Gaza Strip would be "embarrassing" (he had used the
English word). For five months Israel had been resisting
withdrawal from Gaza and the Straits area lest the Egyptians
return and incursions begin again. After a number of exchanges
between President Eisenhower and Ben Gurion, Israel's foreign
minister had been instructed to agree to withdrawal from the
two zones provided that "any proposal for UN evacuation from
the Straits be brought first to an advisory committee
representing the [UN] General Assembly . . . ." [79] This was
promised by the UN secretary-general in a memorandum dated
February 26, 1957. "Considering the . . . arrangements of the
UN and the maritime states, my government believes that Israeli
and international freedom of navigation . . . will be fully
assured following Israeli evacuation."

Ben Gurion did not, however, intend to rely entirely on the
UN, the US and the 15 other maritime powers who had supported
the view that the Straits were an international waterway.

> Israel will defend her ships plying international waterways.
> Any intervention by force in the movement of Israeli ships
> exercising their right of free and innocent passage in the
> Gulf of Eilat and the Straits of Yotvat [sic] will be viewed
> by Israel as an act of aggression entitling it to its natural
> right of self-defense according to Article 51 of the UN
> Charter.

He issued a similar warning regarding the Gaza Strip if the situation were to revert to that preceding the Sinai Campaign. He attempted to point out the difficulties involved in Israeli control of Gaza because of its sizable refugee population. "Whoever speaks about the Gaza Strip without seeing all the complications and dangers inherent in the composition of its population, lives in a fool's paradise."

EILAT AND TWO SEAS

He held out great promise for Eilat's future, with the opening of the Straits to international traffic:

> Eilat will become a port of international importance and with the laying of a larger pipeline [for oil] than the present one from Eilat to Beersheba, with construction of a railroad and the widening of the road to Eilat, Israel's entire geopolitical position is changed and wide horizons for the economic development of the Negev and Israel's economic progress will be opened. [80]

More will be said later about Ben Gurion's view of Israel as a two-sea power. At this point, one must stress his pragmatic adjustment to the international pressures, including the threat of sanctions, which he faced.

> . . . the arrangement reached last week [regarding withdrawal] was, in the opinion of our friends in the world, the only possible arrangement . . . . There is no dogmatic or static policy, and one cannot ignore the changes . . . which take place in public opinion and relations between nations. [81]

Ben Gurion spelled out this last point: Israel's dependence on the West for arms had forced his hand. From the wine of victory, he had extracted the not negligible lees of free passage through the Straits and UN presence in Gaza. The army obeyed

and withdrew. But free passage from Eilat port was ensured.
Ben Gurion's geopolitical vision for Eilat was recorded
lucidly in a memo to Justice Louis D. Brandeis in 1933. At that
time Ben Gurion wrote, under the heading "The land problem
and its special relationship to the Negev and Eilat":

> The main importance of the Negev is in the fact that large
> empty areas are uninhabited . . . . Here we can, by means of
> drilling wells, create mass close settlement, impossible
> elsewhere in Western Palestine . . . . Palestine [Eretz
> Yisra'el] is *blessed with two seas,* the Mediterranean, which
> links us to Europe and Africa, and the Red Sea, which
> links us to the great continent of Asia. Palestine, which
> must become an industrial center in the Middle East, will
> particularly need to create commercial ties with the Asian
> hinterland. *Hence the vast importance of the Gulf of
> Eilat* . . . . It is of the utmost political and economic
> moment to found a Jewish settlement here [in Eilat] in
> order to create a *fait accompli.* [82]

This fact was not to be established until the conquest of Eilat
in March 1949. Indeed, the operation was called "Fact." In
May 1949, in a radio address on the occasion of Israel's first
anniversary, Ben Gurion briefly referred to Eilat and the Negev
in the same terms as used in his memo of 15 years earlier. The
Egyptian closure of the Straits deferred the carrying out of the
program, but from 1956 Israel pushed Eilat's development,
stationed naval units in the Gulf, and increased its trade with
East Africa and Asia.

IDF'S ROLE AS EDUCATOR AND UNIFIER

Though Ben Gurion's geopolitical eye was far-ranging, in the
final analysis he was much more concerned with the use of the
IDF as the unifying and state-controlled educator and nation-
builder. The political parties held a partial stranglehold on
education, and essential central services such as health,

employment and, to some extent, housing were in the hands of politicized bodies, particularly in the early years of statehood. Ben Gurion's concept of *mamlakhtiyut,* i.e., the placing of national over sectoral interests, made use of the army as the only non-sectoral body to implement nation-building tasks.

Non-politicization did not mean the removal of ideology. The state had an ideological base — the ingathering of Jews. Ben Gurion and the labor movement had developed a generally accepted subideology of land settlement, "pioneering," and self-defense. These were to be the ideological bases for the IDF. The army was cast in three linked roles, extending beyond its attack-defense, purely "military" functions. These were: absorbing, educating and training the new immigrants of military age; the preservation and continuation of the land-settlement, pioneering tradition; and the fostering of a new definition of ḥalutziyut to include voluntarism in general and volunteering for specialized or dangerous units in particular.

In a speech to the Knesset in June 1950, Ben Gurion, speaking in his capacity as minister of defense, said:

> Our army is attempting to solve another difficult problem: our army must be not only a fortress of security for the state, but because of the historic reality of ingathering the dispersed Jewish communities, the army must be the crucible of national unity. [83]

He said the "return of the captivity [the Biblical term for dispersed Jewry]" was to him "the greatest thing that had happened in Jewish history." The arrival of many illiterate Jews from backward lands made it necessary

> . . . to teach [the new recruits] the alphabet and elementary concepts in the ways of cultured man . . . . I saw how their faces shine from the feeling that each day they are striking roots in the motherland, in its language, they learn things they did not know, they become friends and partners with the native-born . . . . [84]

A year later, he said that the IDF was to be a central factor in educating the younger generation and in forming the national character. "We will accustom the youth to a life of brotherhood and mutual aid; and of themselves will fall the barriers between communities and tribes, and the divisions . . . of the past will be speedily bridged."[85] He used the idea of nation-building: "to convert [the youth] into a nation."

Thousands of soldiers were taught to read and write over the years. A standing order of the IDF's General Staff required the army to bring all recruits to the level of primary school completion.[86] In addition, said Ben Gurion in 1951, the forces, in their natural course of training skilled workmen in their armories, teach many others "vital trades . . . metalwork, electricity, communications, driving, carpentry, etc . . . . "[87]

The provision for agricultural service in the Defense Service Law of 1949 has already been discussed. However, it remained a dead letter due to the pressures of technical specialization.[88] A mere half-year after its enactment, the minister of defense was empowered to postpone the implementation of the farm service provision or to forego it. This empowering legislation was renewed annually until 1957. Then, following an initiative of the right, it was decided that it was to be renewed every three years.

The right had, in the original debate, opposed the law on the grounds of the need for professionalization and because it coerced soldiers to work as farmers. The left had favored continuing agricultural service since it would have "demilitarized" the military. By keeping the law on the books, Ben Gurion paid lip service to the left's ideals, yet adopted the policy of the right for purely pragmatic reasons. In an interview Ben Gurion shrugged off the issue; it was just not practicable in an era of increasing technical specialization.[89]

Only one formation implemented the farm service provision. *Nahal,* the acronym formed from the Hebrew words for fighting pioneer youth *(No'ar Halutzi Lohem),* was established as a volunteer framework at the end of 1949. Its principle aim was to keep intact the groups of pioneer youth movement graduates who wished to form a new settlement or reinforce an existing one. These are known as "settlement nuclei." It was feared that if on reaching military age these youth groups would disband and be dispersed throughout the armed services, the youth movements would lose their sense of purpose. Naḥal soldiers spend part of their service in kibbutzim or in newly established border settlements and the rest on regular infantry duty. This is a limited institutionalization of the original farmer-soldier synthesis. The paramilitary, secondary-school-age youth battalions (Gadn'a, acronym for Gedudei No'ar) embodied the stress on agriculture as well, with "national service" periods in kibbutzim.

Though Naḥal was the only military formation to carry the word "ḥalutz" in its title, the concept of pioneering and volunteering was one Ben Gurion did not want to drop. He broadened its context, to include volunteering for all difficult tasks in the army. At the same time, he was aware of the dichotomy between voluntarism and institutionalization (or étatism), which Lenin had to face and which Mao is still trying to solve, albeit on a far different scale, with regard to their respective revolutions. Ben Gurion attempted to fuse the two. In the fall of 1949, he said:

> IDF's face is turned to the future: to techniques of
> warfare, forms of organization, to equipment and
> most modern operations . . . but the IDF must
> develop within itself the valuable asset of the Haganah,
> whose time is not past nor will it be past, viz. the
> spirit of voluntarism. . . .[90]

Six months later, speaking to leaders of the kibbutz and moshav movements, he said:

> The IDF, although maintaining strict discipline . . . and
> being based on [conscription], is basically built on
> pioneering voluntarism . . . . The permanent army [cadres]
> is entirely an army of volunteers . . . . [91]

In performance, this is quite true. The men in crack units (pilots, frogmen, commandoes, paratroopers, etc.) volunteer for their particular type of service. In retrospect, viewing the general level of performance of the IDF and its specific educational and state-building tasks, it is clear that Israel followed Ben Gurion's 1949 formula rather closely, as phrased by him when introducing the Defense Service Law:

> The purpose of the . . . law is to prepare the entire people to be at the required hour a fighting nation; to give the youth — Israeli-born and immigrant — pioneering and military training; to maintain a permanently mobilized striking force sufficient to drive off a surprise attack and hold out until all reserves are called up; to fashion in the framework of the army the form of a people united, unified, peace-keeping, trusting in its ability and taking its fit place in the society of nations. [92]

In this sense, there is a clear distinction between Ben Gurion's thinking before and after the establishment of the state. Before 1948, it was the Jewish people and the Zionist movement, but particularly the Yishuv, which were building the state-to-be. After 1949, it was the state which was to build the nation, with the IDF in a central nation-building role. For this reason, Ben Gurion could speak of the forces in passionate and unministerial tones.

> I confess that I love the IDF with a strong and deep love, for I see it not only as the fortress of our security, which alone would suffice, but also as an educational force for national unification, and a loyal instrument for welding together the dispersed ethnic groups. [93]

THE LAVON AFFAIR: A PROBLEM IN MANAGING THE IDF

As one who saw such great purpose in the IDF, and who totally identified with its creation and progress, Ben Gurion was not likely to judge lightly any successor to the post of minister of defense. In the first case of substitution, Ben Gurion offered the position to Pinḥas Lavon, who held office for just over a year — from December 7, 1953, the date of Ben Gurion's resignation, until February 21, 1955.[94] The resignation followed a working vacation of several months during which Ben Gurion prepared a three-year plan for defense needs, later adopted by the government. He has written that by that summer (1953) he had already decided to make his home in Sde Boker.[95] This fledgling kibbutz in the arid Negev came to be a symbol for him of Israel's need to settle its southern wasteland.

The reason given by Ben Gurion for his temporary retirement from public life was stated in a warm, human letter to his old comrade and dear friend, the then president, Yitzḥak Ben-Zvi. As it is atypical in that it consciously reveals a great deal about its writer, one paragraph merits citation at length.

> However, for about a year I have felt that I am unable to bear any longer the mental strain in which I find myself in the government . . . . This is not normal tiredness. On the contrary, when I leave my work . . . for a few days, I do not feel at all tired, and it seems to me that I am able to work as I did 20 or 30 years ago, physically and mentally . . . . I attempted to take leave and return to work and it became clear to me . . . that I cannot do so without a long break. I came to the regrettable conclusion that I have no choice but to depart from this work for a year or two . . . . [96]

In the letter he admitted that there had been differences of opinion within the cabinet, both with his fellow party members and with other ministers: "No self-respecting man . . . would work with people who do not have their own opinions."[97] There is undocumented evidence that serious policy differences did exist, possibly in relation to a massive retaliatory action proposed by Ben Gurion, and voted down by the cabinet.

Certainly the eventual resignation (1956) of Moshe Sharett, who had replaced Ben Gurion as prime minister and on the latter's return carried on as foreign minister, was due to Sharett's emphasis on "diplomacy," international mediation and guarantees, as opposed to certain more direct forms of dialogue proposed by Ben Gurion. [98]

At any rate, during Ben Gurion's leave-of-absence before his official resignation, his two tasks were handed over temporarily to Sharett as acting prime minister and Pinḥas Lavon as acting minister of defense. Their permanent appointment to these positions was confirmed in January 1954. Lavon thus served a total period of 13 months with full powers, and prior thereto for a few months in a caretaker capacity. This is the period under consideration.

Lavon, some 20 years younger than Ben Gurion, grew up in Poland, where he was one of the founders of a nondoctrinaire labor-socialist movement based on the teachings of a Tolstoyan Russian-Jewish philosopher of labor, A.D. Gordon. A kibbutz member, he rose rapidly in the ranks of Mapai following his arrival in Palestine in 1929, and served as secretary-general of the Histadrut in 1949-51, minister of agriculture, 1950-51, and minister without portfolio till 1954.

On assuming office, Lavon ran into difficulties in two spheres: his relationship with Sharett and his lack of rapport with his colleagues in the ministry of defense and on the IDF General Staff. Lavon was not particularly cooperative with his prime minister. He was an activist in regard to military action and retaliation raids. Sharett differed with him about the scope and size of actions and their frequency. The relations between Sharett and Lavon were automatically tense. Sharett was the career diplomat and head of the foreign ministry. Lavon was the man who had to follow Ben Gurion as head of the defense establishment, which had developed a deep distaste for diplomacy and diplomats and whose professional interests conflicted with those of Sharett and his establishment. Lavon, apparently in a high-handed manner, tried to keep Sharett out of key decisions. This might have succeeded had he not opened a second front, against his lieutenants who were Ben Gurion appointees and who lost confidence in the new leader.

The Qibiyah action against a Jordanian village, during the Sharett-Lavon interim period (October 1953), resulted in heavy loss of civilian life, supposedly inflicted by Israeli "irregulars," so it was claimed at the time. As a result, according to a distinguished specialist on Israeli decision-making, the prime minister and foreign minister were charged with deciding on retaliation policy, together with the defense minister. In addition a committee of five Mapai ministers tried to work out a system of coordination between the prime minister and the defense minister. [99]

One of Ben Gurion's associates, Pinḥas Rosen, who ten years later clashed with him, gives witness to the strained relations within the cabinet due to Lavon's inability to win its confidence during his tenure as defense minister. Rosen, long-time minister of justice and a non-Mapai politician, said in 1965:

> In the Ben Gurion period, we heard more about what was happening, we asked more questions and matters were brought before us with more frankness and more clarity than in the Lavon period. Everyone who worked with Ben Gurion, whether he agreed with him or opposed him, will admit that Ben Gurion talked with the cabinet. [100]

Moshe Dayan, the chief of staff, and Shimon Peres, the chief civil servant (director-general) of the ministry, initially saw in Lavon an ally in pursuing Ben Gurion's policy in the face of Sharett's attempts at diplomatic conciliation. However, Lavon's efforts to assume control of detailed execution of policy, and of tactical matters, brought him into conflict with these and other subordinates. For example, Shimon Peres stated in an interview that Lavon tended to intervene in highly detailed matters of ministry activity, giving as one instance the case of a purchase of a building. [101] Ben Gurion claimed in a talk with the writer that on two occasions the chief of staff refused to obey extreme orders given by Lavon. [102]

The compounded deterioration of Lavon's relationships with the premier, the cabinet and the staff of the defense ministry and the IDF came to a head with the "security mishap" of 1954. A series of sabotage attempts, particularly in Egypt, on American government property was planned by Israel military intelligence in the hope of damaging US–Egyptian relations. The plan failed; the Egyptians broke the Israeli spy ring, executed some of the leaders and imprisoned others. A dispute arose as to whether Lavon had approved the operation or whether it had been initiated by intelligence officers. (Later it was even claimed that the operation had been planned to discredit Lavon.) Sharett appointed a secret enquiry commission consisting of two highly reputable public figures: Chief Justice Yitzḥak Olshan and the first chief of staff, General Ya'akov Dori. The committee found it impossible to apportion blame and the matter was seemingly forgotten, to be revived in the vicious "second Lavon Affair" of 1960 and later (see Chapter 13).

There is evidence that the Olshan-Dori hearings became, rather than a probe into the euphemistic "mishap", an enquiry into relations between the minister and "his" establishment, as well as into the division of authority between the ministry and the IDF. Lavon demanded that Sharett agree to the removal of some of the principals and to the creation of a national security council consisting of civilian and military figures. Sharett rejected these terms, and Lavon resigned. [103] Ben Gurion, under pressure from his colleagues in Mapai, proposed other candidates to head the defense ministry. Nothing availing, he returned to this office on February 21, 1955. Not until November of that year did he reassume the premiership.

There is a point to bear in mind. In 1954, just six years after independence, only Ben Gurion held the confidence of both the cabinet and the army. The state had not yet become sufficiently routinized and relations not sufficiently bureaucratized for an orderly transfer of power. In the mid-1950s Ben Gurion's chemical interaction with the state civilian authority, the cabinet, and its subordinate military arm was critical. By 1960, when Ben Gurion was accused of being the only man who could rule the army, he was able to reply that he was not irreplaceable. [104]

There were some other attempts to institutionalize the relations between the cabinet and the military. A Cabinet Committee for Foreign Affairs and Security was appointed on April 12, 1953, and functioned in the various governments in office until the end of term of the eighth cabinet in December 1959. At the beginning of the tenth cabinet, it was reborn as the Ministerial Security Committee in November 1961. [105] In its original form, the committee dealt more with foreign policy than with security matters. However, there is one source which states that the committee was charged by Ben Gurion with approving actions outside of Israel's borders. [106]

The Lavon issue was raised once again and led to a public outcry which shook the government and parties of Israel from 1960. This properly belongs in the discussion of party politics, since problems of IDF management were touched upon mainly in retrospect.

CHAPTER EIGHT

The Arabs in Israel

Despite the great Arab exodus from the area that was to become Israel, many Arabs still remained in the new state by the end of the 1948 war. Early in 1949 they numbered 108,000 or almost 15 percent of the population, and by the end of that year, as a result of repatriation and border adjustments with Jordan, the number grew to 150,000 although the percentage remained constant as Jewish immigration grew.[1] Whatever the percentage, they had secondary importance in Ben Gurion's ideological plan for the Jewish state. In the previous two decades he had consistently rejected a collective Arab claim to Palestine and had argued that the Arabs had many homelands and states while the Jews had only one.[2] Their role was to be that of individual citizens with guaranteed civic, cultural and religious rights. Pre-state Zionist rhetoric had promised the Arabs rights and participation in the Jewish state. Testifying before the Anglo-American Committee on Palestine in 1946, Ben Gurion projected the position of the Arabs in a Jewish state as equals in law but they would follow separate cultural patterns.

> We will treat our Arab and non-Jewish neighbors as if they were Jews, but make every effort to ensure that they

preserve their characteristics, their Arab culture, their Arab [sic] religion, their Arab way of life, while doing our utmost . . . gradually to raise their standard of living.[3]

The Proclamation of Independence of May 14, 1948, a document to which he gave final form, asked

> . . . the Arab inhabitants of the State of Israel to preserve peace and to participate in the upbuilding of the state on the basis of full and equal citizenship and due representation in all its provisional and permanent institutions . . . . [Israel] will ensure complete equality of social and political rights of all its inhabitants irrespective of religion, conscience, language, education and culture.[4]

Following the war, his announced major concern was his old vision of realizing "the iron will of the Jewish people" to return to Palestine in their millions.[5]

> Our territorial conquests and redemption will not be assured if we do not succeed in erecting a great and closely linked chain of settlements of ex-soldiers on the borders, in the Negev, on the coast, in the Jerusalem corridor, around Gaza and in all other areas of strategic importance.[6]

The thrust of his thinking was clear: Israel was a Jewish state and the place of the Arabs in it was to be that of a minority.

Furthermore, though Israel was in the Middle East, it was not of it. In 1951 he described Israel as

> . . . geographically part of the Middle East, but ethnically and culturally . . . distinguished from it. [Israel is] essentially different from all its neighbors . . . . Israel was established and built by a nation of high cultural level, one attached to a messianic vision, a vision of redemption of the Jews and of mankind . . . . It is a nation of pioneers

faithful to their destiny, their historical task, and
realization of their vision.[7]

Long before the creation of the state, Ben Gurion had
acknowledged that individual Arabs already resident in Palestine
should be entitled to citizenship in the state.[8] The Nationality
Law (1952) qualified as citizens only those Arabs who had
remained and excluded those who had once lived there. It
required an Arab seeking recognition as an Israeli citizen to
prove that he had been a citizen of Palestine before May 14,
1948, had been registered as an inhabitant of Israel on March 1,
1952, and had been in the country throughout the intervening
period or had legally entered in that period.[9]

Overshadowing the ideological and political question
regarding the place of the Arabs in Israel was the security
question. This was the spectrum through which Ben Gurion
viewed the issue of control of the Arabs in Israel and which
guided national policy in creating areas of Jewish settlement.
Many of the Arabs who remained had been armed enemies in
the 1948 war and, if the armistice agreements had ended the
open conflict, they did not remove the hostility of the
neighboring Arab states which exerted religious, cultural and
political influence on their Israeli brethren. The memories of
the past and the uncertainties about the future augmented the
tendency of Israel's leadership to question the Arabs' loyalty to
the new state and to view them as an internal security threat.

Ben Gurion was particularly prone to this attitude. In
rejecting all claims of Palestine Arab nationalism, he had
associated Arabs in Israel with those across its borders. He
viewed the Middle East situation in terms of the Arab "many"
who might unite some day to wipe out the Jewish "few." The
imbalance between "little" Israel and the "vast areas" of the
Arab peoples was an "iron fact of history."[10] This type of
analysis led to fear of encirclement and the concomitant
apprehension that perhaps the enemy was already within. The
presence of large numbers of Arabs in many strategic border
areas did nothing to assuage these fears. They continued

throughout Ben Gurion's entire ministry. As late as 1957, during a Knesset debate over the internal secret security service, Ben Gurion noted:

> To our sorrow there are in this country groups who potentially or actually constitute a fifth column or are capable of becoming a fifth column . . . we are not yet at peace with our neighbors and this fifth column is a grave danger to our security and perhaps our existence.[11]

For this reason, the treatment of the Arabs was based primarily on security considerations. In terms of overall policy their numbers were to be kept to a minimum and they would be given civil rights to the extent they could be trusted not to abuse them. "Every person living under the flag of Israel and not breaking the law or endangering the state's security received the protection and the blessing of the state.'[12]

THE MILITARY ADMINISTRATION

During Ben Gurion's term of office, Israel's Arabs lived under a system of military administration controlled by him in his capacity as minister of defense. In order to fill in the necessary details, a brief review of the nature and scope of this administration will follow. Its origin lay in the confused and unsettled nature of the 1948 conflict. The relatively rapid victories of the IDF in that war and their consolidation by armistice agreements left Israel in control of considerable areas with virtually all-Arab populations. These included a strip along the northern border with Lebanon and a good portion of the Galilee extending down to the so-called Little Triangle, the area bordering the large Jenin-Tulkarm-Qalqilyah bulge of the Jordan-controlled territories. In addition, there were settled Arabs and semi-nomadic Bedouin living in the near empty Negev and around the Gaza Strip. On the other hand, the Arab populations of Jaffa, Haifa and Ramlah were greatly reduced from their pre-war level and were insignificant in relation to the

Jews who streamed there under the crash immigration program. Although Jerusalem had been effectively partitioned and only 2,000 Arabs remained in the western part of the city under Israel control, mostly in the village of Bayt Safafah, there were scattered Arab villages in the narrow corridor linking the city to the rest of Israel.

Such a distribution meant that the Arabs for the most part were invisible to the Jews, but occupied many areas essential to the defense of the state and were not counterbalanced in these areas by a Jewish presence. The additional fact that many of these people had recently been armed enemies and that almost all had relatives and friends living as refugees across the borders further suggested the existence of an "emergency" situation.

In an almost spontaneous reaction, Ben Gurion's government, which was in office through 1948, left or delegated most administrative functions relating to the Arabs to the army. Under the Law and Administration Ordinance of May 21, 1948, Ben Gurion, as minister of defense, was empowered to create closed security areas in any part of the country. Through Israel's status as a successor state, he also had the right to exercise the British (Mandatory) Emergency Regulations of 1945, designed originally to suppress Jewish terrorism. These 147 regulations permitted surveillance, administrative arrest, imposing curfews in villages, travel restrictions and exile of residents from the country. They also enabled the chief of staff, with the consent of the minister of defense, to appoint military governors over any part of the country. In such areas, the courts of first and exclusive instance would be military. [13]

Use of the powers followed quickly upon their receipt. The first closed security area was declared on May 22, 1948. Although such areas were created piecemeal, by the early 1950s the military administration had a recognizable form. It embraced three principal areas — the northern section (Galilee), the central section (the Little Triangle), and the Beersheba region (including areas around the Gaza Strip) — and had at least 80 percent of the country's Arabs under its control. [14] Movement to and from the closed areas could be restricted and controlled, and persons resident there could be ordered to leave and forcibly ejected if they failed to comply. The minister of defense was empowered, however, to make exceptions and grant settlement rights in the areas to any person or group of his choosing. Since the original legislation contained a time limit, the military administration was ultimately dependent upon periodic acts of the Knesset for its existence. The legislation passed in 1949 was renewed annually or biennially, keeping the emergency regulations in force indefinitely. With the exception of the cities, where military jurisdiction ended early in 1951, security areas and military administration of the Arabs remained on the whole a feature of Israel — slowly shrinking in scope — until the system was abolished by Ben Gurion's successor, Levi Eshkol, on December 1, 1965.

So much for the factual outline. The idea behind all this was clear: to ensure the supremacy of the state over a potentially dissident minority of its population. The laws and the institution they created and perpetuated had several effects. The Arab population came under an administration ultimately guaranteed by the prestige and power of the IDF. The travel and other restrictions limited Arab movement and helped keep the Arab minority for the most part an inconspicuous element in Israel life. The security area policy served as an instrument in discouraging the idea of a return of Arab refugees (both internal and external) to their former dwellings. It also facilitated the occasional transfer of Arab populations from strategic points through evacuation of people and villages. [15]

Over the years, the military administration engendered mounting opposition among both Arabs and Jews. For example, in 1951, Mapam pressed for its abolition on the grounds that it was not in the interests of the state, was not needed for its security, and did not provide any administrative benefit. It was collective punishment, so Mapam claimed, and only limited the freedom of the citizen. [16] Later that year the General Zionists called for partial abolition of the military administration. An Arab spokesman for Mapam voiced his criticism of it as a political instrument. One of the members of a pro-Mapai Arab

party also called for its total abolition.[17] In effect, the issue
was raised almost regularly, and in the course of time the
various opposition groups drew closer over the question of
terminating military rule. By 1959, the Knesset, with the
exception of the Ben Gurion-led Mapai, decided that there was
a need to end the military administration, but again no action
was taken.[18] Throughout this period, the Communists and the
Zionist far left (Mapam) based their opposition on libertarian
grounds, claiming that the military administration was a denial
of equal rights for the Arabs. In a 1962 debate, Moshe Sneh of
the Communist Party (Maki) implied that the military administration was merely an expression of Arabophobia on Ben
Gurion's part. He condemned the prime minister for having
categorized, in a foreign press interview, the majority of Arabs
in Israel as "enemies of the state."[19] Both Sneh and Menaḥem
Begin, whose right-wing Ḥerut Party opposed the emergency
regulations for historical reasons — they were originally used by
the British against Etzel — voiced their suspicions that the
military administration was being used for political purposes,
i.e., to influence Arabs to vote for Mapai or Mapai-affiliated
Arab parties.[20]

The inability of the opposition to do away with the military
administration has been attributed to the fact that in the 1950s
Jewish public opinion largely supported its existence.[21]
However, on the political level, a more important cause was Ben
Gurion's unswerving commitment to its preservation. In the
early years, he linked the continuance of the Mandatory regulations to the "emergency" (war) situation, so that in early 1951,
for example, he could explain to the Knesset that the original time
limit on the law, then about to expire, was because

> We were evidently optimistic and hoped the emergency
> would soon pass. To my sorrow, this optimism has been
> misplaced. The present situation obliges greater concern
> for our security than was necessary a half-year ago, and
> the validity of the regulations must be extended until the
> end of the emergency.[22]

At the end of the year, in the debate on extending the emergency regulations, Ben Gurion made a number of revealing statements. Knesset members had complained that the inhabitants of a number of Arab border villages had been vacated against their will. He replied:

> The inhabitants of Bar'am and Ikrit received other land.
> They received the same area [as they had possessed] . . . .
> For security reasons they were not permitted to
> return . . . . They may demand land of the same quality and
> the same conditions. They cannot demand the same
> explicit place. I lived in Tel Aviv and it was necessary that
> I move to Jerusalem. What is the tragedy? . . . . To [the]
> question, how do we want to bring about cooperation
> between the Jewish people and the Arab peoples, there are
> two answers: a) by ensuring the Arab minority in our
> country a better standard of living than that of Arabs in
> any Arab country. I know that the Arabs do not like
> military government, that it limits their freedom of
> movement to a certain extent. I know that security zones
> are not pleasant for them, but they must understand that
> the State of Israel has a grave security concern . . . you
> must recognize that there is a need for security zones . . . .
> [This, to an Arab member of Mapam.] b) The second is
> that we are ready to make peace with the Arab states as
> they are . . . . We want peace with Egypt, its people and
> government without interfering with its internal
> rule . . . . [23]

In later years, when the memories of 1948 had faded and fidaiyun raids were rare, Ben Gurion had begun to treat the military administration as an integral and permanent part of Israel's security position. In 1960, for the benefit of his left-wing partners in government (Mapam and Aḥdut ha-'Avodah), he had made it clear that he could have no part in a government which would abandon the military administration because he would consider this as sabotaging Israel's security. [24] In response to the opposition in the 1962 debate, he declared that the military government, by then much diminished in scope, was "subject to the IDF and to the civilian authorities entitled to give instructions to the IDF," and was "essential for the security of the state, and the well-being of the Arabs in Israel." The institution was needed to quell unrest or open revolt in the Arab districts and the absence of such attempts at insurrection only proved its success. Furthermore, since the propaganda of the neighboring Arab states stirred up Arab youth, and there were Arabs in Israel who "hoped for the day when Nasser and other Arab leaders would attempt to carry out their plan to destroy Israel," there was a continuing need for the restraining force of the military administration.[25] It was "to suppress destructive elements, to prevent infiltration and spying, to prevent injuries to Arabs desiring peace within Israel and between Israel and her neighbors" — that is the military administration was carefully designed, normal, beneficial and necessary for the internal security of Israel.[26] By threatening resignation, he had forced his party and his coalition partners to go along with this view and support the retention of the institution. In the 1962 vote, he demanded and duly received the support of the Arab Mapai-affiliated members of the Knesset.

Yet Israel's experience, following the termination of the military administration, suggests that Ben Gurion's support for the institution was predicated on other than purely objective grounds. As with other matters related to the army, he seems to have had a deep emotional involvement with it. In the 1962 debate he insisted that only he and Mapai "have succeeded in being consistently right in building and planning Israel," and he flatly accused all opposition of "not understanding defense affairs or [being] negligent of the state's security." He stated that opposition to the military government and emergency regulations was to "abandon the state to the intrigues of the enemy in the neighboring countries and those who hate the State of Israel from within."[27] The implication was that in security matters his judgment was best. On the one hand, his profound concern with security in part explains this attitude. On the other hand there was complete identification of himself and his role with all parts of the defense establishment. Therefore, Ben Gurion could easily interpret any criticism of the institution as an attack on his personal integrity and morality.

INFILTRATORS AND REFUGEES

Ben Gurion and his colleagues wished to keep the Arab presence in Israel to a minimum. They therefore refused to readmit most of the refugees who had fled the state in 1948 and took action to deport those who had illegally filtered back across the ceasefire lines. The implementation of the latter policy was occasionally questionable in terms of the origin of the deportees. On February 28, 1949, 700 refugees were reportedly expelled by the army from Kafr Yasif across the border into Jordan. According to one Arab source, these people were actually internal refugees who had come from the Western Galilee.[28] In a more publicized incident in 1950, 150 alleged infiltrators were deported from Abu Ghosh, a village in the land corridor linking Jewish Jerusalem to the central area of Israel. Ben Gurion, as the responsible minister, defended this action in the Knesset and threatened his resignation if the policy of deporting infiltrators were to be changed. In response to criticism of the government's policy of imposing collective punishments upon places concealing infiltrators, he affirmed that the government would continue to act in this fashion. He charged that the Arabs were using the tactic of first sending their women and children back to Israel to act as moral hostages weighing on the Israeli conscience. In regard to Abu Ghosh, which had been friendly to the Jews during the War of Independence, he observed that the village was being used as a base for infiltrators:

> At the beginning of the war . . . there were people who demanded we undertake, on the termination of hostilities, to return all the refugees to the country.

The government rejected this. If the Knesset wishes
to change this policy and to permit infiltrators to
return, and not hundreds but hundreds of thousands
would return, it would be better that the Knesset
immediately elect another government.[29]

The policy continued. It was buttressed by the Nationality Law
of 1952, designed in part to prevent granting Israeli citizenship
to any refugee who had returned illegally.[30]

Not many of the estimated 539,000 to 726,000 Arabs who
left what was to become Israel territory, returned legally.[31]
While the war raged, Israel refused to discuss their repatriation.
Shortly afterward, at the end of 1948, Ben Gurion was asked by
Mark Ethridge, chairman of the UN-appointed Conciliation
Commission for Palestine (CCP), about Israel's acceptance of
the repatriation principle stated in UN Resolution 194. The
prime minister stressed that a large-scale return of Arabs must
be conditional on a final peace settlement. Yet, he added that
although he personally thought that the resettlement of Arab
refugees in the Arab states was the ideal solution, Israel would
be willing to cooperate when the time came.[32] Apparently this
was not his final stand, for his reply of May 1949 to US
President Harry Truman (who sent a personal letter) and other
American officials, then exerting pressure for the repatriation of
200,000 refugees, is couched more strongly and indicates less
flexibility. Again he hinged repatriation on a final peace
settlement and insisted that there would be no admission of
fifth columnists. He explained that "Israel is a small and weak
[country]. We can be crushed, but we will not commit
suicide."[33]

While the view that readmission of refugees was a form of
national suicide became the conventional wisdom of Israel, Ben
Gurion, the man who had most succinctly articulated it,
remained open to refugee negotiations when other advantages
could be gained, particularly in the early stages. Essentially he
saw the refugees as one element contributing to an unsettled
situation and was willing to make concessions provided that

Israel's security would simultaneously be strengthened. The transfer to Israel of the Little Triangle, an area of land facing the narrow waist of Israel roughly between Tel Aviv and Haifa, as part of the armistice agreement with Jordan, broadened Israel's difficult-to-defend, narrow coastal strip. It also added about 40,000 Arabs to an Arab population which then numbered approximately 100,000.[34] The strategic gain was worth the price. At the Lausanne Conference (April 27–September 15, 1949), conducted under the auspices of the UN General Assembly Conciliation Commission, in an early move that seems to have originated with the strategically-minded Ben Gurion, Israel offered to accept Gaza's 200,000 refugees and 70,000 inhabitants on condition that the Gaza Strip would also be incorporated in the new state. The Arabs rejected this proposal. At the end of July 1949, following the replacement at Lausanne of Walter Eytan, a Sharett associate, by Reuven Shiloah, Ben Gurion's trusted lieutenant, Israel, in response to American pressures, agreed to the return of 100,000 refugees. The CCP considered the proposal unsatisfactory, while public opinion in Israel attacked it as too generous. Within the government coalition, the religious party expressed its dissatisfaction. Within Mapai, veteran leaders characterized the proposal as endangering the security of the state and reducing Israel's capacity to absorb Jewish immigrants.[35] Ben Gurion kept silent, the proposal was rescinded and Sharett bore the onus for its inspiration.[36]

Within a very few years the refugees became less of a problem awaiting solution and more of a propaganda issue. By 1951 Israel was set in its principle determination that no refugees would be admitted, except in cases of family reunion. In its first five years, Israel admitted over 30,000 refugees under the family reunion plan.[37] The government informed the UN Commission that Israel was prepared to conduct separate negotiations on the question of compensating Arab property owners whose lands were held by Israel. Frozen Arab bank accounts were also released. In other words, there was no possibility of physical return, but there was willingness on Israel's part to settle accounts fiscally.[38]

A speech in 1961 reveals Ben Gurion's matured attitude on the refugee issue.[39] In contrast to Sharett, who earlier had predicated Israel's refusal on immediate security and economic conditions and thereby implied the possibility of reconsideration if these conditions were to change, Ben Gurion then phrased the refusal as valid under all conditions. He attempted to fit the refugee question into a historical and international framework. He first observed that there had been no repatriation of the 20 million refugees created by World War II and he denied Israel's responsibility for the plight of the Arab refugees. Almost all these people left before the establishment of the state, under orders from Arab leaders. Moreover, the Arab exodus must be seen in conjunction with Jewish immigration to Israel from Arab countries, because the exodus and influx actually constituted a *de facto* population transfer. In addition, there were also Jewish refugees from those parts of Palestine which had fallen under Arab rule. Consequently, Israel was under no obligation to admit any refugees and compensation would have to be reckoned in both directions. In conclusion, Ben Gurion blamed the Arab leaders for not resettling or absorbing the refugees.

> If the problem of the Arab refugees still exists, it is
> because of the breach of the UN Charter by the Arab
> states and their cruelty to people. Israel did not wait for
> the Arab states to restore the property of Jewish refugees,
> but saw them as living people, brothers . . . . The Arab
> rulers acted toward the Arab refugees not as if they were
> their own and living people, but as if they were arms to use
> against Israel. Israel rejects with all its might the intrigue
> inherent in the proposal of free choice by the refugees
> [which] is designed . . . only to destroy Israel . . .
> [there] . . . is only one practical and fair solution: settling
> them amongst their own people in countries rich in good
> land and water, which require additional manpower.[40]

This is a condemnation of the Arab leaders for not

implementing what 13 years before Ben Gurion had told the head of the CCP was the ideal solution and what for the past decade Israel had maintained to be the only possible solution for the refugee problem. On Ben Gurion's part there was a natural tendency to view the Arabs on the scale of Jewish values: to assume for them the same patterns of mutual aid and responsibility developed to a fine art by the Jews, and therefore to find the Arabs contemptible when they did not act accordingly. The major point of the speech, however, was not so much to blame the Arabs as to vindicate the Jews, to deny any responsibility for the refugees. Such a blanket denial enhanced the policy of the Arab states to use the refugees as pawns against Israel.

EXPROPRIATION OF LAND

The confiscation of refugee property, particularly of farmland and urban dwellings, which Ben Gurion defended in 1961, was originally a pragmatic solution to an urgent problem. Faced in 1948 with the Arab exodus on the one hand and the beginning of mass Jewish immigration on the other, Israel moved quickly to nationalize the abandoned Arab property. On June 23, 1948, a little more than a month after the declaration of the state, Ben Gurion as defense minister ordered the registration of all abandoned property with the police. The police were also instructed to seize all unregistered property. Additional regulations published the next day gave the minister of finance, under the directive of Ben Gurion as prime minister, power to dispose of movable and real property in the "abandoned areas." Such areas, according to an ordinance published at the end of the month, were defined as "any area or place captured by armed forces or surrendering to them or left by its inhabitants or part of its inhabitants and which has been proclaimed an abandoned area [by the defense minister]."[41] These regulations effectively gave the government the legal basis to proclaim almost any area of its choice "abandoned" and to transfer its property to the state. The power and its purposes were clarified by subsequent legislation.

In October 1948, the minister of agriculture assumed the authority to seize and work land or water resources not being exploited by their owners. At the end of the year, an emergency regulation entrusted abandoned and absentee-owned property to the Custodian of Abandoned Property, a newly created department in the ministry of finance. The latter category included by definition property whose owner had left it after November 29, 1947 (the acceptance of the UN partition plan) but had remained within the territory of Israel. [42] As a result any Arab land or house not actually inhabited by its owner, regardless of where the owner was, became liable to confiscation. In the same way, villages and other areas whose Arab residents had been evacuated for security reasons could pass over to the "Custodian." A 1950 law gave this office the right to sell the property under its control to a projected Development Authority or to government ministries, e.g., the ministries of immigration, housing and defense. Finally, these institutions could allocate, give or sell the property to Jewish settlements and immigrants. The 1953 Land Acquisition Law confirmed the above law and the actions of the Development Authority which had by then begun operating.

Although Ben Gurion's insistence on the mass immigration policy had created the need for the expropriation program, and although he had initiated it and closely linked it to his plans for Israel's security, from the end of 1948 he played only a peripheral role in its day-to-day development.

During the 1959 Knesset election campaign, Ben Gurion met with leaders of the Mapai-affiliated Arab list. Among the first grievances they presented was a demand for the return of the land, and an appeal that the government should soon announce a plan for the resettlement of displaced Arabs in other parts of Israel. [43] As far as Ben Gurion was concerned that settled the matter. His assessment of the security situation had not changed; the land in question was occupied by Jewish settlements populated by immigrants or had been added to the resources of pre-1948 Jewish agricultural villages. Perhaps realizing that the expropriations had limited the traditional pursuits of the Arab community, he advised them to industrialize and promised government assistance to this end. At the close of the meeting, the prime minister prophesied that if cooperation between the Jews and Arabs in Israel increased, there would be cooperation between Israel and its neighbors.[44]

ATTITUDES AND COUNTER-ATTITUDES

The military governors initially appointed councils of local Arab advisors but eventually local councils were elected. Nevertheless, the system of government was unquestionably a source of irritation to the Arab citizens of Israel. A visiting scholar summarized the Arab complaints as follows: The military government affected only Arab communities; the regulations placed restrictions upon movements of Arab citizens; searches were at times a method of intimidation; the laws were discriminatory and permitted confiscation of land and expulsion.[45] Some critics of Israel's treatment of the Arab minority have attributed the policies as much to Ben Gurion's personal attitudes as to his concern with security. They point to his well-publicized refusal to accept his identity card because it was printed in Arabic as well as Hebrew.[46] One may well ask whether these supposed attitudes caused Ben Gurion to overestimate the Israeli Arabs as a security risk and whether the measures taken against them were excessively stringent. As the cited 1962 speech on the military administration indicates, Ben Gurion was convinced that it was both necessary and effective. Although it is an argument *ex silencio,* the record of generally peaceful coexistence, unmarked by violence, sabotage, demonstrations and riots, supports this view. The military government itself did not generally achieve its results by obtrusive methods. One study of the Arabs in Israel pointed out that the military administration "consisted of a few dozen employees in civilian garb; but behind it were the strength and prestige of the army and the possibility of military intervention if all else failed."[47]

In an address to the Knesset in mid-1955, Ben Gurion suggested that one could obtain a measure of the Arabs' status in Israel by comparing it with the position of political dissidents in Arab countries, or the rights of Jews in these states. The reference to political opponents is significant. Ben Gurion must have felt that the Israeli Arabs, seven years after statehood, had not accepted and come to terms with the fact that Israel was a Jewish state and would remain so.[48]

His misgivings are borne out by the voting patterns of the most important all-Arab city in Israel, Nazareth. The citizens of Nazareth, the population of which is about evenly divided between Muslims and Christians, have fairly consistently given about half their votes to the Communists, and following the 1967 split in Israeli Communist ranks along pro- and anti-Soviet lines, have favored the pro-Soviet *Rakah (Reshimat ha-Kommunistim ha-Ḥadashah* — New Communist List). Even allowing for personal, clan and religious considerations which play a role in Nazareth politics similar to the Lebanese and Syrian clan-confession axes, the trend to "vote against Israel" by supporting a pro-Soviet, hence pro-Arab grouping is clear. Added to this is the small but regular support for Mapam, which has always been sharply critical of Ben Gurion-Mapai Arab policies, internal and external.[49]

The case of Nazareth further demonstrates that Ben Gurion saw political opposition to the Jewish state and threats to Israel's security as two sides of the same coin. An attempt was made there in 1955 to offset "Communist influence and pro-Nasser nationalist sentiment at a time when the border situation was precarious," by establishing the all-Jewish town of Upper Nazareth.[50] In its early years, Upper Nazareth was the child of the ministry of defense, and its role was to establish a Jewish physical presence in the predominantly Arab central Galilee, towering over the area and overshadowing Lower Nazareth. Although other hopes may have animated the planners (e.g., to prove that "Jews and Arabs could live and work side by side in harmony and cooperation"), the security motivation predominates.[51] The action fits Ben Gurion's approach of viewing the indigenous Arab population as a potential danger, now become actual due to pro-extremist political activity, and of using Jewish settlement as a defense mechanism.

An equally valid reason for discounting the opinion that animosity inspired Ben Gurion's public policies concerning the Arabs is that he never espoused a racist philosophy, i.e., the Arabs were never considered *Untermenschen,* nor were the Arabs in Israel publicly accused or condemned *in toto.* On the contrary, his actions and reactions following two serious incidents affecting Israeli Arabs in 1956 and 1958 witness concern for and a desire to be fair to the Arabs.

On the day of the launching of the Sinai Campaign in 1956, a unit of Border Police, which under war conditions comes under the command of the IDF, was ordered to implement a curfew at Kafr Qasim, an Arab village in the Little Triangle. The unit opened fire on a group of Arab men, women and children returning from the fields unaware of the imposition of the curfew; 51 innocent people were killed. Six weeks later Ben Gurion officially notified the Knesset of what he called "the horrifying occurrence." Immediately upon learning of the incident he had appointed an investigation committee. Charges had already been brought against those responsible and compensation paid to the families.[52] Ben Gurion's Knesset statement went on to express again his sentiments concerning the value of human life and the traditional commandments to treat "the stranger" as an equal and to love one's neighbor. "The Arabs in Israel," he added, "are not strangers but equally privileged citizens."[53] A study of Ben Gurion's statements leads one to believe that his advocacy of the traditional respect for human life and the equality of civic privileges (wherever security permitted) was both consistent and sincere. They were spoken in the tones of an educator, a role Ben Gurion consistently stressed as an aspect of leadership.[54] Yet, as a politician, he made sure that all legal aspects of the case (investigations, charges, compensations) were well in hand before presenting them to the Knesset.

Early in May 1958, a chain of street demonstrations and riots occurred in Nazareth, Um al-Faḥm and other Arab localities and resulted in injuries to both Arabs and police. The disbanding of an illegal May Day parade in Nazareth, which had been staged by the Communists as part of a drive to organize the Arabs, was the immediate cause of the incident. In the background, though, was the general unrest in the Middle East and the Soviet Union's recent, very audible support of Nasser, all of which had been stirring nationalist sentiments among Israel's Arabs.[55] Nevertheless, Ben Gurion tried to isolate the perpetrators of the incidents from the bulk of the Arab public by blaming the clashes on the Communists. The note of fairness was struck by pledging that the accused in these cases would be treated strictly according to the law.[56] In the light of this incident, Ben Gurion's response to Sneh's 1962 charge that the prime minister had termed "all Israeli Arabs enemies of the state" takes on significance. Ben Gurion carefully and simply asserted that he had not said *all* Arabs in Israel were enemies.[57]

Of course, Ben Gurion had little love to spare for the Arabs. They were not Jews willing to implement Zionism, and they were not easily integrated into a Jewish state. Yet he did not want to consider them permanently estranged from the Jews. In the midst of the War of Independence, he cautioned his people against considering the Arabs as historic enemies and insisted that they be treated with morality.[58] He hoped to instill a modicum of Arab allegiance to Israel by improving their material condition and thereby giving them a vested interest in the state's survival. In 1952 he noted with pride and satisfaction "that the Arab laborer and peasant in Israel have better conditions than in any Arab state and the status of the Arab woman in Israel is better than in any Arab country."[59]

Although the military government, responsible to Ben Gurion in his capacity as minister of defense, was his primary tool in relating to the Arabs, another unit functioned under his control as well: the prime minister's advisor on Arab affairs.[60] It was used to advance the welfare of the Arabs. The advisor, who was a senior official of the prime minister's office, acted as the chairman of the interministerial committee for Arab economic affairs and the government's liaison with the UN Arab Refugees' Resettlement Authority which operated in Israel.[61] In conjunction with his office, the ministry of agriculture, under Moshe Dayan, at the end of 1961 undertook a five-year program to provide expanded services, approach roads, electricity and piped water to rural Arab localities.[62]

As leader and prime minister of a democracy, Ben Gurion was likewise concerned about safeguarding the theoretical right of the Arabs to civic equality, notwithstanding whatever measures the minister of defense was obliged to take for the sake of security. In the early years of the state he occasionally emphasized that Arabs were entitled to the same benefits that Jews received from the state and to educational, cultural and religious equality (within the traditional Middle Eastern framework of cultural separatism and Arab-language schools).[63] Concomitantly he attacked discrimination against the Arabs. The same 1952 session of the Knesset Committee on Security and Foreign Affairs which demanded the retention of the military administration also adopted Ben Gurion's resolution "to abolish all traces of discrimination whatever against the Arab population in any area."[64] The resolution further stated:

> The defense minister is himself at present investigating
> every incident and arrangement in order to prevent
> cultural or economic discrimination. The prime minister is
> in contact with all institutions involved and a new
> controlling agency has been established. But these actions
> do not rule out the need for the establishment of a
> particularly secure regime.[65]

Ben Gurion's doctrine of equality within the bounds of security resulted in the treatment of the Arab minority as a "Jewish problem" in reverse. The status accorded to the Arabs becomes a test of the Jews' morality, as much for their sake as for the Arabs. The analogy may even have been present in Ben Gurion's mind when he suggested the comparison of the Arab minority with the Jews in Arab states. However, for him, the minority was not "his Arabs" or "Israel's Arabs" alone. They were also representatives of a people living across the border. Because of this Ben Gurion explained that he could not force on the Israeli Arabs the universal military service incumbent on all citizens. The Israeli Arabs should not be placed "in the tragic position of having to fight Egyptians, Syrians and so on . . . . "[66] But as representatives of a people hostile to Israel, the Arabs could not be full psychological partners in Israel's statehood. Ben Gurion later explained that the exemption of Arabs from the draft disqualified them from full citizenship rights.[67] The key to full equality and the dispelling of suspicion, the removal of the internal border in Israel, Ben Gurion believed, lay across the borders, in the chanceries of Arab governments, within whose power it was to concede Israel's right to exist and to make peace with it. In the final analysis, the Arabs in Israel were viewed in the light of Israel's security needs and the broader context of the regional conflict.

PART THREE

External Affairs

CHAPTER NINE

The Arab Neighbors

Following the 1948 hostilities, Ben Gurion and his fellow decision-makers in Israel entertained the possibility that war, in accordance with the universal custom, would be followed by an armistice, and armistice by peace. The prime minister might have momentarily doubted that the Negev battles with Egypt, which ended on January 7, 1949, were to be the last phase of open warfare, but he was prepared to consider the option that peace might come to the Middle East.

At the very least, he was ready to make an offer: " . . . on the basis of existing realities [i.e., the post-war borders], we are prepared both for peace and for cooperation with the Arab nations, and differences in regime will not stand in our way."[1]

He repeated the offer regularly; for example in late 1951, in the Knesset he said:

> I want to realize cooperation between the Jewish nation and the Arab nations . . . by two means: 1) through our promise to the Arab minority in our land of a condition better than that of the Arabs in all the Arab lands . . . . 2) The second point is that we are prepared to make peace with Egypt, with her people and her government, without intervening in her internal regime or questioning her integrity.[2]

According to his outlook, Israel could and should find its way as an integral part of the Middle East, and thus his desire that it play a role in a program of regional cooperation and development. This is not a new element in his thought.

Years before the creation of the state, he had rejected a European orientation for the country, however consistent it would have been with the origins of its Jewish settlers. He wrote in 1930:

> If we wish to be an Eretz Yisra'el [Palestine] nation we
> must link ourselves with the new geographic and
> ethnological conditions which surround us. The Jewish
> people in Eretz Yisra'el will be linked with Europe only on
> the west via the Mediterranean. On the north, east and
> south it will come into contact with Arabic-speaking
> nations.[3]

In 1947, as the decision on partition approached, he returned to this theme and explained to the Yishuv's leaders (no doubt hoping the Arab states were also listening):

> In order to develop our country thoroughly, we need
> mutual relationships with our neighbors — economic,
> political and cultural. We have much to give our neighbors
> and they on their part have much to give us.[4]

To return to the post-independence period, in line with the peace option and possibility of cooperation, Ben Gurion called for a "Jewish-Arab agreement" which meant to him "economic, social, cultural and political cooperation with neighboring states." He declared the effort to reach such an agreement to be one of the principles of Israel's foreign policy.[5] Although he did not spell out the details at the time, later statements and actions suggest that he had considered offering Jordan a free port area in Haifa; Egypt transit rights through the Negev and use of Israel's expertise to solve that country's medical problems; and committing Israel to joint exploitation of the region's water resources.[6] In return, Ben Gurion sought Arab recognition of Israel as an equal and the respecting of the borders to be determined by the armistice agreements. Above all, he wanted quiet so that the new nation could face its problems, which, as he envisaged them, were to be difficult but internal, arising from the commitment to the "ingathering of the exiles" and the need for economic development.[7]

Nevertheless, he realistically acknowledged that even if a peace treaty were to be signed in "good faith and sincerity" Israel's place in the sun would not be guaranteed. He always foresaw the other option: no peace, or further war. Shortly after the armistice with Jordan was signed in early April 1949, he warned his people against relying on the "wondrous victories" of the recent past, since geopolitical conditions would continue to operate to the new state's detriment. In particular, he pointed to Israel's territorial smallness in relation to the vast expanses controlled by the Arab peoples, an imbalance he called "an iron fact of history."[8]

Striking a more ominous note, he stressed another iron fact of history, that there is no such thing as a frozen situation. A weak and corrupt regime may be replaced by a powerful and strong one. Implicit in this statement was the fear that under strong leadership the tens of millions of Arabs might unite and, aided by their geographical deployment, overwhelm in one way or another the demographically and territorially tiny Israel. Characterizing the possibility of this scenario as part of "the military danger" confronting Israel, Ben Gurion, while he was elsewhere calling for peace, appealed to his nation for internal consolidation: "Let us not congratulate ourselves that our security is assured and standing . . . our defense will demand immense efforts and means, for upon it depends our entire existence."[9] A month later, in May 1949, he again spoke of Israel's disadvantages in relation to its neighbors and used a metaphor which would be repeated many times. In defending the policy of unlimited Jewish immigration, he said, "Immigration is the foremost factor for our security . . . . Without immigration we are destined for destruction: 700,000

Jews surrounded by a sea of Arabs will not survive. " [10]

There is no reason to interpret these statements as belligerent or at cross-purposes with Ben Gurion's stated desires for peace. He believed that a strong Israel would be less easily opposed and more readily accepted by the Arab states than a weak one. In this sense, of creating incontrovertible facts, he is consistent. This is the way he had responded to the Balfour Declaration 32 years earlier: "It is not in England's power to return the Land to us . . . the Hebrew people itself must turn this right into a living, established fact."[11] He now sought to make Israel's statehood a fact not dependent upon the actions of its neighbors. However, in the absence of peace, the cool appraisal of the state's geopolitical disabilities could give way to a fear of encirclement and isolation.

Within the framework of being both open to peace and militarily vigilant, Ben Gurion was ready to negotiate with the Arab states in 1949. By the middle of that year, separate armistice agreements had been signed with the neighboring states who had been directly involved in the conflict.[12] The efforts of a UN Conciliation Commission (composed of representatives of the United States, Turkey and France), appointed by the General Assembly, brought forth the Lausanne Protocol of May 12, 1949. It laid a foundation for future negotiations on the two central issues: borders and refugees.[13] The Israeli acceptance of the first point, which posited the 1947 partition plan as a basis of negotiations, theoretically committed the country to territorial concessions and certainly negated any supposed expansionist desires. Ben Gurion's exclusion from his cabinet of the irredentist Ḥerut Party and the leftist Mapam, which were concerned with the territorial integrity of Mandate Palestine, reflected to some extent his own attitude on borders. His acceptance of the partition of Jerusalem, which entailed the loss of the Old City (of great symbolic importance to the Jews), his drive to settle the Negev, and his concern for new settlements elsewhere were further demonstrations that control of a given area was more important than its size.

On the second basic issue, the refugees, he had less room for maneuver. Despite his conviction that readmission of the refugees would jeopardize the state, he tried to maintain some flexibility in their regard (see previous chapter). The Lausanne Conference bogged down as the Arab states least involved in the Palestine issue came to realize that they had not much to gain and perhaps something to lose from peace and recognition of Israel. [14] 'Abdallah, the Arab ruler who stood to gain most from peace and who was the primary physical partner in the now-partitioned Palestine, did pursue serious negotiations.

In his own analyses, Ben Gurion attributed the failure to reach peace to Arab "delusions" about the outcome of a second war and the economic viability of the new state. World tensions and the nonsettlement of the Arab refugees in the neighboring countries were also seen as factors complicating relations with the Arabs. [15] But a more basic factor, he thought, was that the anti-democratic, anti-liberal internal character of the neighboring regimes, combined with their inability to solve immediately their myriad social and physical problems, was responsible for "foreign adventurism" which proclaimed the destruction of Israel its principal aim. In other words, the existence of Israel was a false problem for the Arab leaders and their concern with it was an evasion of responsibility to their people. He suggested in the early 1950s that the possibilities for peace were dependent on the democratization and liberalization of the Arab countries.

> I am certain that if two conditions will be met, there will be a real possibility not just for formal peace but also for continuing cooperation and trust between the Jewish nation and its Arab neighbors. The first condition is the strengthening of the State of Israel, both politically and economically, which will root out from the hearts of its enemies any thoughts that this state can topple under the weight of the burden which looms over it, and which will remove the grounds for discord, between it and its neighbors . . . . The second condition is the liberalization

and democratization of the Arab states. This too will come
sooner or later. And for both the Semitic peoples, the
Jewish and the Arab, there is a common destiny in their
part of the world . . . . [16]

In this light, he at first welcomed the Naguib-Free Officer's
putsch of July 23, 1952, and later, in apparent exasperation,
bitterly castigated Nasser as a dictator who did not attend to
Egypt's needs.[17] Therefore, as he noted in the middle of 1952,
Israel would be in a no-peace, no-war situation for a long time.
In terms of security, it would have to be strong, and in terms of
foreign policy, in control of the situation and retaining the
initiative.[18]

In May 1950, a year after the ill-fated Lausanne Protocol was
published and shortly after Foreign Minister Moshe Sharett had
unsuccessfully tried to buy arms in the West, the United States,
Britain and France issued their Tripartite Declaration. They
undertook to limit the supply of arms to the Arab countries and
to Israel, in order to prevent an arms race. They also became the
guarantors of the armistice borders against any attempt at
alteration by force.[19] Ben Gurion greeted the Tripartite
Declaration with some reserve. He admitted that Israel
depended on its relations with the big powers as well as on itself
for its security. However, he urged the powers not to content
themselves with preventing hostilities but to help speed the
signing of a peace agreement between Israel and the Arabs.
After this statesman-like bow in the direction of the Big Three,
he proceeded realistically to evaluate the declaration in the
tones of a minister of defense:

Both an enemy or a friend of the State of Israel
could sign the Tripartite Declaration. In accordance
with the Declaration, a friend could supply us with
weapons and an enemy could withhold arms from
us . . . . The Declaration . . . might possibly improve
our position but it depends how the Declaration will
be implemented.[20]

The second part of the document, which hinted at "strengthening the defense of the area by bringing all the parties together into a regional defense organization," elicited more interest. A few months later, after the United States, Britain, France and Turkey proposed a Middle East Defense Command, the Israeli government was unofficially reported as being willing to join. However, the Egyptian rejection of the program (for reasons not primarily related to the Israel conflict) negated Western efforts.[21] Despite the lack of results and Israel's assurances that it would not join an anti-Soviet pact, the Soviet Union seized upon Ben Gurion's welcome of the Tripartite Declaration as a pretext for estrangement of Israel. Its leaders, Sharett in particular, were depicted in the Russian press as cringing before the West. Relations between the USSR and Israel would have worsened anyhow as the outcome of internal developments in both countries (e.g., the Soviet attitude to Zionism as a bourgeois ideology and the resurgent anti-Semitism there, and Israel's concern for the rights of Russian Jewry and its desire for immigrants), but Ben Gurion was to be criticized by the leftists in his country for having alienated Russia. The history of steadily deteriorating relations, including a period (1952-3) in which diplomatic ties were broken, enabled the Soviet Union to begin wooing the Arabs at the end of 1953, thus heralding a break with the embarrassing past of friendship toward Israel and the espousal of a new pro-Arab orientation.

The Tripartite Declaration and its aborted offspring, the Middle East Defense Command, represented the only attempt by the West to treat Israel as a politically integral part of the Middle East. Later attempts to weld the region into a defense organization, such as American Secretary of State Dulles' Baghdad Pact, were to ignore the country. These actions eliminated pressure on the Arabs from an outside force to accept Israel as a neighbor and implied that Israel was *sui generis* in but not of the Middle East. Israel's political leadership had little choice but to make the necessary inference. The resultant attitude was crystallized in 1955 when, in order to offset Iraq's participation in the Baghdad Pact, Israel first attempted to join NATO and failing that tried to conclude a mutual security treaty with the United States. However, prior thereto Ben Gurion had rethought the position of his country vis-à-vis the Arabs and the world. (This is discussed above in the Sinai section of Chapter 7.)

ISRAEL'S POSITION: ISOLATION AND ENCIRCLEMENT

Between 1950 and 1956, the lack of peace in the Middle East was accompanied by a constant escalation of bellicose statements from the Arab states, increasing infiltration and armed clashes, and a mounting economic boycott. The first were designed to undermine the psychological and physical security of Israel. The last was intended to hamper its economic development and condemn it to economic isolation. The material effects of the boycott on commercial and industrial enterprises dealing with Israel "are not susceptible to accurate estimation."[22] For the same reasons, the Egyptian regime over the years effectively tightened its control over the Gulf of 'Aqabah and kept the Suez Canal closed to Israel traffic, in spite of great-power and UN pressures. The Canal was sealed not only to war material, but to all goods bound for or leaving from Israel, even when carried in non-Israeli vessels. The UN was unable to enforce its resolutions on freedom of passage through the Canal, and in March 1954 the Soviet Union, by then firmly pursuing a pro-Egyptian policy, vetoed further action. These maritime blockades to some extent closed off Asia and Africa to Israeli trade, while simultaneously forcing the country to reroute its oil purchases, or find more distant and more expensive sources of supply.

The Arabs also practiced boycott on a political level. Directing themselves to the new countries of Asia and Africa, and particularly to the growing Muslim communities there, they lost no opportunity to brand Israel a "tool of imperialism."[23] Thus, not content with keeping Israel out of the Middle East, the Arab states sought to deprive it of contacts with the Third World, at a time when the country was being greeted with coldness from the West and outright animosity from the Eastern bloc. The resulting feeling of isolation experienced by Israel is highlighted by the sense of celebration which swept the country when in 1953 Burma established diplomatic relations with Israel.

Playing the good clubman at the UN to overcome this isolation was impossible. On the one hand, the Arabs had managed to exclude Israel from the Afro-Asian caucus; on the other, the United Nations Organization had little popularity in Israel. The December 6, 1949, resolution to internationalize Jerusalem and the various UN condemnations of Israel's retaliatory raids had engendered resentment, while failure to prevail upon Egypt to observe the armistice agreement or to permit Israel use of the Suez Canal had earned it contempt. Some of the feelings toward the international body were given expression by Ben Gurion in a 1956 speech.

> There is not a statesman in the world who does not know that the war in 1948 was a malicious attack against Israel by Egypt, Iraq, Syria, Lebanon and Jordan. And even though the two great powers in the world, America and Russia, were partners in the decision on the establishment of a Jewish state in Israel — and this partnership was perhaps their first and only since the founding of the United Nations — and the two of them were the first to recognize Israel immediately after its establishment, first the US and then the USSR, and even though the UN Charter was then in force and required of its members to aid an attacked nation, not a single state lifted a finger in defense of Israel . . . . [24]

He drew the conclusion that:

> . . . we do not see in the UN Charter by itself any real guarantee for the security of Israel or deterrent to the aggressors plotting war against us. [25]

The recognition of Israel's near-universal pariah status must have contributed to Ben Gurion's pre-1955 reformulation of his country's place in the world. His writings of 1954, at which time his leave from the government freed him for long-range thinking, reveal an attempt to find new patterns of international associations for the state. He did not altogether drop the idea of a "Jewish-Arab" agreement or the belief that the state would some day have to integrate with its Middle East surroundings, but he now considered such developments dependent on greater reciprocity on the part of the Arabs.

> . . . not only is it up to Israel to integrate into the Middle
> East, but . . . it is also up to the Arab states to recognize
> the State of Israel as a fact and to be reconciled with this
> fact, and only in this way will the road to rapprochement
> be opened. [26]

However, if the Arabs did not accept Israel, the Middle East was *faute de mieux* not the only possible locus of definition for Israel.

> But from the geographical aspect one cannot ignore the
> sea. Our close neighbors in geographical terms are not only
> those nations which border on Israel by land, but also
> those which border on us on the sea . . . . According to our
> geographical position, we are a Mediterranean nation
> and all the nations bordering on the shores of the
> Mediterranean Sea are our neighbors. [27]

Having found a second tier for national involvement and integration, Ben Gurion depicted a third one, which he considered more important than the others: the Jewish people. In fact, he compared the relation of the state to the Jews as an international body with that of a member state in the British Commonwealth or the Soviet bloc or NATO. There are some differences, for "the nation [Jews] in Israel regards itself as but a part, a pioneer and delegate of the entire Jewish nation," but on the question of integration and isolation, the result is the same:

> More than any other tie, the tie of the nation in Israel to the entire nation of Israel will define and determine the "integration" (in regional and bloc terms) of the State of Israel. The fact that the Jewish nation is a world nation makes the State of Israel the state of a world people and for a world people. [28]

Whether or not the Jewish people could offer Israel the same benefits that NATO could is not really relevant. The embracing of an ally (and a dependable one at that) relieved some of the *angst* of isolation and strengthened Israel's determination to "go it alone" when necessary. At the same time, the conscious recognition of this alliance would have ramifications in Israel's foreign policy. An orientation to the Western countries, where the Jews were free to support Israel, and opposition to the Soviet bloc, where they were not, had been inevitable. Nevertheless, the self-proclaimed alliance could not remove the fear of encirclement which was to grow in direct proportion to Nasser's rise in the Arab world.

In 1952, notwithstanding Ben Gurion's earlier warning that corrupt Arab regimes could give way to strong ones, Israel could take some comfort from the fact that the surrounding Arab states were disunited and, in a way, psychologically distant. There was a certain amount of tension with Jordan over infiltration and terrorist acts whose perpetrators had come from Jordanian territory, but these incidents in themselves did not put the existence of Israel into question. Besides, Jordan itself was going through political perturbations in the wake of 'Abdallah's assassination the previous year and it was doubtful whether the raids represented a policy of aggression against Israel. The other borders were relatively quiet.

The situation was sufficiently relaxed in the summer of that year for Ben Gurion to extend a sincere welcome to the new regime in Egypt, a scant four weeks after Naguib's takeover. He blandly assured it that Israel would disregard Pharoah's ancient misdeeds, and even Farouk's invasion of the new state four years earlier, since it wished to see "an Egypt free, independent, progressive . . . . To the extent that Egypt's present rulers attempt to uproot corruption and advance their country . . . we can only bless them wholeheartedly . . . . "[29] This public signal for a *détente* was apparently accompanied by diplomatic approaches, yet in itself it was loud, clear and unmistakable.[30] Ben Gurion stressed that

> . . . no doubt there was not then [1948] or now [1952] any reason for a dispute between Egypt and Israel. A wide, large desert stretches between the two states, and there is no place for border disputes; there was and is no reason whatsoever for political, economic or territorial disputes between the two neighbors. On the contrary, the cooperation between Egypt and Israel would help Egypt to overcome its political and social difficulties.[31]

What comes through here is a feeling of the distance of Israel from Egypt and vice versa. Ben Gurion was in effect saying "good fences make good neighbors and there is no better fence than the Sinai Desert." But he did not speak in a spirit of fending off Egypt or even admonishing it. Rather he seems to be taking note of an existing situation and proposing that it become a basis for peace.

Within three and a half years the situation had worsened radically, and the feeling of space had given way to claustrophobia. Under the Anglo-Egyptian Treaty of July 1954, the British troops whose physical presence in the Suez area had acted as a buffer between Israel and Egypt were withdrawn. Shortly afterward an Egyptian military presence began to develop in Sinai and in late 1954 the Egyptian military intelligence organized so-called *self-sacrifice* squads *(fidaiyun)* which probed deep into Israeli territory. Their aim was not only to terrorize civilians but also to gather useful military information. By then, the Israeli attempts at conciliation by

Sharett were balanced by the Israeli sabotage ring broken in 1954 (see Lavon Affair section of Chapter 7), and by the Israeli attempt to force the Suez Canal issue through the UN by dispatching an Israel flag vessel to attempt to enter the canal.

Toward the end of 1955, Egypt's leader and General Muḥammad Naguib's successor, Gamal Abdel Nasser, his prestige heightened in Arab eyes by his removal of the British, by the friendship displayed him by the Soviet Union and by the attention paid to him by the West, and, perhaps most of all, by the Russian (Czech)-Egyptian arms deal announced in September 1955, began tightening the noose around Israel. Syria hastened to toe the Nasserist line and by the summer of the next year had placed its troops under Egyptian command. Jordan seemed likely to follow suit.

In the meantime, the situation on the border with Egypt, unsteady since the beginning of fidaiyun activity, rapidly deteriorated. On October 7, 1955, Egyptian troops entered the de-militarized Nitzanah area, in violation of the 1949 armistice agreement. UN efforts to dislodge them unavailing, they left only after the Israeli Sabḥa Hill action of November 3, which cost them heavy casualties. The international response to this incident was given expression in UN Secretary-General Hammarskjöld's suggestion of a buffer zone for the borders, and in British Prime Minister Eden's call for Israel to make territorial concessions to the Arab states, Egypt in particular.[32] Both ideas were, of course, anathema to Ben Gurion. Their proposal heightened his awareness of how hemmed in and alone Israel was.

The prime minister acted out this awareness by projecting a picture of a beleaguered and encompassed Israel. On November 15, in Churchillian khaki battle dress, he addressed the Knesset and officially rejected Eden's proposal. He repeated his past offers to meet face-to-face with the Arab rulers. There was "room for local frontier rectifications accepted by and beneficial to both sides, carried out as a result of mutual agreement," he admitted, but he declared that there was "no room for the truncation of Israel." He then went on to describe

Israel as a victim of aggression.[33] A few days later he characterized both Britain and Russia as pursuing policies leading to the destruction of Israel.[34] An analogy with the Czechoslovakia of 1939 was obvious enough to be left unmentioned.

At the beginning of the following year, he discussed the problem of Egypt. That country was now the principal enemy; it was responsible for most of the terrorist activities occurring on all sides. Fidaiyun units had been sent to Jordan and Lebanon in order to strike at Israel. Behind these machinations stood the ambitious Nasser. Ben Gurion reported that from his reading of Nasser's book *The Philosophy of the Revolution* he had learned that the "Egyptian dictator" was motivated by three goals: "1) to stand at the head of the Arab peoples; 2) to be the leader of the Muslim peoples; 3) to be the spokesman of the African continent." The attack on Israel, then, was not an end in itself for Nasser, but merely "the easiest and cheapest means" to achieve the first goal.[35] Elsewhere Ben Gurion remarked that when he first learned of Nasser's ambitions he knew that peace with Egypt would be impossible. Nasser would try to unite the Arab states by playing upon the one point on which they were all agreed, opposition to Israel. Arab unity would lead to the encirclement of Israel, and encirclement to its destruction.

Thus, the early fears of isolation and encirclement were fully justified by the end of 1955. These apprehensions and the geophysical and political realities which fed them precluded Israel, not only in 1956 but in preceding years as well, from pursuing a normal foreign policy with its Arab neighbors. In effect, they made the diplomatic efforts to reach peace seem quixotic. For Ben Gurion, probably from the time of 'Abdallah's assassination in 1951 and certainly after his own return to the government in February 1955, the major policy question vis-à-vis the neighboring states was not one of peace but of the survival of Israel. On January 2, 1956, he told the Knesset that the watchword of Israel must be "strength and peace."[36] He was giving expression to his practice, of several years standing, of downgrading foreign policy in favor of defense policy and of frequently using military means to convey Israel's message to its neighbors. The heightened sense of Arab encirclement and hostile intentions, coupled with lack of support from the great powers and UN impotence, proved, so it seems, that diplomatic and political action would not lead to negotiations with the Arabs. This strengthened Ben Gurion's basic attitude that deeds, not words, really count.

BEN GURION AND SHARETT

The attitude just mentioned highlights the policy differences between Sharett and Ben Gurion. There were also basic personality differences between the two. An aide of the latter has referred to this clash as "chemical."[37] In a pioneer study on Israel's foreign policy, Michael Brecher cites an interview with Sharett, some years after his dismissal, in which the former foreign minister described Ben Gurion's key attribute as "Courage," and his own as "Caution."[38] Brecher, adapting a classification proposed by a senior Israeli foreign ministry official, suggests that both Ben Gurion and Sharett wished to achieve reconciliation with the Arabs, but the former sought to do so "from superior strength" (Ben Gurionism) and the latter "through a rational search for moderate solutions" (Weizmannism).[39] The key differences may be seen in the frequency and especially the forcefulness of Israel retaliatory raids against Jordan and Egypt under Ben Gurion and during the period when Sharett was prime minister and Ben Gurion was not defense minister. Sharett tried to curtail the use of armed Israeli replies and questioned their value.

Essentially, the deterrent raids were the expression of Ben Gurion's foreign policy vis-à-vis the neighboring states. They began shortly before he announced, in June 1951, that the no-peace, no-war situation in the Middle East would continue for a long time, but they were probably predicated on an earlier decision to that effect. Although 'Abdallah was still alive on February 8, 1951, when, following incursions, and the murder of an Israeli, a small Israeli force dynamited several houses in the Jordanian-controlled Jerusalem suburb of Shu'afat, he had not found a prime minister willing to sign a peace treaty with Israel, and it seemed certain that he would not.[40]

Thus the policy operated on the understanding that the sides involved saw the Arab-Israeli conflict as an established fact and within that framework tried to improve their strategic position. The international community, on the other hand, preferred not to recognize this situation and viewed the reprisals as disturbances of the peace. Ben Gurion consequently had to take into account the status of international relations and estimates of international reaction in his planning of the reprisals. However, this stock-taking did not dissuade him from acting. Sharett's starting point was different. He used the difficult-to-define term "atmosphere" to summarize his attitude.

> The problem of peace will not be solved either by material arguments or by logic . . . . It is ultimately a matter of willingness . . . whether we create an atmosphere conducive to peace or at least remove mental obstacles to peace.[41]

"Atmosphere" called for a lessening of the frequency and strength of retaliation; attempts to reach out to Arab diplomats through carefully unpublicized contacts; gestures with regard to the refugees; an attempt to use the UN forum, the Truce Supervision Organization and its Mixed Armistice Commissions, and Western, particularly US, influence to create a mood in which Israeli and Arab diplomats would slowly find ways of initiating contacts and tenuously working out the stages of an agreement. "Atmosphere" could also mean a willingness to offer the Arabs partial settlements which could conceivably satisfy them more than they would Israel, as when Sharett declared Israel willing to grant Jordan free port facilities in Haifa as soon as Jordan stopped the boycott and opened itself to Israeli trade. No formal peace settlement would be necessary.[42]

Ben Gurion, the deed-oriented pragmatist, was concerned with strength and tangibles; he demanded that foreign policy be a facet of security needs. Sharett, the word-oriented diplomat, though not unaware of defense factors, felt that safety lay in a satisfactory international climate and cautious steps toward reconciliation. "I do not believe," Ben Gurion said, "nor did I believe . . . that by ideological disputation will Jewish-Arab understanding arise."[43]

With the return of Ben Gurion to the cabinet in 1955, Sharett managed from time to time to rally a majority to vote down Ben Gurion's proposals (such as the Straits of Tiran plan), a practice which had been followed on occasion prior to Ben Gurion's resignation. This was one of the major reasons if not the paramount one for Sharett's dismissal. (The others, particularly the practical relations between the defense and the foreign ministries, are dealt with in the next chapter.) The final break came over preparations for the Sinai Campaign. Sharett told a Zionist Congress in April 1956, just two months before his resignation, that Israel's "spiritual superiority might be lost, if instead of a war being forced upon us, we launch a war initiated by ourselves."[44]

Ben Gurion's position, to lead from strength, did not prevent him from searching for lines of approach to the Arabs and particularly to Egypt. On many occasions both before and after the Sinai war he offered to meet Arab leaders any time, anywhere, even if this meant going to Cairo.[45] In 1951 through Sharett and in 1955 and 1959 personally he offered any interested Arab government a non-aggression pact. Sometimes these offers were a bit anomalous. He once said that Israel was not satisfied with the anarchy which prevailed in its relationships with Egypt and therefore desired peace with that country. The date of this speech was November 4, 1956.[46] This and similar statements, not obviously consistent with his acts, resulted in the projection of an attitude which, as one scholar describes it, seemed to be saying: "Talk peace as if you were acting tough, and act tough as if you were not talking peace." To the Arabs, he continues, "the toughness seemed the essential and the peace talk mere eyewash."[47] To Ben Gurion, they were one; he who desires peace prepares for war, is the Roman equivalent.

The attitude of toughness is further demonstrated by Ben Gurion's handling of the Arab-Israeli negotiations on the exploitation of the Jordan River. Several days after the Qibiyah raid in October 1953, the United States, in an effort to cool the area, recommended a new program for development of water resources on a regional scale in the Jordan Valley.[48] The initial Israeli reaction was cool, particularly since Israel's own water diversion work at the Bnot Ya'akov bridge had been stopped by a Security Council resolution, enforced by cancellation of an American loan.[49] Moreover, Israel favored a plan quite different from the one proposed, which was designed to benefit the refugees primarily.

However, negotiations did get underway; Eric Johnson, the US appointed mediator, made four extended trips to the Middle East between October 1953, and September 1955. By 1955, a compromise plan, the Main-Clapp Plan, had been worked out and was all but agreed upon by both the Israelis and the Arabs. The Israelis were ready to drop their demand for the inclusion of the Lebanese Litani River: the Arab states (Syria, Jordan and Lebanon) were almost willing to accept the necessity of the Kinneret (Sea of Galilee) as a storage area although the entire lake was under Israel's sovereignty. The differences over water allocations under the plan had been narrowed.[50] Thus it appeared at the time that the Israeli-Arab conflict could be alleviated to some degree through cooperation in regional development. However the general heightening of tensions in 1955 (results of the arms race, the Baghdad Pact, etc.) led to the abandonment of negotiations.

Although Ben Gurion had often declared that development of water resources was part of Israel's overall security posture, he refrained from giving the American proposal his blessing. His role in the negotiations was at best peripheral. When Johnson first came to Israel, Ben Gurion was still prime minister (the news of his retirement was already known), but he did not meet with the American mediator. On the occasion of Johnson's fourth visit to Israel, Ben Gurion found many excuses for not seeing the diplomat: Johnson had acquiesced to Arab demands for changes in the program; Ben Gurion was having trouble putting together a coalition government; the border situation with Egypt was worsening. In any event, he chose one of them. During secret talks held the following January (1956), President Eisenhower's emissary, Robert Anderson, tried to revive interest in the project. The prime minister made no response.[51] Later in the year, when the subject was mentioned at the Histadrut Convention, he did reply:

> I feel obligated to tell the members that we must try — although there is no assurance that the attempt will succeed — to exploit the Jordan under terms of agreement with our Arab neighbors, if the agreement will be reached in the shortest possible time. I think that it is better for us to get a little less water through an agreement, than a little more water through a quarrel. But if no agreement is reached in the near future, and we will have wasted precious time for nothing, we will do the work in any case, and whoever interferes with us will have to bear the consequences.[52]

The attitude is typical of Ben Gurion: "We prefer an agreement with some concessions, but we are not going to sacrifice our rights or waste our time. If necessary we will go it alone." In terms of the Jordan River exploitation plan, that is what actually happened. At the end of 1960, Minister of Agriculture Moshe Dayan received a large budget for work on the northern section of the National Water Carrier, a project designed to use water pumped out of the Jordan—Sea of Galilee system. The Syrians who tried to interfere with these operations were ultimately meted out their punishment in a series of retaliatory raids dating from 1962-7.

In the last six years of Ben Gurion's term in office, the Middle East hung in a tenuous balance of power. Nasser's rise, set back by the Sinai Campaign, was further blocked by the Iraq-Jordan coalition until 1958, and then by the Iraqi politicians who opposed Nasserist policies. Israel itself had broken out of both encirclement and isolation. The French honeymoon was on and continued beyond Ben Gurion's 1963 resignation. The Israeli demonstration of strength in Sinai made the world take both the country and its leader seriously. This must have been a source of great satisfaction to Ben Gurion. In the post-Sinai period, he discovered the art of personal diplomacy and visited Burma, Sweden, France, England, Canada and the United States. Through his contacts with foreign heads of state, he tried approaching his old enemy Nasser with offers of peace. In December 1961, U Nu, the Burmese premier, took word to the Egyptian president that Ben Gurion sought a meeting with him. There was no nibble. The following year, Ben Gurion wrote to Tito proposing that the Yugoslav president, who was known to be a good friend of Nasser, arrange a meeting between the two. Tito turned the idea down. [53]

To some extent Ben Gurion's actions in terms of the Middle East seemed to be proving the thesis, or at least recognizing the fact, that Israel is in but not of that region. The formation of the United Arab Republic on February 1, 1958, was greeted with great reserve. Israel announced that it did not see this development as affecting the *status quo*. [54] The Arabs did not quite know how to take this; Syria rather hysterically accused Israel of plotting military activity against it and Egypt. [55] The reaction to the Jordan-Iraqi Federation, formed in response to the UAR, was almost equally mild. Jordan was warned that an Iraqi presence in the West Bank would be construed as a violation of the 1949 armistice. Although the message went through the foreign ministry, Jordan got it. There was no Iraqi presence in the West Bank during the short-lived Federation. The unrest in the neighboring Arab states in the middle of 1958 — the civil war in Lebanon, incipient insurrection in Jordan, and the revolution in Iraq — did direct Ben Gurion's attention to his neighbors. He described the situation as dangerous because he believed at the time that the Iraqi revolution would strengthen

Nasser, the principal enemy. He appealed for internal consolidation and strength "in order to fend off danger and protect [our] independence."[56] But Israel waited quietly for further developments and did not loudly protest the British overflights bringing troops and supplies to bolster King Hussein's regime against pro-Nasser dissidents. The American overflights to Lebanon were not protested at all, and even tacitly approved.[57] Evidently the question of internal Arab politics only bothered Ben Gurion when it seemed that Nasser would stand to gain. This was in line with his considering Egypt the chief adversary. In such cases, he was willing to assist his enemy's enemies, provided that such help did not require Israel's open or direct involvement. Enemies' enemies are after all not friends.

Ben Gurion remained unswervingly committed to the idea of the *status quo* and the need to defend it whenever it was threatened. There were no retaliation raids from the Sinai Campaign until February 1960, when the IDF routed Syrian troops who, masquerading as Arab peasants, had taken control of the demilitarized zone. After the raid, Ben Gurion said that Israel would make every effort to preserve quiet but it would not allow Syrian troops in any area where they had no right to be and would act on its own if the UN refused to or could not evict them.[58] Tension did mount along the Syrian front and, in somewhat of a surprise move, the Egyptian army moved into the Sinai Desert for the first time since the 1956 war. Ben Gurion urged the nation to be calm and charged Egypt with inciting war. A few days later, on February 29, 1960, he announced that he was flying to the US to receive an honorary degree.[59] The tensions dissipated. A repetition of Syrian provocation evoked another retaliatory raid two years later (March 17, 1962). Ben Gurion himself was on vacation at the time, which suggests that he may no longer have taken an active part in the planning of the raids.

Ben Gurion's tough policy ensured survival. In the long run the policy shows negative results as well. The rapid Sinai victory increased Arab anxiety about Israel's power. Its collusion with

France and Britain lent a semblance of veracity to the claim that Israel was a bridgehead of imperialism (a term reserved for Western influence in Third World litany in general and in the Arab lexicon in particular). The expansionist image was enhanced, even though Israel at last grudgingly evacuated territories (Sinai and Gaza) it had occupied. The road to negotiations was never opened. The infrequent post-Sinai raids were a dialogue of last resort.

CHAPTER TEN

Arms and the Powers

In a lengthy address to the commanding officers of the IDF in 1950, Ben Gurion stressed the value of physical strength in the life of the nation. To reject the use of strength or power would mean "rejecting Jewish history from the days of Joshua to the Israel Defense Forces." According to his Bible-centered historiography, this would also constitute a denial of the basic doctrine of the indivisibility of matter and spirit.[1] That year he told the Knesset: "I see in Jewish strength a precondition for mutual understanding with the Arabs . . . . We believe in . . . strength and peace, and our policy can be summed up as follows: 'Supreme military preparedness; sincere readiness for peace.' "[2]

At the time of Israel's Declaration of Independence, the infant state faced grave problems in the realm of "matter" and strength, or more precisely, arms materiel. The inventory before the war in 1948 was scanty: no artillery, no armor, a few hundred two- or three-inch mortars, several thousand machine guns, and about 10,000 rifles.[3]

Israel's problem was to obtain arms, which meant building up sources of supply. The first and instinctive reaction of the fledgling defense system, beginning in the pre-state period when it was not yet free of the mentality of the underground, was to rely on itself. Attempts were made, especially in the United States, to obtain war surplus, tool, die and other basic equipment, and to design an infantry weapon which could be produced in quantity locally. This of course turned out to be quixotic since it required too long a lead time.[4] Heavier equipment — beyond a rudimentary three-inch mortar manufactured in Israel, along with inefficient homemade Sten guns and some grenades — would have to be imported. The three Western powers had imposed an arms boycott on the Middle East but since Britain had been supplying most of Israel's neighbors, its strictures were felt principally by the new state. The solution lay in smuggling arms from the West, especially from the United States, and in opening a line to the Soviet East, whose interest lay in easing out the British as a first step to establishing itself in the Middle East. In either case, large sums, astronomical in relation to the pre-state Jewish Agency budget, would be required.

Earlier, in the summer of 1945, Ben Gurion had thrown himself into the efforts to prepare for the anticipated military showdown with the local Arabs and the neighboring states. His initiative, in New York, led to the organization of a group of Jewish supporters who conducted unpublicized fund-raising for the acquisition of American war surplus and other supplies, as well as for financing the purchase of materiel from other countries. Some of these supplies were smuggled into Palestine in the final stages of British rule, but bulkier and more obvious items had to be stored in Europe and the United States, in anticipation of the British departure.

Ben Gurion personally directed these arms purchases. He was prepared to buy arms anywhere to create and protect the Jewish state. This outlook was given explicit expression a few years later, when he told the Knesset:

> The present point of departure of Israeli policy is not our relation to the ideology of one state or another — but only the fundamental values of Israel and our present and historical needs. Our needs are security, immigration, developing the land . . . .[5]

His representatives secured an effective line of supply from Czechoslovakia. A rudimentary airlift, begun while the British were still in control of Palestine, picked up steam with their departure. On occasion the newly arrived arms turned the balance of battle, as in the case of a few field pieces rushed to the Deganiah area, south of the Sea of Galilee, which helped rout a Syrian advance in 1948.[6]

Once the War of Independence was won and the IDF began to take on form and shape, procurement continued along the lines developed before and during the war. Vast stockpiles of unused or rebuilt arms were still available in the West; and the Arabs showed no signs of introducing more sophisticated materiel into the area. In the early 1950s, the IDF's ordinance was a mixture of what had been and was still readily available: Czech (ex-German) light weapons, British and American armor, and British and German planes.

In the 1949-55 period, Israel's major problem was to find a stable and ready source of relatively unsophisticated arms. Britain, France and the US had subscribed to the Tripartite Declaration which stated their intention to prevent the creation of an imbalance in armament. During the early 1950s Israel attempted to obtain arms from the West with limited success. On various occasions, diplomatic efforts were made by the foreign ministry to gain Israel's entry into a regional alliance or a Middle East Defense Command, both under Western sponsorship.[7] The attempts failed as Ben Gurion informed the Knesset at the end of 1951:

> We have turned to all countries from whom it is possible to obtain our requirements [in arms]. Not from any single country did we receive all our needs, and it will do us no good to be angry with the whole world . . . . [8]

However, conditions began to change in the Middle East and by 1955 new Israeli successes in acquiring arms supplies were becoming evident. As Egypt drove the British out, procurement from the former Mandatory power became easier. In the mid-fifties Israel commissioned a few dated British destroyers to augment its tiny corvette fleet, and obtained a small number of British jet aircraft. The destroyers arrived in June 1956.[9]

Following French disenchantment with the Arabs over Algeria and the Suez Canal nationalization, and the entry of Russia into the Middle East through its arms deal with Egypt, the French interest in Israel increased. The French opening was pursued by Ben Gurion's aide Shimon Peres, whose role will be discussed later in this chapter.

These developments followed Ben Gurion's return from Sde Boker to replace Pinḥas Lavon in the defense ministry. As mentioned above, Ben Gurion had reached the conclusion that Arab acceptance of Israel's permanence in the Middle East hinged on their recognition of Israel's indestructibility. Events in the Middle East, such as Egypt's arming and increased Arab infiltration, moved him to act. When exactly he first decided on a preventive war with Egypt is not clear, although by October 1955, a full year before the Sinai Campaign, he had proposed the seizure of the Straits of Tiran, a plan worked out by his chief of staff, General Moshe Dayan, which his cabinet rejected.[10]

The menace of a mightily armed Egypt was never far from Ben Gurion's thoughts. In April 1956 he said in the Knesset: "Let it be told to the people of Israel: We shall ceaselessly augment our ability to defend ourselves . . . ."[11] A voluntary defense fund was encouraged and then transformed into a tax. The security question had become "the center of our concerns," Ben Gurion told the Zionist Congress that spring.[12]

In June 1956 Sharett was ousted from the foreign ministry following conflict over the role of diplomacy as opposed to military action, and Ben Gurion's hands were freed to carry out his policies. The question of arms supply had become the crux of Sharett's dismissal, as part of the overall policy which was to lead to war. Ben Gurion just about said this to the Knesset:

> But the crux of our efforts is, and this in my opinion is the
> key point in our policy . . . the constant strengthening,

ceaselessly and without pause, of our internal strength here in this country; this is the center of our foreign policy; this is the center of our security policy. This is the entire *Torah* [teaching]; strengthening of our moral, economic and military power. For this power, and only this in the final analysis, will be the determining factor in all the talks and disputes and possibly also in the battles which we will be forced to face. [13]

In July, August and September, the efforts to obtain supplies from France were crowned with success. (The parallel foreign service section of this chapter will touch on these efforts.) As a result, the "French deal," as Ben Gurion termed it, reinforced the Israeli army with tanks, jets, machine guns and ammunition. The supplies arrived clandestinely, usually in the dead of night and often at improvised harbors, and Ben Gurion enlisted the cooperation of the newspaper editors to keep the secret. [14]

The Ben Gurion-Peres-Dayan trio was in full control of the entire defense establishment, and an uncanny rapport existed between the then septegenarian and his two decidedly younger colleagues. The evidence is incontrovertible that Ben Gurion participated in the secret negotiations near Paris preceding the Suez-Sinai operation, which was the end product of the arms procurement policy. [15] French aircraft and armor were the tools for Israel's hundred-hours' victory in 1956, and the victory was Ben Gurion's vindication of his supply policy.

The build-up of Egypt's defeated forces after 1956 continued apace with massive Soviet aid, which had shed its Czech cover. The arms race entered a stage of heightened sophistication and augmented quality. The arms of the World War II period were left behind because of the rapid advances in weapon technology. While Ben Gurion continued to seek French arms, he also attempted to gain access to the major source of Western arms, the United States. An initial breakthrough had occurred in the months preceding the Sinai Campaign, when Canada was permitted, if not encouraged by the United States to sell Sabre jets to Israel. The deal fell through apparently due, first, to the

Israeli Air Force's unwillingness to introduce a new line of more expensive aircraft, and secondly, to the American-Canadian reaction to the Sinai Campaign.[16]

The policy of trying to obtain US arms through third parties later succeeded in securing an arms agreement with an embarrassing source, West Germany. Since 1952, West Germany under Adenauer had been making reparation payments to the Jewish people and to Israel as the beneficiaries of the heirless Jewish victims of the Nazi Holocaust. A brief review of this agreement and the surrounding controversy is necessary at this stage, in order to obtain perspective for reviewing the later internal conflicts over German arms.

Following behind-the-scenes diplomatic contacts and clarifications, the Israeli government presented notes to the four great powers, the US, USSR, Britain and France, concerning reparations from Germany and the restoration of Jewish property. This démarche, of January 1951, was followed by another in March, setting forth a demand for $1.5 billion as reparations, not including stolen Jewish property. The demand was to be made upon both East and West Germany. The second note states that "the State of Israel is entitled to, and commanded to protect the honor, rights and property of the millions who were slaughtered, since it is the only incarnation of statehood (mamlakhtiyut) of the people who were slaughtered and burned in the ovens and gas chamber, their property having been confiscated and robbed."[17]

These reparations were to take the form of a block payment, regardless of individual restitution still to be claimed by survivors and their heirs. Reparations for heirless property were to be paid to the collective heir to prevent the "murderers and their successors in East and West Germany" from inheriting former Jewish possessions. The biblical overtone was apparent in Ben Gurion's dictum, "Let not the murderer also be heir."[18] He told the Knesset that the state had undertaken, in concert with world Jewish communities, to absorb and rehabilitate in Israel the survivors of the Nazi period.

The Soviet Union and East Germany ignored the note. The

Western Powers, though recognizing the special Jewish case against Germany, were prepared to help press Israel's claim on an unofficial basis only. During 1951, the Jewish Agency and particularly its chairman, Dr. Naḥum Goldmann, and the newly-constituted Jewish Material Claims Conference, together with Israeli diplomats, helped create the political climate and public pressure which made it possible to open direct negotiations with the West German government. Chancellor Adenauer agreed (both for practical as well as moral reasons, whose delineation lies outside the framework of this study) to meet representatives of the State of Israel and of the Claims Conference.

The issue reached the Knesset in January 1952. Menaḥem Begin, former commander of the Revisionist-oriented Etzel and leader of the Ḥerut Party, rallied the opponents of negotiations with Germany, which they viewed as the successor of the Nazis. He said, in reference to the 1948 *Altalena* incident in which Ben Gurion used force to prevent the landing of arms by the Etzel (see Chapter 7): "When you fired on us with artillery I then gave the command 'No! ' Today I shall give the command 'Yes! ' This will be a war for life and death."[19] From a balcony in Jerusalem's Zion Square, Begin issued this challenge; below were gathered thousands of enraged Israelis, members of Ḥerut, or sympathizers with its anti-German line. The mass demonstration was blocked from disrupting the Knesset session by helmeted Israeli police. The ensuing riot could have shaken the nation, shattered civic unity or deterred the government from pressing its claims on Germany. Mapam and the Communists also opposed the negotiations.

Ben Gurion took to the air in a brief (750 words) radio broadcast. He hit back with the forceful words of a tried orator.

> Yesterday a criminal hand was raised against the sovereignty of the Knesset. A beginning was made of destruction of democracy in Israel. It was announced that not the elected representatives of the nation will determine Israeli policy, but men of the fist and of political murder.[20]

Ben Gurion claimed that ex-Etzel soldiers and Communists had banded together, "the impure ideology of Fascism in its varying manifestations on the right and the left," in order to demolish "the freedom of the people and its sovereignty." He threatened to use "all means" to prevent this, and promised that

> Israel will remain a free and democratic state, and the sovereignty of the Knesset, the authority of the elected government and the rule of law will not be upset; terror against the sovereignty and freedom of the State of Israel will be eradicated, without hesitation and without compromise. [21]

The agreement with West Germany, concluded on September 10, 1952, at a silent ceremony in Luxembourg, called for the payment of a sum exceeding 3,450 million marks over a period of years as reparations for material damages suffered by the Jews. [22]

The reparations agreement naturally led to a growing import of German goods and equipment to Israel, and as a result trade relations slowly normalized and technical interchange grew. Given this development, and the rising eminence of West Germany ("the economic wonder") in Europe, the ground was laid for the later Israeli-German rapprochement. In terms of arms supply and sales, this proved to be of particular importance in the late 1950s and early 1960s. In view of the growing importance of the Federal Republic in the West European community — in economics and defense matters, and especially joint European arms production — Israel had been striving to build contacts with Germany. Shimon Peres, then responsible for day-to-day operations of the ministry of defense, has stated that "in the late 1950s, we resolved to make a serious effort to secure a new source of arms supply — West Germany." [23] Peres is extremely cagey about dates, possibly due to censorship restrictions, but it seems likely that the efforts began shortly after the Gaza withdrawal in March 1957, and perhaps even earlier. At any rate, by the end of 1957 the outgoing chief of staff, General Moshe Dayan, had been invited to pay an official visit to West Germany.

The Mapam—Aḥdut ha-'Avodah left axis was then in the coalition, and had been since 1955. The two former wings of the old Mapam Party raised objections to any dealings with West Germany, on Jewish grounds in particular, but also in the context of East-West relations. The new relationship with Germany was being worked out through ministry of defense channels, and without the official knowledge and approval of the entire cabinet. In this way Ben Gurion wished to lay the foundations for the relationship without having to face a battle on the home front, beginning in his own cabinet. When the issue was finally brought before the cabinet, the story of Dayan's forthcoming visit was leaked to the press, apparently from Aḥdut ha-'Avodah ministerial sources.[24] Since military censorship forbade the mention of Dayan's name, esoteric methods of communication were used: a newspaper headline speaking of a "V.I.P." visit to Germany, and elsewhere on the page a photograph of the one-eyed hero. Of course, in the inner sanctum of opinion makers in the Knesset and press circles, the name became known, and through informal lines of communication, was passed on to the general public.

Ben Gurion resigned on the last day of 1957 and by January 7, 1958, a new cabinet, identical in membership to the previous one, was formed. He was forced to cancel Dayan's visit but received reassurances concerning the secrecy of deliberations in the cabinet and joint cabinet responsibility.

It became clear that within the cabinet there was a not-very-loyal opposition. The issue of Germany came to a head 18 months later. In June 1959, the West German press carried reports that Israel was exporting arms to Germany. Peres explained that Israel was the party which stood to gain more from this than Germany.[25]

The debate in the Knesset was a strange one. Were it not for the solemnity of the attendant circumstances — the historic memory, still fresh, of German mass murder and genocide, the deep rift within the Israeli public, and the vital need for arms supplies — the debate would seem high comedy. Though the issue was whether the government had approved, as the law required, manufacture of arms for sale to Germany, and the actual export itself, the mechanics of the debate hinged on whether the dissident ministers had actually heard Ben Gurion use the word Germany in the cabinet discussion held months earlier. Apparently the deal with Germany had been effected and shipments were proceeding with Ben Gurion's approval and full knowledge, when the legal advisor to the ministry of defense notified his minister about the law requiring cabinet approval for export of arms.

Ben Gurion stated in the Knesset that at that time, December 1958, Israel was "negotiating large sales." The use of the word "large," and the fact that Peres in his book refrains from giving any dates whatsoever raise the question whether the matter was not brought before the cabinet *post factum,* after "small" deals had already been consummated.[26] The point is important in that it may show that Ben Gurion had refrained from consulting with his not-so-loyal left-wing cabinet partners.

At any rate, the Mapam and Aḥdut ha-'Avodah ministers claimed that the cabinet approval of the sale, and the subsequent approval of manufacture for the purpose of these sales, also given at the request of the minister's legal advisor a few weeks later, had not specifically included Germany. They had not heard Germany mentioned, otherwise they would never have agreed. The traditional Mapai supporters, the National Religious Party, were in opposition at that time due to the "Who is a Jew? " crisis of a year earlier, and were able to cast their arrows in all directions. One of their leaders interrupted the statement by Aḥdut ha-'Avodah with the cry, "Why say this is a security problem? It is an acoustical problem."[27]

On formal grounds, the left position was based on a Knesset resolution declaring opposition to the re-arming of both Germanies, adopted in November 1954.[28] Ben Gurion's stand was that the left's refusal to support the government was opposed to the Knesset law of collective responsibility, the coalition agreement on the same subject, and a further undertaking made at the time of the previous crisis a year-and-a-half earlier that abstention by a minister from a vote supporting a cabinet decision meant the automatic resignation of that minister.

Ben Gurion told the Knesset that in the new world situation, Germany was "one of the many members of NATO." He added:

> The small State of Israel does not belong to any alliance or bloc. I state this out of great regret and deep concern . . . . Belonging to a bloc increases security, supplies, arms . . . . But we are alone . . . and more than any nation, need friends . . . . They tell us . . . we would even accept arms from the Devil . . . . In matters of international relations we ask one simple question: What is good for Israel? And if it is good — all my Jewish and human instincts tell me: do what is good for Israel and necessary for its security. And if the lips of the victims of the Holocaust move in their graves, they say, "Be strong and of good courage."[29]

Ben Gurion won the close vote in the Knesset with the support of the General Zionist opposition members and the pro-Mapai Arab lists, while the two Agudah parties abstained.

A few days after the vote, on July 5, 1959, since the opposing ministers did not tender their resignation, Ben Gurion submitted his, causing the automatic resignation of the entire government. Elections were held in November 1959. Ben Gurion received a significant increase in support (up from 40 to 47 seats), Ḥerut a slight increase (15 to 17), and Aḥdut ha-'Avodah suffered a distinct setback (from 10 down to 7). The more ideological parties — Mapam and the religious — held their own.[30]

During this period of crises, Ben Gurion had been evolving the philosophy of "another Germany" — that the West Germans were not only seeking to make material amends, but also to reform spiritually.[31]   In any event, West Germany was

America's favorite child on the continent, and its economic miracle had kept pace with or even outstripped its rehabilitation in the eyes of the West. Furthermore, the rapprochement between France and Germany was leading to cooperation between the erstwhile enemies in a number of technical and military fields, and good relations with both partners was dictated by a strategic reading which saw Western Europe as a potential super-power.[32]

Some of Ben Gurion's traits show through clearly in this key issue: Israelocentrism, extreme pragmatism, illustrated by his acceptance of the realities of Israel's need for funds and friends, and stubbornness and courage in facing the possible civil disturbances stemming from his unpopular decision. The Jewish state's rapprochement with Germany came about *in spite* of its recent Jewish memories and *because* it was a state. *Raisons d'état* overrode other, perhaps more human considerations.

In 1960, Ben Gurion adopted a new course in Israeli foreign relations — personal diplomacy. In 1960 and 1961, he met with two American presidents, Eisenhower and Kennedy, with De Gaulle and Adenauer (the latter meeting taking place on American soil), as well as political heads of Canada, Burma and Western European states. During this period, he cemented the Peres-initiated policy of the tacit French alliance, and the German grant of arms, then worth about $277 million. Finally, the first dent was made in the standing American policy not to be a major supplier of arms to the Middle East.[33] President Kennedy agreed to sell Hawk anti-aircraft missiles to Israel.

HOME PRODUCTION OF ARMS

Ben Gurion had never been happy about Israel's dependence on foreign arms suppliers. The underground Haganah workshops had turned out small arms, handgrenades, rudimentary Sten submachine guns (the latter almost as dangerous to the user as to the target), light mortars and ammunition. As the War of Independence approached, Ben Gurion sent a number of key aides to the United States "to secure not only arms but the means of producing them."[34] Their success was so great, since they were buying surplus equipment by weight at 19 cents a pound, that by 1970, according to Peres, "the last of the crates were . . . opened only a short time ago and were pounced upon by Israel arms technicians as upon hidden treasure."

In 1949, Ben Gurion called for "development of home production of defensive weapons so we may be independent of import."[35] The implication was clear: arms supply by foreign states is a function of the suppliers' politics. It is a faucet which may be opened or closed at will. Peres relates that over the years production included ammunition and then artillery, machine guns, heavy mortars and even the rebuilding of tanks. The industry developed rapidly and part of its production was earmarked for export.

Ben Gurion personally approved the establishment of an aircraft industry and invited the subsequent head of Israel Aircraft Industries to the country in 1951. In 1955, the plant started operating a rudimentary servicing and repair department, and over the years it began to assemble jet trainers and other aircraft.

Ben Gurion used the defense establishment as an instrument toward realizing his dream of Israel as a great scientific nation. In presenting his government to the first Knesset he had said:

> Like the best of the nations of the world we must bring
> scientific research, pure and applied, to its highest
> achievement . . . . All that we shall do . . for the
> strengthening of our security and expanding our
> economy . . . will be based on the latest and finest results
> of pure and applied science and the most advanced
> technology . . . .[36]

No attempt will be made here to catalog Israel's scientific successes in defense technology, nor is it news that modernization often results from defense needs. It is clear that in arms production, aircraft, electronics and other sophisticated fields Israel has built up an efficient and advanced military industry. One specialist on the military in the Middle East has written that "Israel produced almost all its needs in light and medium weapons, developing in the process the most elaborate military industry in the region."[37] One example will suffice. On July 5, 1961, Ben Gurion presided over the launching of a "meteorological" rocket, Shavit II. It has since been learned that Israel's Gabriel sea-to-sea missiles, now fitted on small and speedy pocket vessels of the Israeli navy, owe their origin to the Shavit.[38] The ministry of defense maintains a large scientific staff in its Authority for Weapons Development, known by its acronym of Rafael. The incidence of the use of angelic names bears no relation to the end product.

The development of weaponry in Israel is more shrouded in secrecy than is the case in most Western countries. This is in part a tradition dating back to the underground, and in part due to the military doctrine of preserving the element of surprise. With regard to the Shavit, the writer had the opportunity of witnessing Ben Gurion's reaction on the morning of the launching, and his delight was clearly evident. His cabinet colleagues, particularly of Aḥdut ha-'Avodah, were angered over the timing of the publicity and, presumably, over the fact that they had not been photographed alongside the rocket with Ben Gurion. He told the cabinet that the timing was determined in order to forestall a reported Egyptian launching scheduled a few weeks later.[39] It is a fact that national elections were held six weeks later, on August 15, 1961.

Sooner or later, the web of secrecy is lifted, but in one area, the nuclear, secrecy has been even greater than usual. Israel's Atomic Energy Commission is under the minister of defense. It began with a small 1–5-megawatt experimental reactor constructed with US cooperation at Naḥal Ṣorek near Rishon le Zion in 1950. The swimming-pool type reactor went critical on June 16, 1960.[40] At a later stage, while the French-Israel honeymoon was yet in bloom, a larger reactor was established in secrecy near Dimona, apparently in 1958.[41] Ben Gurion was taxed with its existence by the Americans in 1960 and at that time tried to fob it off as a textile factory. A number of cabinet ministers also claimed that they had not been informed of the details.[42]

In a Knesset statement, Ben Gurion admitted that a 24-megawatt reactor was being built "in the Negev," for peaceful purposes. The report that Israel was producing an atomic bomb was, he said, "either a deliberate or unwitting lie." He related the new reactor to plans for developing the Negev. It would "serve the needs of industry, agriculture, health and science." It would take three or four more years to complete, he added. Ben Gurion did not mention any cooperation with the French.[43] The Dimona reactor uses uranium and heavy water and went into operation in late 1964.[44] One scholar has described it as "capable of producing enough fissionable material for making one or two nuclear bombs a year."[45]

The Israeli government has constantly stressed that its policy is "not to be the first to introduce nuclear weapons into the Middle East."[46] In this context, it is of some interest to note Shimon Peres' remark of February 1963. Israel, he is reported to have said, could do nothing to prevent the Arabs from acquiring nuclear technology. It was no longer a question of "where" but of "when"; of who will be the first to amass this knowledge and to what use it would eventually be put.[47] Late in Ben Gurion's ministry there were complications with the Americans, who demanded some form of inspection rights. The difficulties with the United States were reportedly straightened out before Ben Gurion resigned.[48]

A PARALLEL FOREIGN SERVICE

The search for arms suppliers as well as for states which would cooperate in scientific development was conducted by the ministry of defense, which set up a network of purchasing missions in major Western capitals. The increasing contacts established over the years, the desire for secrecy, the lack of experience of regular diplomats in this particular area and, one may also assume, institutional rivalry — all these led to the creation of a kind of parallel foreign service. The development seems to have been for pragmatic rather than policy reasons.

Relations with France before Sinai are a key example. Official diplomatic approaches, that is Israel embassy requests to the Quai d'Orsay in 1954-5, seemed to get lost in the polished verbiage of the profession. In order to give a balanced view, it must be stressed that the first purchase of French jets was negotiated by Foreign Minister Sharett and the Israeli ambassador. However, the young defense ministry representatives, headed by Shimon Peres, and with Ben Gurion's blessing, sought and found unofficial contacts. Peres recounts some of these probes, and they make exciting reading: contacts with friends of friends, introductions to highly placed officials, and so on. Since Peres writes rather discreetly, there may be even more which he has not disclosed.[49] For our purposes the details are not important. The technique and the results are. The outcome was the tacit French-Israeli alliance which saw Israel through the Suez period and into the 1960s. The technique was summarized by a leading French civil servant in a conversation with Peres in 1955: "Keep away as far as possible from the diplomatic crowd — they don't make foreign policy, but policy that is foreign. We must establish direct contact between us, get to work, and stop pampering dictators all over the place."[50]

Ben Gurion gave the policy an added dimension of primacy and of legitimation. In early 1956, he told the Knesset:

> Security problems are firmly linked to foreign policy and
> they constitute perhaps the central axis of this policy;
> however for reasons with which I shall deal, the problems
> of security have been aggravated recently, and they require
> special clarification by themselves, and I shall limit my
> words to the question of security.[51]

This centrality of security was bound to lead to an institutional clash with the foreign ministry.

On the French issue, this came at a time when Ben Gurion's relations with his foreign minister, Moshe Sharett, were already strained. This was due in part to differences in orientation, with

Sharett preferring diplomatic to military efforts, and consequently clashing evaluations regarding reprisal actions against the Arabs as well as a difference in "chemistry." According to former aides of Ben Gurion, the practical expression of this was Sharett's ability to lead an opposition within the cabinet, which voted down Ben Gurion's operational proposals. The question of "direct contacts" by the defense ministry was a major issue of controversy in this overall context, as was the matter of who would speak for Israel in the Mixed Armistice Commissions (Israel-Jordan, Israel-Egypt, etc., presided over by an officer of the UN Truce Supervision Organization). Both foreign ministry and military representatives sat on these bodies and the contest between the two was another source of friction.

In the light of this clash, the Knesset debate in which Ben Gurion informed the legislature of Sharett's resignation is instructive. Sharett indicated that his collaboration with Ben Gurion had been "put to severe tests" in the past.[52] Ben Gurion, under sharp and often sarcastic attack by the opposition, explained that he had retained Sharett in the government

> . . . not in spite of differences of opinion, but to a great
> extent, because of them . . . . However, recently, since the
> state's security situation has been exacerbated in a most
> unusual manner . . . I reached the conclusion that now
> there is a need for full coordination — to the extent
> humanly possible — between the ministry of defense and
> the ministry for foreign affairs . . . . [These ministries]
> actually deal with what is almost the same thing, for those
> matters of foreign affairs which are not security issues have
> no great value at this time. In normal times foreign policy
> does not deal exclusively with problems of defense; not so
> today . . . . There is a need that harmony reign between the
> executors of both offices, whose content is one. And
> therefore Mr. Sharett told you yesterday that he found it
> necessary to leave the government.[53]

Sharett's successor, Golda Meir, also clashed with Peres; obviously it was no enviable task to be head of the ministry of foreign affairs but to have effectual control over only one of the two establishments dealing with foreign relations. The opening up of lines of communication between the Israel defense establishment and a European power was repeated later in the case of West Germany. Peres specifies that the "special relationship" with Germany was established through then German Defense Minister Franz Josef Strauss on the basis of "direct contact between our two ministries."[54] Many observers relate the later break between Ben Gurion and Golda Meir in part to these activities and the theory seems highly plausible.

In reviewing Ben Gurion's policies one sees that pragmatism dictated the means of implementing the principle of increasing Israel's strength and ability to survive. No internal crisis or intramural tension was allowed to stand in the way of obtaining arms. Arms supply and security in general became the supreme factor in Israeli foreign policy. This subject, foreign affairs, is not included in the purview of the present study, nor is there great need for such treatment considering the massive and detailed work recently published .[55] The key to understanding the policy is this singularity of purpose, bridging the institutional duality (foreign affairs and defense ministries).

In briefly summarizing Ben Gurion's world outlook, it can be said that he had great respect for Britain and more than that for the US. Furthermore, his anti-Communism was bolstered by Russian anti-Zionism, while in the US he had access to a powerful and wealthy community of Jews, the largest in the world. With the shifting of Russian interests in the early 1950s, Ben Gurion came to lean more and on the US in the international arena. However, American unwillingness to supply arms to Israel and Dulles' wooing of Egypt, until the Aswan financing fiasco in 1956 and the internationalization of the Suez Canal, coinciding with the decline of Britain, prompted him to adopt Peres' pro-French and later pro-German policies.

The relationship with the UN, which must be mentioned briefly if only in passing, was at best one of ambivalence, at worst, of disdain. Ben Gurion never lost sight of the importance of big-power support and world public opinion. Nonetheless, the UN, whose decision had legitimated Zionist aspirations, had not helped Israel establish itself or defend itself. Ben Gurion said in early June 1948: ". . . we know that not by the loving-kindness of nations was our independence renewed, and not on their goodness of heart does it depend."[56]

As the UN, through its mediators and in its councils, pressed for the internationalization of Jerusalem, Israel tended to reject this solution. Since this is an early example of conflict between the UN and Israel it will be briefly treated here as an indication of the future policy. Late in June 1948, the Provisional State Council debated Jerusalem's beleaguered status and future. Ben Gurion asked Sharett to deliver the statement regarding "rumors about Jerusalem's special status." He told the Council that such proposals were being mooted by the Mediator's staff, but that "no proposals have been made and there was no discussion or negotiation in this respect." In other words, the options were open, but Israel was delaying taking any of them.[57] Ben Gurion closed the debate by announcing that *de facto,* pending agreement between the parties and international accord, "Jerusalem (for the moment regrettably without the Old City) is within the realm of the Jewish government [as distinct from the Jewish State] just as is Tel Aviv."[58]

The *fait accompli* policy regarding Jerusalem became clearer on September 3, 1948, when, in the IDF's first proclamation *(minshar)* on military rule, the minister of defense published a map designating "occupied areas" in which Israeli law applied. The second proclamation of the same date appointed military governors, in Jerusalem's case, Dov Joseph, who had been asked to hold this position by Ben Gurion, *de facto,* on April 10, 1948. The Jerusalem Military Government Ordinance (Confirmation of Acts), 1949, validated all acts, laws, regulations and orders issued by the military administration in the Jerusalem area. Military government in the capital ended on February 2, 1949.[59]

The UN's efforts to internationalize Jerusalem were based on its partition decision of November 29, 1947, according to which Jerusalem was to be a *corpus separatum* from the future Arab and Jewish states.[60] *De facto,* Jerusalem had been partitioned in the 1948 war — its new Jewish and a number of Arab quarters were in Jewish hands, with the Old City (including *its* Jewish Quarter) and connected areas under Jordanian control. Israel had no intention of changing its status of effective control over the New City. At the end of 1949, the Jerusalem issue was raised at the UN General Assembly. By then, Israel had proved its strength by concluding armistice agreements with its neighbors. Ben Gurion was therefore able to state from the rostrum of the Knesset that Israel would honor all the existing rights regarding the Holy Places and religious buildings in Jerusalem and guarantee freedom of worship and of access without discrimination. He further announced Israel's intention to withstand any UN decision aimed at weakening the young state's control over its part of the city.

> Jewish Jerusalem is an organic and inseparable part of the State of Israel, just as it is an inseparable part of Jewish history, the religion of Israel and the soul of our people. Jerusalem is the very heart of the State of Israel . . . . We do not for a moment suppose that the United Nations Organization will attempt to remove Jerusalem by force from Israeli hands. We declare that Israel will not of its own volition give up Jerusalem . . . . [61]

To mollify world public and official opinion, he did agree that the United Nations maintain "effective supervision over the Holy Places and existing rights, as will be agreed by the UN and the State of Israel."[62] (Most of the Holy Places were under Jordanian control, particularly in the Old City of Jerusalem.)

Within the week, following the UN General Assembly vote to establish an international regime for the *corpus separatum,* Ben Gurion announced on December 13, 1949, the Israeli government's irrevocable decision to ignore the Assembly's resolution.

> This resolution cannot be carried out under any
> circumstances, if only due to the firm and resolute
> opposition of the inhabitants of Jerusalem . . . . The first
> Knesset opened in Jerusalem on February 14, 1949, . . .
> but it was necessary to transfer its seat temporarily to Tel
> Aviv. With the completion of the necessary arrangements
> in Jerusalem there is no further cause to delay the
> Knesset's return to Jerusalem. [63]

He further announced that the transfer of the government
ministries from Tel Aviv to Jerusalem would proceed as
planned. Though most foreign representations have continued
to maintain their missions in Tel Aviv, and a considerable part
of the government apparatus, particularly of the defense
ministry, was to remain rooted in the coastal city, the transfer
of the legislature and the executive established the fact that
Jerusalem was not only an integral part of Israel, but its capital
as well.

In 1957, it was not the UN decision calling for Israeli
withdrawal from Sinai but pressure from the US and, for that
matter, other friendlier states which forced Ben Gurion to roll
back his forces. It was the power of the powers, so to speak,
rather than the words of the UN which determined his decision.

The pendulum of Israel's relations with the big powers thus
went through the following oscillations: reliance on or
exploitation of the two great powers in the first stage
(1948-50); a cooling-off of relations with the USSR and
attempts to enlist US aid, or even to enter an alliance with the
US and NATO; the opportunistic coincidence of Israel-French
interests and the unwritten alliance with France; rapprochement
with Germany and an eventual strengthening of US-Israel ties as
the US drew its conclusions from its 1956-7 Egyptian fixation
and particularly following President Kennedy's assumption of
office. The UN counted only when the major powers were
following a consistent policy to enforce its decisions.

The thrust was clear and consistent. Ben Gurion desired the
highest possible technical level, possession of the most

sophisticated weapons, and qualitative superiority of manpower for purposes of deterrence or for determining the course of eventual warfare. By building a machine manned by dedicated lieutenants (aptly called *"bitzu'istim"* — a word which encapsules both the concept of pragmatism and the idea of the executive and technocrat), he applied the principle of building strength through arms as a guarantee of survival. The essence of the policy was to exploit any source which would enable Israel to offset Arab hostility and rejection of Israel's existence, a policy still pursued today. It has indeed not led to peace, but has provided interludes of no war. Ben Gurion often cited Psalm 29: "The Lord will give strength unto His people; the Lord will bless His people with peace."[64] This was said not as a pious platitude or politician's ploy, but as an expression of the firm and deep conviction which guided his acts.

CHAPTER ELEVEN

The Jew Who Left
the Zionists Behind

In 1945-8, myriads of Western Jews, shocked beyond complacency by the impact of the European Holocaust on their fellow Jews, joined the world Zionist movement. On the eve of Israel's statehood, the movement could claim two million members and many more Jewish and non-Jewish sympathizers were ready to lend political and material support and aid.[1] Weizmann had effectively been neutralized at the World Zionist Congress in Geneva at the end of 1946, and had been denied the presidency of the movement. Ben Gurion led the large labor bloc, and had become the key figure in Palestine, arena of the coming showdown with the British and the Arabs. Though formally "only" chairman of the Jewish Agency—World Zionist Organization Executive in Jerusalem, the Jewish quasi-government, his preeminence was enhanced by his growing control of defense matters (Haganah and weapons purchase and production). His position was further strengthened with statehood and the positions he filled. Therefore, his role in determining Israel's relationship with Zionism, as well as Israel's place in world Jewish affairs, is central, and will be examined in this chapter.

Ben Gurion's attitudes rested on a basic line he had evolved in his early years; his interpretation of reality reinforced his theoretical conclusions. In the debate between practical and political Zionism, Ben Gurion had inclined heavily to the practical side: he preferred real or material progress in establishing settlements and reclaiming land to international statements of support, guarantees and declarations. As a realist, he recognized the importance of moral and political support, but felt that such declarations would be meaningless without a physical land base in Palestine. This is the way he had greeted the Balfour Declaration of 1917, in which the British government recognized the right of the Jews to establish a National Home in Palestine.[2] This practical *Palestinocentrism* had expressed itself even earlier, when the emerging Labor Zionist groups in Europe and Palestine united in the worldwide Po'alei Tziyyon organization and set up a fund for constructive purposes in the formative years preceding World War I. Ben Gurion refused to see the Po'alei Tziyyon in Palestine as merely another local "branch" of the worldwide party, sharing control of the fund with the others, but the one which was central. Therefore the fund "must be an institution of all Palestine laborers and be conducted by them . . . ."[3]

His road to a Labor Zionist state was laid out in 1917: to make the labor element the leading force in world Zionism, and through the World Zionist Organization bring about Jewish statehood, as and when possible. With statehood, the need for a Zionist Organization would disappear.

> With the formation of a Jewish majority in Eretz Yisra'el, the task of the Zionist Organization will end, and the independent Hebrew nation in Eretz Yisra'el, together with the other non-Jewish communities, which will have equal rights, will become the absolute owners of the country.[4]

This Palestinocentrism was strengthened for very practical reasons in World War II. Communications and travel were difficult, and the Palestinian members of the world Zionist leadership had great freedom of action, which was exercised by the Jewish Agency—World Zionist Organization Executive, headed by Ben Gurion. Nonetheless, he was aware of the political and financial supportive role the Zionist movement could continue to play after statehood, and seemed prepared to let it stand the test of time, a departure from his views about the movement's disappearance, expressed some 30 years previously.[5] This was a pragmatic recognition of the fact that the Zionist movement existed and its disbanding would create new difficulties at an already difficult time. It may also have been a tactical delay, to postpone the showdown. Certainly he had clear doubts about the movement's ability to adjust to new realities and to be able to redefine itself. These thoughts and the embryonic outline of his future attitude toward the organized Zionists are embodied in an address to the Zionist General Council (the so-called Actions Committee), which is the governing body of the movement between World Zionist Congresses, in May 1949, on the day after Israel's first anniversary.[6] Because of its importance, the speech will be summarized and cited extensively.

"The State of Israel has become the leading factor in the realization of Zionism from henceforth onwards," Ben Gurion said. Previously, of course, this role had been played by the Yishuv. But the state is not the "final aim of Zionism, the aim is ingathering the exiles." This required cooperation between the state and the World Zionist Organization, with each body playing an exclusive role in some areas and collaborating in others.

Israel was a sovereign state; its sovereignty, he said, was the exclusive responsibility of its citizens. "No Jew in the Diaspora, Zionist or non-Zionist, may share in this." The state did not represent world Jewry, and it should not come between its Jewish citizens and their ties with Jews outside of its borders. The areas of collaboration between the State of Israel and the Zionist Organization included Israel's security and foreign policy, immigration of Jews to Israel, fostering Jewish culture, and settlement of the land.

Both security and foreign affairs were, he stated, seemingly under the exclusive jurisdiction of the state. Nevertheless, the state was not intended only for its own present inhabitants; all Jews have a stake in its existence. They should therefore provide financial and economic aid to strengthen Israel and ensure its existence, and help explain Israel's foreign policy in the countries in which they dwell.

The question of immigration, Ben Gurion said, is a paradoxical one: from where, on the one hand, will Israel take its immigrants? how, on the other hand, will it be able to absorb those who do come ? The slaughter of six million European Jews was followed by the prohibition of Jewish emigration from certain European and Arab states. Ben Gurion said:

> We are confronted with a bitter question: Whence will we take Jews for the State of Israel? This is not simply a question, but a demand, a demand upon Zionists who inhabit free lands — if Zionism is not lip-service but a revolutionary historical vision, whose end is ingathering the exiles.[7]

This demand was coupled with one for extensive financial participation in the great cost of absorbing the immigrants, in the form of contributions, investments, and loans.

Almost subsumed under the question of immigration was that of Hebrew language and culture, which Ben Gurion saw as the cornerstone of national unity, then endangered by the influx of immigrants who did not know Hebrew. Ben Gurion accorded a special and separate place to this vital issue, and urged that Hebrew be taught "to the people, the youth, the masses" in the Diaspora, as a major undertaking of the Zionist movement.

A further extension of immigration, but again given separate prominence as the fifth point in the address, was the expansion of pioneering in Israel by young people who would settle the wasteland. There was also a call to include under the old heading of "pioneering" new concepts regarding visits to and study in Israel by young Diaspora Jews, a subject which will be considered later in this chapter.

Three of the five points in the May 1949 speech dealt with one or another aspect of immigration. Defense and foreign affairs policies were completely under Israel's sole sovereign jurisdiction; Ben Gurion was calling only for financial and moral support of these policies. The remaining issue really was whether Zionists would immigrate to Israel, encourage immigration to Israel, and create new frameworks and methods for making Israel more central in the life of Jews abroad, with the hope that immigration would evolve from all these activities. Ben Gurion did not mince words. In addition to presenting the choice Zionists must make regarding immigration as either "lip-service" or a "revolutionary historical vision," he said:

> The Zionist movement must understand that Zionism is no
> longer that which it was, that dimensions have changed,
> the essence has changed, the pace has changed, the needs
> have changed. And if Zionism will not be able to meet the
> new needs in new dimensions and at a new pace, it will go
> bankrupt and disappear from the stage.[8]

The veiled or not-so-veiled threat implicit in this explains Ben Gurion's seeming ambivalence, and his departure from his earlier position regarding the disappearance of the Zionist movement once the state was achieved. His position at the 1949 assembly was a conditional acceptance of organized Zionism, provided it would provide political, financial and *manpower* support for Israel. It was a completely pragmatic approach. The organization existed and it would be difficult to dismantle it. If it would change and become more effective, it could be an additional avenue of support for the weak and struggling state.

This attitude had been foreshadowed in 1937. The British Royal Commission's conclusion that the Mandate was unworkable and that a Jewish state would arise in partitioned Palestine seemed to indicate that independence was near. At that time, Ben Gurion outlined the future cooperative functions of the state and the Zionist Organization in terms similar to those of 1949.[9] The intervening years had shown him the limitations on material help the organized Zionist movement was able to give Israel. Ben Gurion had turned to non-Zionists, especially in the United States, to finance the arms purchases in the pre-state struggle (see previous chapter) and the majority of overseas volunteers who had fought in Israel during the War of Independence had not been Zionists.[10]

The debate with Zionists in the early years of the state was conducted on two levels: the operative and the ideological. The first sought to define the areas of cooperation and collaboration as well as the areas of the exclusivity of function. The second demanded a redefinition of the purpose of Zionism: its aims, the actual responsibilities of Zionists to their movement, the "dosage" of "self-realization" of each member — must he move to Israel?, and so on. On both levels these questions were complicated by the personal relationships between Ben Gurion and the Zionist chiefs: Silver, Goldmann and later Sharett.

On the operative level, the questions of collaboration and exclusivity were raised early in statehood. The unified *personnae* of the Jewish Agency Executive and the government underwent the kind of operation reserved for Siamese twins. In August 1948, Ben Gurion resigned his chairmanship, and other ministers surrendered their membership in the Jerusalem Executive. In spring of 1950, the relationship between the state and the World Zionist Organization again formed the core of the discussion at the Zionist General Council meeting in Jerusalem.[11] Two central issues emerged: first, the Israeli demand that overseas Zionists make immigration to Israel their main goal, as opposed to the stand of most non-Israeli, and especially US Zionists, who saw their role as political spokesmen or "interveners" on Israel's behalf, and as leaders of general educational activity toward increased identification with Judaism and with Israel. The second issue was the formal, official relationship between the government and the WZO—Jewish Agency, considered from the aspect of Israel's sovereignty and the extent that it might be impaired by the status and activities of the Zionist Organization. Ben Gurion was, naturally, on the side of the Israel-centered "Zionism-means-immigration" group, and opposed giving the Zionist Organization any status of equality with the state.

> 'Aliyah [immigration] precedes everything else . . . . For in
> 'aliyah there is security, in 'aliyah there is renaissance, in
> 'aliyah there is ingathering of the exiles, *and there is
> nothing without it* . . . . The Zionist movement will be
> tested from now on by deeds and an ability to act *(bitzu'a)*
> by standards which reflect the needs of our times. But in
> this partnership, the first and decisive place is reserved for
> the State of Israel. In it the vision is being realized, and
> only in the state framework *(mamlakhti)* is activity
> possible. [12]

The General Council heard many proposals for regulating the relationship between the Zionist Organization and the state. Some called for the appointment of an observer by the Zionists who would sit in on cabinet meetings of the government, others for the granting of a special status by law to the World Zionist Organization. The debate had its touching, and comic parts. One delegate, comparing the Zionist movement to a parent and the state to its offspring, said: "I have known of legislation allowing fathers to legitimize their sons, but I have never heard of the need for laws allowing sons to grant recognition to their parents."[13] Most important was the plan outlined by Dr. Nahum Goldmann, chairman of the Jewish Agency Executive in New York. Goldmann wanted the Zionist movement to become "the sole authorized representative of the Jewish people in its work in Israel." It was to be the channel through which "everything must go."[14]

The 1950 meeting decided to establish a coordinating committee together with the government and stated that it was "essential that the Jewish Agency be granted legal status . . . in Israel," and that it be authorized "to regulate activities in Israel of Jewish organizations abroad and coordinate their plans . . . with the Jewish Agency."[15] A few weeks later, Ben Gurion presented the Knesset with a proposal, agreed upon by the cabinet and the Zionist Executive, to establish a joint body for "development and coordination," consisting of representatives of both who would deal with day-to-day practicalities and planning in the fields of "immigration, absorption, housing of immigrants, land settlement and agricultural development." The body would operate until the next World Zionist Congress.[16] There was no mention of the exclusive role the Zionists desired, to represent all Jewish organizations vis-à-vis the Israel government. Ben Gurion had blocked this monopoly desired by Goldmann, and would continue to prevent any such development.

At the first Zionist Congress to be held after the establishment of Israel, in August 1951, it was Abba Hillel Silver who formulated the Zionist demand, which had been expressed in memos prepared by the Organization Department of the Executive two years previously.[17] Silver, the leader of US Jewry's pre-1948 political fight for Israel, had been Ben Gurion's partner in sidetracking Weizmann. He had resigned two years earlier from his post as head of the American Executive of the Jewish Agency, ostensibly over a battle between the Jerusalem and New York bodies regarding Zionist control of fund-raising for Israel. Although the struggle seemed to be between American Jewish representation on the one hand and American national Zionist leadership on the other, for control of the United Jewish Appeal, behind the scenes the Agency Executive members in Israel were supporting the group interested in increasing local community representation. Silver's irritation mounted. He saw a trend by the state (and the Israeli members of the Executive, who, he felt, were being directed by the state's leaders) to bypass the organized Zionist movement. His resignation may be seen as an outcome of Ben Gurion's consistent refusal to grant the Zionists exclusivity in "representing" Jewish communities vis-à-vis Israel and vice-versa.[18]

In this sense, Ben Gurion's policy, though, as far as can be ascertained, never stated explicitly, was to retain a direct relationship with those raising and contributing funds to the Jewish Agency and other Israeli bodies. He would reason that to permit this to remain in the hands of the organized Zionists might subject Israel to interference or an attempt at control by overseas Zionists. These men were not "equal" to Israelis, in Ben Gurion's view: "Only here in the Land did I learn that the realization of Zionism is a matter of life and death."[19] Furthermore, the organized overseas Zionists were of the right wing, and did not share his party's social and political views. The non-ideological pro-Israeli Jewish contributors would therefore be more convenient partners. Here ideology and practical considerations again were wed.

To return to the thread of the organizational question, Silver, already "burnt" as it were, in 1952 proposed a two-directional function for the World Zionist–Jewish Agency Executive: "the right of direction and coordination of all activities in the Diaspora for the benefit of the State of Israel" and that the Israel government should "channel its requirements . . . from Diaspora Jewry through it [the World Zionist Organization]." One of the most reliable reporters on the Israeli scene tersely summed up the prime minister's position on this issue:

> Ben Gurion had been opposed to exclusive status [for the Zionist Organization] *even in Israel* . . . . The Organization would merit a special status only if they pledged "unconditional cooperation" with whatever government was in power.[20]

The latter point would seem to bear out Ben Gurion's fear of having "outside" control by political rivals.

In May 1952, Ben Gurion presented the Law of the Status of the Zionist Organization in Israel to the Knesset. In his introduction, he spoke of the central point of the law, that the State of Israel

... as a unit of statehood *(yeḥidah mamlakhtit)* has a connection with the Jewish people .... There exists a mutual link between the fate of the state and the fate of the Jews of the world; the destiny of the Jews depends in a number of aspects on the destiny of Israel and the destiny of Israel depends on the destiny of the Jews. [21]

This was to be expressed through cooperation and coordination in "ingathering the exiles," in immigration and development. The speech pays tribute to the Zionist Organization and its role in helping bring Israel into being. But "the state itself has become the leading and major instrument for realizing the Zionist vision . . . ." Therefore, just as one does not envy one's son or pupil, so must the Zionist Organization recognize, "with love and with will" — a phrase culled from Hebrew liturgy — the primacy of Israel in the "net of instruments of redemption of the Jewish people."[22]

Under the pressure of debate, Ben Gurion admitted that two points which the 1951 Zionist Congress had demanded, both relating to exclusivity of status, were not included in the law. The Organization was not recognized as "the representation of the Jewish people, for the Jewish people is dispersed throughout the world and the state has not the power or authority or possibility to determine" such representation. Furthermore, the state would not conduct its activities amongst Jewish communities overseas, "in consultation and coordination with the World Zionist Organization."[23]

In November 1952, the law again came up for debate. Ben Gurion refused to entertain any clauses which would enhance the status enjoyed by the World Zionist Organization, but, typically, did agree to delete one phrase that limited Israel's role. The draft began: "The State of Israel, which represents only its own residents, sees itself as the creation of the entire Jewish people . . . ." The prime minister agreed to delete the words "which represents only its own residents."[24]

The debate is important because Ben Gurion, while proclaiming a special relationship between the state and the

Zionist Organization, in effect considerably limited the relationship and downgraded Zionism as an organized movement, foreshadowing his later abandonment of the name Zionist. "The name 'Zionist' is not enough . . . . Many who call themselves Zionists have lost their Zionist faith . . . to be a Zionist means first and foremost to live and to work in the Land of Israel." [25] The movement would be judged by action, and it was this which would ensure that its vision "would not be emptied of content and turn into a hollow phrase." For this reason, the state was ready to share its jurisdiction over immigration and land settlement with the Zionist Organization. Nonetheless, the state takes precedence and priority over the Zionist movement.

> If this be a sin, I confess it this time . . . . The State of
> Israel is the greatest happening in Jewish history during the
> past three thousand years . . . . The superiority of the state
> over the Organization is not only its state powers, its
> international standing, and its deep influence on all parts
> of the Jewish people . . . . The preeminence is qualitative
> and in effect was in existence before the creation of the
> state . . . . Here in the Land is located the forge of
> pioneering ḥalutz Zionism . . . . [26]

The law, as passed, was almost identical with the one proposed some months earlier.[27] Ben Gurion had his way. When, during Moshe Sharett's stewardship as prime minister, the state and the Zionist Executive signed an accord or Covenant ('amanah), it essentially contained the same points as the law. The Zionist movement was not given the status of representing Diaspora Jewry in Israel, nor the function of channelling Israel's relations with the overseas communities.[28] Somewhat later, in November 1953, Ben Gurion wrote that the state had "granted special status to the Zionist Organization within the State of Israel . . . in order to strengthen the position and prestige of the Zionist Organization . . . ." even though the state would probably be able to do the same work "more efficiently and without duplication."[29] The state took primacy over the earlier "rival" framework not only in Ben Gurion's design and thought, but in practice.

The agreement between the state and the Organization was to be effected by a Coordinating Committee. Ben Gurion's priorities did not give this committee pride of place. For example, at regular intervals, in the years 1957-1960, the president of the World Zionist Organization, Naḥum Goldmann, expressed his disappointment with its work, both publicly and at meetings with the prime minister. [30]

The problems between Goldmann and Ben Gurion were compounded by personal differences concerning Zionism, Israeli foreign policy and, basically, perhaps by an unbridgeable gap between Israelocentrism and Diasporism. For example, in 1957, Ben Gurion objected to Goldmann's pronouncements on such subjects as neutralism and Israel's foreign policy; Goldmann used an old Ben Gurion ploy and retorted that "his views had been personal" and did not necessarily represent the World Zionist Organization. According to the press, Ben Gurion asked Goldmann to refrain in the future from dealing with matters that were purely the affair of the state, to which Goldmann reportedly agreed. [31] For his part, Goldmann wished to sit in on cabinet meetings, a desire to which Ben Gurion never acceded. [32]

Parallel to and much more important than Ben Gurion's relations with Goldmann was his evolving disenchantment with organized Zionism, which was finally clearly voiced. His initial caution, the principle of Israelocentrism, and the policy of state primacy over the Zionist Organization have already been shown. The development continued. In December 1953, Ben Gurion wrote a brief note to the Zionist General Council from Sde Boker. His message, on the need for Zionists themselves to immigrate to Israel, was interpreted as: "a man who did not come to Israel could not be a Zionist." This was what distinguished a Zionist from any Jew who helped Israel. [33]

Ben Gurion continued his call, irritating to many Zionists, for immigration to Israel. At the World Zionist Congress in 1956 he said:

> The security of Israel is first of all dependent on the
> continuation of immigration . . . and not only a
> quantitative, but a qualitative increase. That is to say a
> moral and intellectual strengthening by the addition of
> professionals and intellectuals.[34]

To another forum that year he said that "Zionism today is only
pioneer immigration and Hebrew education. Only those who
themselves carry these out, or have their children do so, deserve
the name Zionist."[35]

In July 1957, he restated sharply his interpretation with
regard to the responsibility for the creation of Israel. It was not
the Zionist Organization *per se,* but the ḥalutzim, the
immigrants, who had built the state. (This further
demonstration of Israelocentrism had been foreshadowed in the
debate on the status of the World Zionist Organization, but not
stated as baldly, possibly for tactical reasons.) A month later, in
August 1957, Ben Gurion spoke at an ideological conference in
Jerusalem and was interpreted as having said he was "not a
Zionist."

> I absolutely reject this thing that is now called "Zionism"
> by most of the "Zionists" in the Diaspora . . . . As for the
> Jews who consider themselves a part of the American,
> British or French people, who do not feel and understand
> that they are living in exile . . . I have no part in this
> "Zionism."[36]

At the World Zionist Congress of 1960, he again spoke out
sharply about Zionism and immigration to Israel. He was
concerned about Israel's staying power, the asymmetric ratio of
population between the Arab states and Israel.

> I must state clearly: our limited strength in this country
> will not suffice to correct historic wrongs if we do not
> receive enlightened pioneer immigration from developed
> countries rich in intellectual forces . . . . The question

which those who are assembled here are called upon to
resolve and to respond to not only in words and in
resolutions, but in deeds — is whether you intend . . .
whether you have the will and ability . . . to ensure the
required immigration to Israel in large and growing
dimensions . . . . A personal tie with Israel . . . is the first
responsibility of those who bear the name of Zion.[37]

Finally, in April 1961, Ben Gurion wrote that since the term
Zionism had been emptied of content (that is, there was no
distinction between Zionists and other Jewish supporters of
Israel, since the Zionists were not required to immigrate to
Israel), the Zionist Organization should change its name to "The
Jewish Organization." This would "do away with the artificial
wall between Zionists and non-Zionists and free its members
from the burden of an 'agreed lie.' "[38] Moshe Sharett, then
chairman of the Jewish Agency–Zionist Executive in
Jerusalem, responded sharply: "It is surprising that a man of
such great achievements and creative powers as David Ben
Gurion should be wasting his energy on such meaningless
semantic polemics."[39]

The broader context of Ben Gurion's historiography and
motivation has been discussed elsewhere, but here the polemic
raised by Naḥum Goldmann will be considered. He wrote that
Ben Gurion "lost all interest in the Organization as soon as the
General Council decided, at its first meeting after the
establishment of the state, to transfer all functions concerning
the inhabitants of Israel to the Israeli government." Goldmann
opposed this, but delegates from Israel voted for the division
of functions (between the Zionist Executive and the new state's
government) "out of enthusiasm for statehood, and the
non-Israelis out of fear of dual loyalty." The veteran Zionist
leader adds that as a result, Ben Gurion, "self-centered as ever,
turned his back on the Zionist Organization."[40]

The process though had begun earlier, as we have shown, in
the battles between the Palestine-based and overseas Zionists,
and in the conflict between pragmatism and the limited Zionist

political and economic strength — limited as compared with the broader avenues of Jewish non-Zionist wealth and influence.

BEN GURION AND THE NON-ZIONISTS

Ben Gurion's disenchantment with organized Zionism rested on two pillars. One was "the old debate between ḥalutzic Zionism and Congress-type Zionism *(tsiyyonut congressistit),* or between the Zionists in the Land [of Israel] and Zionists in the Diaspora." [41] It can be traced back to the cold reception he was given by the Lovers of Zion Committee in Odessa before his emigration to Israel. [42] In his view, Congress (or political as opposed to practical) Zionists were more involved in external relations and internal political machinations than in the true messianic content of Zionism: settlement and restoration of the land. The second pillar was the vast strength and financial power which lay beyond the framework of Zionism. The two merge when he describes the help he asked from American Jewry for defense, before the state was founded.

> I demanded aid for defense, but not from the great public and not from the Zionist leaders. This aid required unpublicized modest work, and leaders in America are not accustomed to or able to do work without "publicity." [43]

The remark about "publicity" does not cover the entire truth: beyond security considerations, the Zionist movement did not have access to some of the wealthier elements of American Jewry. Thus, the launching of the Israel Bond effort by Ben Gurion in a triumphal coast-to-coast visit to the United States in 1951 was in a sense a bypassing of normal Zionist channels, and a reaching-out to wider circles of pro-Israeli Jews. Ben Gurion's attitude to non-Zionists is perhaps more clearly illustrated by his relationship with the American Jewish Committee.

The Committee, founded in 1906, was made up of well-established American Jews, often of German origin or descent, who through public pressure and behind-the-scenes lobbying attempted to ensure Jewish civil rights in the United States and to protect their co-religionists in other countries. A major concern of the Committee, which had after much deliberation finally supported the emergence of Israel while continuing to adhere to its definition as a non-Zionist body, was the "need for a clear understanding that Jews outside Israel owe that country no political allegiance," and "that Israeli officials speak only as representatives of their own citizens."[44]

While these were "operative" concerns, in that they affected the legal status of non-Israeli Jews, or could be seen as liable to injure this status (through claims of dual loyalty on the part of Jews outside of Israel to their country of abode and to Israel), there were also areas of ideological or moral conflict. The Committee resented "the continued insistence of leading Israeli spokesmen that Jews must emigrate *en masse* to Israel, and that Jewish survival could never be assured except in a sovereign state."[45] The Committee leadership had made known its views in a statement issued in January of 1949 and followed this by a visit to Israel in the spring of that year. However, the Committee reached the conclusion that further clarification and more binding commitments were required. In 1950, the late Jacob Blaustein, then president of the American Jewish Committee, drafted, together with Ben Gurion, complementary statements. Had they been negotiated between sovereign entities, they would have to be considered as treaties. The statements were taken up in the cabinet, and "made public at an official function attended by all high-ranking government officials." According to the Committee, the president of Israel, Dr. Weizmann, was shown both statements by Blaustein, and gave his concurrence. This, it is stated, was done "at Mr. Ben Gurion's suggestion."[46] Considering relations between Ben Gurion and Weizmann, one wonders just exactly how the suggestion was proposed to Ben Gurion and by whom. Because of its cardinal importance, the statement by Ben Gurion will be given at length.[47]

The prime minister welcomed Blaustein as befitted an

exilarch of old, roundly praising American Jewry and Blaustein personally. Israel was described not as the messianic goal of Jewry, but in pragmatic tones. It had shouldered "the major share of providing permanent homes under conditions of full equality to hundreds of thousands of our brethren who cannot remain where they are and whose hearts are set on rebuilding their lives in Israel." This philanthropic-humanitarian language is closer to the lexicon of the Committee than to Ben Gurion's. Ben Gurion continued by referring to "some confusion and misunderstanding" regarding the relationship between Israel and Jewish communities abroad.

> The Jews of the United States, as a community and as individuals, have only one political attachment and that is to the United States of America. They owe no political allegiance to Israel . . . . The State of Israel represents and *speaks only on behalf of its own citizens* and in no way presumes to represent or speak in the name of Jews who are citizens of any other country. We, the people of Israel, have no desire and no intention to interfere in any way with the internal affairs of Jewish communities abroad.[48]

Ben Gurion went on to define his demand for immigration to Israel in terms which are closer to his "Zionist" addresses.

> We should like to see American Jews come and take part in our effort. We need their technical knowledge, their unrivalled experience, their spirit of enterprise, their bold vision, their "know-how." We need engineers, chemists, builders, work managers and technicians . . . . But the decision as to whether they wish to come — permanently or temporarily — rests with the free discretion of each American Jew himself. It is entirely a matter of his own volition. We need *ḥalutzim,* pioneers, too . . . . The essence of *ḥalutziyut* is free choice. They will come from among those who believe that their aspirations as human beings and as Jews can best be fulfilled by life and work in Israel.

In the latter passage, the change in style and language (it seems to show signs of having been drafted originally in Hebrew) indicates that Ben Gurion was not prepared to concede his right to call for immigrants, but, to make it more palatable, did stress the obvious voluntaristic aspect of such appeals. This was sheer realism; he had no means to enforce his pleas. On the other hand, the first part of the statement does show that Ben Gurion was willing to find the lowest common denominator, in the name of unity and joint action, particularly in fund-raising, in order not to jeopardize the messianic vision which he did not feel it wise to proclaim on that specific occasion.

Ben Gurion's dichotomy is noteworthy: the demand on Zionists was not based on voluntarism; they *must* come to Israel; non-Zionists *should* come, because they are needed by Israel and because they need Israel to fulfill themselves as Jews.

The relationship between Ben Gurion and Blaustein became a close personal friendship. The Israeli labor leader and the American industrialist exchanged long letters over the years. Ben Gurion insisted on writing to Jacob Blaustein as "Dear Ya'akov," signing *"David"* (both names in handwritten Hebrew) and Blaustein, in rather stiff and untried Hebrew calligraphy, followed suit.[49]

The position was reiterated in 1957, on the occasion of another visit by an American Jewish Committee delegation. There were no serious problems until the winter of 1959-60. There then occurred a number of anti-Semitic incidents across the world, including the daubing of swastikas on Jewish community buildings and synagogues. The Israel foreign ministry reacted with a series of notes to the governments concerned. This act, in defense of Jewish rights in countries outside of Israel, was interpreted as Israel assuming "the role of spokesman for Jews everywhere."[50] (The incidents and Israel's reaction will be discussed below.) The Committee complained that the 1950 agreement (statements, rather) had been violated. This incident was followed by another.

At the end of 1960, in an address to the Zionist General Council, Ben Gurion (asked by his cabinet to speak in a personal and non-official capacity because of his "extreme" views on the Zionist Organization), created a storm in Israel and in the world press.[51] In fact, Ben Gurion said nothing he had not said before. Calling for mass immigration to Israel, he particularly pointed his finger at orthodoxy. Ten years earlier he had taken the American Mizrachi (orthodox Zionists) to task for not settling in the Land of Israel, "even though this is an explicit positive commandment" of the Torah.[52] In 1960, he tried to hoist the orthodox with their own petard, by quoting the Talmud. However, the translation of his Hebrew speech rendered the Hebrew *dati* as "religious" whereas in the context, the intention was "orthodox." Thus the statement read:

> Since the day the Jewish state was established and the gates of Israel were flung open to every Jew who wanted to come, every religious [*dati*] Jew has daily violated the precepts of Judaism and the Torah by remaining in the Diaspora. "Whoever dwells outside the Land of Israel is considered to have no God," the sages say.[53]

Israel at that time had little experience with religious, non-orthodox Jews, Liberals, Conservatives or Reform, and thus the context was clear to Israelis. For American Jews, who particularly see themselves as the flagbearers of the Judaistic part of the three-religion American society (the trinity of Protestantism – Catholicism – Judaism), to be called "Godless" was a blow, especially considering the wide publicity in the American press. Obviously, the fact that Ben Gurion was quoting the Talmud was not stressed in the headlines, nor for that matter was the citation always bound in quotation marks, as it should have been. Ben Gurion's jeremiads concerning the danger of cultural assimilation of Jewry in lands of freedom gave the speech an added goad. "Jewish life [outside of Israel] . . . is compressed into a small corner . . . . Judaism . . . in free and prosperous countries . . . faces a kiss of death – a slow and imperceptible decline into the abyss of assimiliation."[54]

The Committee "immediately pointed out that Mr. Ben Gurion's speech was 'a violation of the explicit understanding' reached with Mr. Blaustein in 1950, and of 'the basic spirit of understanding' inherent in the agreement."[55] Here the Committee abandoned its earlier terminology of statements and spoke of understanding and agreements. Blaustein, by then honorary president of the American Jewish Committee, was dispatched to Israel, and in April 1961, a joint statement was released. Referring to the 1950 "Agreement" — now sanctified by a capital letter — Ben Gurion and Blaustein reaffirmed its spirit and content. They admitted that there was room for different interpretations "on the essence and meaning of Judaism and Jewishness," and pointed out that some misunderstandings "might have arisen owing to the fact that Mr. Ben Gurion now and then takes the liberty of expressing views . . . that are his own rather than those of the government of Israel."[56]

There is some difference between the 1950 and the 1961 statements. All the participants were ten years older, true. But this also meant that Israel was six times older; and Ben Gurion was harrassed by internal problems, party pressures and external affairs. Perhaps the chronicler reads these problems into the second statement, or gives them more weight than their due. It would nonetheless seem that Ben Gurion reitereated his undertaking, and called for its honoring by Israeli officials more out of a desire to soothe Blaustein than out of heartfelt agreement with his premises. He had never abandoned his stand on immigration, even in the first statement. He had indeed spoken of Israel's role as exponent and tribune for its own citizens only and not for other Jews. Juridically, of course, the argument cannot be faulted. However, partly because of Israel's increased strength, proven viability and growing importance (if not centrality in the Jewish world), and partly because Ben Gurion was preoccupied, one has the distinct impression that the second statement was almost *pro forma,* or that at the very most it was designed to disembarrass. Ben Gurion continued to speak and to act as a (perhaps *the*) leader of world Jewry, whether or not he had the blessings of his cabinet, the American Jewish Committee or others. And he treated his non-Zionist friends and allies with more consideration and care than his Zionist colleagues who did not live up to his understanding of Zionism.

As could have been anticipated, Nahum Goldmann took up cudgels against the 1961 Ben Gurion-Blaustein agreement. He claimed that Blaustein was "not representative of US Jewry." Furthermore, before reaching the 1961 agreement, Ben Gurion did not see fit to consult with American Zionist leaders, or the Jewish Agency, which "according to the spirit of the covenant and the law governing the status of the Zionist Organization is the body linking the state with the Diaspora."[57] Goldmann carefully referred to "the spirit" of the state–Zionist Organization Covenant, because, as has been shown, the letter of the accord reflected Ben Gurion's consistent refusal to grant such status to the Jewish Agency–Zionist Executive. His attack was motivated by a desire to protect a new American Jewish representative body. Goldmann had succeeded in bringing the major Jewish organizations, with the exception of the American Jewish Committee, into a Conference of Presidents which was coordinating US Jewish political representations.

Ben Gurion bypassed the Zionist movement on a number of occasions. In addition to his relations with the Committee and Blaustein, he had fostered direct links between Israel and the fund-raising arms of American Jewry. In September 1950, he convened American Jewish leaders in Jerusalem to "sell" them on a drive to float Israel Bonds to be sold on a community-wide basis. The Jerusalem Conference adopted a four-point program: continued raising, in larger amounts, of "philanthropic" funds, or contributions, through the United Jewish Appeal; the new Israel Bond Drive; direct investments in Israel's economy; and intergovernmental or international grants and loans.[58] In spring 1951, Ben Gurion personally launched the Bond Drive, while not neglecting the other three aspects of the Jerusalem or King David (Hotel) program, as it came to be known. The direct links fashioned with the heads of the UJA and the Bond Organization remained in the hands of the government, with the Zionist Organization involved but not decisive. For the record, it should be noted that this policy was followed by Ben Gurion's successor, Levi Eshkol, who called Jerusalem Economic Conferences in 1968 and 1969 to increase investment and the transfer of know-how to Israel. The 1969 meeting took place after Eshkol's death, under Mrs. Meir's ministry.

There is probably a link between the "ideological" or principle agreements between Ben Gurion and the non-Zionists, e.g., Blaustein, and his intense concern for sufficient funds to finance the fledgling state's imposing programs for immigration and development. Having gone beyond the organized Zionists in a number of fields, Ben Gurion turned to the broad spectrums of Jewry with what was the key question in the relations between Jews and Israel: immigration.

INGATHERING

At this point, it would be salient to discuss briefly the state's role in implementing the basic Zionist tenet. "The State of Israel will be open for Jewish immigration and for the Ingathering of the Exiles . . . ." This principle was embodied in the Declaration of Establishment of the State of Israel on May 14, 1948.[59] Two years later, the Knesset was presented with the Law of Return, which Ben Gurion called "one of the foundation-laws of the State of Israel. It contains the central purpose of our state, the purpose of ingathering the exiles."[60] The law states that every Jew has the right to come to this country as an immigrant ('oleh, from 'aliyah, "going up" or settling in Israel).[61] In this sense, it grants an option to each Jew outside Israel to live in the country "because he is a Jew, if only he wishes to join in settling the Land."[62]

The law is an expression of basic Zionist ideology. Ben Gurion undertook to give it content by a program of mass immigration designed to double the Jewish population of Israel within four years.[63] The practicalities arguing against such a policy were clear: war and its aftermath, lack of housing, lack of finances, shortages of food, and the like. In face of doubts expressed within the cabinet and the Knesset, Ben Gurion insisted on a policy of non-selective mass immigration.

Ben Gurion linked the need of Jews in countries in which they could no longer dwell with the need of Israel for a greater population for defense and development. " 'Aliyah to the Land and the rate of 'aliyah are matters of life and death . . . for the Jews in several countries in the Diaspora and . . . for the State of Israel. Not under all circumstances will we be able to stand, if, over the long run, we remain defending ourselves against many attackers."[64] This was in 1949. That year, at a gathering of American Jewish leaders in Jerusalem, Ben Gurion stated: "Be what may, we shall not limit or decrease immigration. This may be illogical, but a mother does not ask about logic when she wishes to rescue her child." On moral and political grounds, he rejected the thesis that Israel could "close its gates" to the Jews of Rumania or Iraq.[65]

By early 1952, "three years and nine months less a day" from the establishment of the state, as Ben Gurion reminded the Knesset, the aim of doubling the population had been over-achieved.[66] Austerity and rationing, housing in abandoned Arab dwellings, in tents and in wooden and tin huts were the more visible extreme steps taken to tide over the country and provide rudimentary arrangements for the immigrants. At that time, Ben Gurion had to come to the legislature with a drastic economic program, based on devaluation of the Israeli pound. Accused of not seeing to it that the import of capital matched the immigration of Jews, Ben Gurion said:

> Of course one might say, "we will move Jews to Israel in
> proportion to the movement of capital." This approach
> was adopted, and may still be followed, by many. I reject
> it totally. Our entire fate could have been determined at
> any given moment by the addition of one hundred or two
> hundred thousand people.[67]

The policy of mass immigration was rooted then in a central

concept, to maximize the Jewishness of Israel by importing the maximum number of Jews, from wherever they were ready to come, in whatever condition they were, and regardless of the economic ability of the country to absorb them at that time. The policy served defense purposes as well as political and Zionist aims. In overriding the skeptics within and without his party, Ben Gurion gambled dangerously, but the state weathered the gamble and even prospered. And as usual, pragmatic considerations of demography and defense were combined with the Zionist ideal.

ZIONISM WITHOUT THE ZIONISTS

Ben Gurion's ideological conflicts with organized Zionism, his impatience at the lack of large-scale immigration of Jews from Western countries, and his intense and overwhelming Israelocentrism led him to a pragmatic program of practical Zionism, which he presented to the many Jewish groups with which he met during his thirteen years in office. In 1950, at the Zionist General Council he had outlined a six-point series of activities which every Zionist movement should undertake, in particular the American Zionist group.[68]

Two of the six points were related to immigration: one was the creation of a ḥalutz movement, that is of "pioneers" who would settle the wasteland and the border areas; the second was the encouragement of a transfer of professionals and technicians. The other four points were all aimed at widening and deepening the contact of Jews outside of Israel with the Jewish state. These points included the demand that every Jewish student abroad study at least one year in an Israeli university; the renewal of the pilgrimage rite, of tourism, or of a visit to Israel by every Zionist and every Jew at least once in his lifetime; investment in Israel either by creating new enterprises or through purchasing shares in existing ones; and finally Hebrew education for Jewish young people.

No longer feeling any particular obligation to the organized Zionists, he carried his campaign for the six-point program to every Jew he could reach. During his term of office (as well as when out of office) he received many groups of Jewish leaders of varying degrees of importance, or was invited to address them. Ben Gurion ceaselessly propagandized in this personal way the fashioning of new chains of communication which would link the Jewish communities outside of Israel, and especially their young people, with Israel.

This effort, apparently arrived at instinctually, shows great parallels with Karl Deutsch's studies of the role of social communication in the formation of nationalities. Deutsch's theories, for the purpose of the present study, may perhaps be best represented in the words of another student of nationalism who wrote:

> Deutsch's major premise would be obvious if it had not been so consistently disregarded by the classic nationalist writers and by earlier scholars. Nationality is not an inborn characteristic but the result of a process of social learning and habit forming. Such learning typically resulted from a marked increase of social communication (that is, of trade, travel, correspondence and the like) within a network linking a number of cities and each of these with its rural hinterland.[69]

The premise was apparently obvious to Ben Gurion, who recognized that exposing more Jews to life-experiences in Israel through a limited stay for study or touring, as well as increased investment and trade, would forge the desired thought habits and enhance social learning. Just as obviously, Deutsch's analysis must be modified somewhat to take account of the geographic spread of the Jewish people.

In 1961, Ben Gurion's aide, Teddy Kollek, added to the prime minister's staff an expert in overseas Jewish affairs, whose function was to establish close contacts with the non-Zionist organizations and religious movements, particularly in the United States, directly on behalf of the state.[70] The appointment may not have been made in consultation with Ben

Gurion, but was definitely in the framework of the policy being implemented under his overall direction by Kollek, his loyal lieutenant.

A few years before this, Ben Gurion had emended the original 1950 four- or six-point program to reflect one of his increasing intellectual preoccupations and an ideological point rapidly assuming centrality in his thinking. At a world conference of Jewish youth held in Jerusalem in 1958 (ironically, it was organized by the very Zionist Organization he condemned), he recast the program of building social and educational ties. The study of the Hebrew Bible took pride of place. Next came education in the messianic vision, and finally, visits to and study in Israel. [71]

The role of the Bible and the messianic vision has been treated in Chapter 3, in the context of Ben Gurion's overall historical views; however this chapter would be incomplete without some reference to them. Whether consciously or unconsciously, Ben Gurion was using the Bible to create or to further national identity in the new state. Thus, for example, in a radio address marking Israel's second Independence Day celebration, there are, in the space of not quite five printed pages, five rather lengthy biblical quotations, as well as one citation from the *Aggadah,* or homiletic tradition. [72] An analysis of Ben Gurion's writings and speeches, excluding normal political polemics, shows that he consistently sprinkled them with biblical excerpts, often in the same high proportion.

With the achievement of statehood, the messianic message became more pronounced in his speeches. "I am one of the believers that in the creation of the State of Israel there is the beginning of redemption, but as redemption grows so will its pangs . . . ." [73] The "beginning of redemption" — *reshit ha-ge'ulah* in Hebrew — or more commonly, the Aramaic term, domesticated into Jewish thought, *althalta de-ge'ulah* — means the beginning of the messianic era. With the advent of the Messiah, or rather preceding it, the world and the Jews will experience, according to tradition, travail and pain: *ḥevlei mashiaḥ* (literally the birth-pangs of the Messiah). These concepts too figure largely in Ben Gurion's writings, in particular in the earlier years of statehood. In the later years of the state, his addresses and writings dwell less on the messianic theme in the present state, and more as a chiliastic aim, due undoubtedly to the wearing off of the new gloss of statehood and the wrestling with day-to-day problems.

The theme of Bible and Hebrew language studies, coupled with the call to greater direct involvement through visits to or study in Israel, and direct investments in Israeli industries, has led to a new type of practical Zionism, adopted by Zionists and non-Zionists alike. The large synagogue and rabbinical movements, "general" Jewish organizations such as the giant B'nai B'rith and the smaller American Jewish Congress — all have joined the regular Zionist constituent organizations in holding conferences and conventions in Israel. Study programs in Israel sponsored by the World Zionist Organization, by universities and talmudic and rabbinical schools are multiplying. Ben Gurion's immense practicality, his understanding that a people's existence beyond territory depends on communications and personal experience have made their contribution to a new Israelocentric non-party Zionism, a Zionism almost beyond ideology. In a sense, this may be Ben Gurion's triumph over the machine he could not or would not control.

ISRAEL THE PROTECTOR OF THE JEWS

Reference has already been made to the fears of Western Diaspora Jews that Israel would become their spokesman and compromise their image as loyal citizens of their home countries. On at least two occasions during Ben Gurion's stewardship, Israel did indeed act in a way which seemed as if it were representing all Jews. One, regarding the Jews killed in the Holocaust, concerned the capture of one of their murderers, and did not create tension among Jews, though it did with the Argentine government. The other, the swastika daubing incidents of 1959 and 1960 and Israel's notes to the countries in which these took place, helped occasion the 1961 Ben Gurion-Blaustein statement. [74]

That Israel should see itself protector of those Jews who had no recourse to the legal systems of their lands of residence was implicit in Zionist ideology and in the ancient tradition that "all Jews are responsible for one another." The opening of its gates to immigrants from the European displaced-persons' camps or from countries like Iraq and Yemen was an expression of this responsibility. Difficulties arose when Israel acted formally and publicly because of its natural identification with Jews who were suffering or whose status and honor were adversely affected, as in the concerted swastika smearing, which at the time led some Jewish organizations and possibly Israeli officials to fear a rise of neo-Nazism.

According to a recent and authoritative study, the protests lodged by the Israel foreign ministry were initiated on the highest administrative level of the civil service almost as a matter of course. They were approved by Ben Gurion, also as a matter of routine. [75] Nonetheless, the action shows a basic Israeli government line; not to interfere in the Jewish communities in free countries, or act on their behalf vis-à-vis their respective governments; but to act on behalf of defenseless communities or all of Jewry on certain matters.

This was certainly the case with the capture (or kidnapping) of Adolf Eichmann, who was apprehended by Israeli agents (called volunteers by the Israeli ambassador to Argentine; and doubtless they had volunteered for the specific assignment).The prime minister had stressed the national and historic significance of the event. [76] A few days later, in a personal letter to President Arturo Frondizi, Ben Gurion wrote:

[The survivors of the Holocaust] regarded it as their mission in life to bring the man responsible for this crime, without precedent in history, to stand trial before the Jewish people. Such a trial can take place only in Israel. [77]

The equation of Israel with the survivors of Nazi murder had been made earlier, in the negotiations with West Germany over material reparations (see preceding chapter). Here the equation is made between the Jewish people and Israel, in that the only "Jewish" court in existence was that of the State of Israel.

Ben Gurion sharpened the point in rejecting a proposal by Nahum Goldmann (again speaking as an individual, and not in the name of the two organizations over which he presided, the World Zionist Organization and the World Jewish Congress) that non-Israeli judges be invited to join the Israeli panel which was to try Eichmann.

> It is . . . the duty of the State of Israel, the only sovereign authority in Jewry, to see that the whole of the story, in all its horror, is fully exposed . . . . Historic justice and the honor of the Jewish people demand that this should be done only by an Israeli court in the sovereign Jewish state.[78]

This rejection is in line with his basic approach to Diaspora Jewish, as distinct from Israeli, interests. In a retrospective interview, Ben Gurion said:

> It was *always* my view that we have always to consider the interests of Diaspora Jewry — any Jewish community that was concerned. But there is one crucial distinction — not what *they* think are their interests, but what *we* regarded as their interests. If it was a case vital for Israel, and the interests of the Jews concerned were different, the vital interests of Israel came first — because Israel is vital for world Jewry. I cannot remember any conflict of *interests*. And their *views* I need not accept.[79]

There is a double dynamic in the progress of Ben Gurion the Zionist leader to Ben Gurion the Israelocentric spokesman. On the one hand, the rival pre-state center, the World Zionist Organization and Jewish Agency Executive, was placed in a secondary role. "[To] the terrible sin of preferring . . . the state over the Zionist Organization, if this be a sin — I confess my guilt."[80]   On the other, the state assumed functions of practical Zionism both in relation to Jews overseas, as shown, and in regard to foreign nations.

In the case of organized Zionism, the principle of state primacy coincided with the pragmatic need to strengthen Israel through implementing Zionist programs through non-Zionist frameworks. Ben Gurion never left Zionism; his Israelocentrism is his Zionism. To preserve, enhance and strengthen it, he left the Zionists behind.

PART FOUR

Withdrawal from Power

CHAPTER TWELVE

Coalition Partnership

The United Nations resolution of November 29, 1947, had called upon each of the two proposed states to be formed in Palestine (Arab and Jewish) to draft "a democratic constitution."[1] Indeed the Provisional State Council had considered a draft constitution prepared by Dr. Yehudah (Leo) Kohn.[2] In February 1950, the First Kenesset began to debate the issue. The orthodox opposed the adoption of a constitution, claiming that the Mosaic law was already Israel's constitution. As one Agudah speaker put it: "A secular constitution may be seen as an attempt to give a bill of divorcement to our holy Torah."[3] The left (Mapam) and right (Ḥerut) were in uneasy — and often acrimonious — alliance over the need for a constitution or bill of rights: the one, to enshrine its labor ideology as a national heritage, the other, to protect itself and other minorities from deviation from constitutional freedoms through a parliamentary "mechanical majority."[4]

The gradualist line won. Left and right (including the General Zionists) voted against, the orthodox abstained from voting on the "compromise" proposal, adopted in June 1950. This directed the "Constitution and Law Committee to prepare a draft constitution for the state ... [which] shall be constructed chapter after chapter in such a manner that each shall in itself constitute a basic law . . . all the chapters together shall comprise the State Constitution."[5] This of course meant that the dreaded *Kulturkampf* had been postponed, and that piecemeal legislation on specific fundamental or "constitutional" issues would be enacted.

In the debate, Ben Gurion differentiated between nations which had wrested their freedom from foreign rulers and the Jewish revolution "against historic destiny, the destiny of an exiled nation, far-flung, without a homeland, language, culture and independence." The State of Israel was engaged in a lengthy struggle for its redemption, which was a "process of 'aliyah, settlement and security efforts. . . ."

> Our state is the most dynamic state in the world . . . . Every day more Jews are freed as they immigrate to Israel; every day new areas are liberated from desertion and waste . . . . The laws of the State of Israel must adapt themselves to this dynamic development.[6]

Ben Gurion's pragmatism became a principle in this issue: a Fabian policy of deferring decision on state-religion or on labor-capital relations while both the state and its people were in the making. Ben Gurion briefly summarized his views on this gradualist strategy in a clearer form on another occasion, in early 1951. Though cited earlier (Chapter 6), it bears repetition at length at this point. Characteristically, the rationale is *raisons d'etat.*

Whoever now wishes to stir up a war of religion or of classes to bring about a final disposition . . . strikes at the soul of immigration and sabotages the security of the state . . . . Saving the nation and preserving its independence and security in this conflict-ridden and storm-tossed world have priority over any religious or anti-religious ideal. Necessarily, in this period of laying foundations, people of differing principles and varying interests must work together . . . in an effort to concentrate the people in its land . . . and when the great

hour comes the ingathered nation will decide the great
questions. Until then, we must all . . . display the wisdom
of compromise in all questions, economic, religious,
political and constitutional which bear delay.[7]

The delaying of major decisions on constitution and
governance perpetuated the proportional representation system,
with its multiparty, coalition system. Though Mapai provided
the essential pre- and post-state continuity and stability,
nonetheless the coalition partners demanded their price: access
to resources, patronage and symbols of power.[8] Ben Gurion
attempted, not always with success, to impress the principle of
collective cabinet responsibility on his non-Mapai cabinet
colleagues. Following the first elections to the Knesset in
January 1949, Ben Gurion announced on the radio that he
would try to form a government based on four points.
"Collective responsibility for the policy line of the government
on the part of all parties and individuals who would participate
in the government" was the first.[9] This was enacted into law in
February.[10]

In the Basic Principles proclaimed by Ben Gurion while
presenting the new government in March 1949, the first chapter
read:

> The government is based on collective responsibility of all
> the members and parties participating in it. This . . .
> applies to the agreed coalitionary program and to cabinet
> decisions. [It] does not prevent freedom of discussion by
> MKs of any proposal . . . or freedom of criticism of the
> government if it stray from the line determined by the
> Knesset and coalition.[11]

The coalition's parties were pulling in conflicting directions and
by October 1950, on the occasion of orthodox ministers
boycotting cabinet meetings, Ben Gurion said:

> The burden imposed on [the prime minister] is not light
> and not lightened by the fact that this is a coalition

government. I have been tested perhaps more than any of those seated in this house in coalition affairs . . . . It has not been easy for me in these two governments [the provisional and the first cabinet after the elections] . . . .[12]

It was not much easier later, as has been described above (see Chapters 6 and 10). Crises cropped up with the religious parties at fairly regular intervals between 1950 and 1954; and again in 1958. The problems with the left began in 1957, a year after Aḥdut ha-'Avodah and Mapam entered the government, and continued with mounting frequency until 1963. In this respect Ben Gurion's description of his partnership with the left in 1948 is apt for the later, post-1957 period. "It was not easy . . . because part of the opposition sat in the provisional government and they know the details as well as I do."[13]

Following the cabinet crisis over the planned dispatch of General Dayan to Germany in late December and early January 1957-8, the five coalition partners agreed to form the same government as before but strengthened the definition of collective responsibility which

> . . . will bind all members of the cabinet and the coalition
> partners to vote in the Knesset in support of government
> decisions and laws which will be proposed by it to the
> Knesset. The government may permit a party to abstain
> from voting, under certain circumstances . . . . If a minister
> or ministers should find it necessary to abstain from voting
> without cabinet agreement, that minister or those
> ministers are required to resign from the government. A
> vote against a government proposal by a party shall be
> deemed as abstention by the minister without government
> agreement.[14]

This was presented again as the first point of the basic lines of the new government in late 1959 by Ben Gurion in the Knesset and was also proposed as legislation.[15]

The record of struggle is a clear indication that the problem was never solved. It also shows Ben Gurion's consistent attempt to apply the principle of collective responsibility as a means of providing minimal effective governance. This was called by Ben Gurion, "unity of action, not unity of thinking."[16] Its lack of success led Ben Gurion to propose a change in Israel's electoral system.

It was not a slow awakening. In 1949, he told the Knesset

> I do not think that the appearance of 21 competing
> [party] lists in the Knesset elections in this little country
> of six or seven hundred thousand inhabitants, is the
> expression of democracy or social maturity. As a Jew,
> I am ashamed of this sick phenomenon.[17]

A few years later he wrote that the "Anglo-Saxon genius" which had fathered and developed parliamentary democracy had evolved the two-party system and the majority constituency elections as opposed to the European proportional representation system.

> The two-party system places full responsibility vis-à-vis the
> people on the majority party and educates the opposition
> party which desires to become the ruling party to
> responsibility in word and deed even when in the minority,
> and thus parliament acts as a national (mamlakhti)
> educational factor for the entire people.[18]

This somewhat idealized view of parliamentary democracy led Ben Gurion to advocate introducing such a system in Israel. He was aware of the resistance which might be met. In reference to his successful attempt to unify the army and create a national framework for its control and support, he had said in a Knesset debate, using a kabbalistic term to describe the breaking of established forms and the forging of new ones:

> It is not easy to "shatter vessels" even if they are
> outmoded; for even the "revolutionaries" among us are

basically staunch conservatives . . . it was not easy to
"shatter vessels," but it was no wit easier to . . . establish
new vessels.[19]

His trial balloon was launched in 1951 and again in 1953. His
praise of the "Anglo-Saxon" system at that time has been
mentioned above. It is hard to say that there were many takers.
The parliamentary majority necessary to change the system
would have to come from the small parties that would
themselves be the first to suffer from any departure from
proportional representation. Their vote would have to be added
to a Mapai that was itself convinced. But though within the
party there were some who honestly believed that proportional
representation would give minorities a fair measure of
representation, many in the party machine preferred the known
technique of management through the coalition procedure to an
unknown system which might produce individualistic or
independent leaders chosen by geographic constituency.

In September 1954, Ben Gurion told the Mapai party council
that

> There is no electoral system which can provide a
> mathematical reflection of opinions in a nation. A good
> electoral system is obliged to ensure effective conditions
> for the survival of democracy and civil liberty:
> a. Providing the nation with the opportunity to decide
> from time to time on central questions pressing the
> state . . . .
> b. Providing the elector with the opportunity to elect a
> representative directly responsible to him . . . .
> c. Providing the nation with the opportunity to decide
> which government is desirable for the nation . . . . These
> three vital conditions can only be ensured through the
> British electoral system. In the Israeli electoral system
> there is no relationship between the elector and the
> elected; he elects candidates, most of whom he does not

know, and only the party apparatus decides who will be on the list and in which position . . . . The government is formed only after the elections through negotiations between the party machines.[20]

He convinced the council to vote in favor of changing the electoral system to the "British" format. The Knesset rejected the change in October 1956.[21]

The coalition situation was confused in the first half-dozen years of the state's existence. From March 1949, when the cabinet responsible to the first elected Knesset was formed, until the elections to the Third Knesset in late 1955, six government coalitions were in office. One lasted one month and 18 days, the longest in office was 14 months and 11 days.[22]

In January 1958, Ben Gurion unleashed a sharp attack on the

> . . . rotten and destructive electoral system . . . which in addition to [perpetuating] the Diaspora culture, useless disputation and hair-splitting, increases party splinterization . . . . In a bad democratic system such as under our electoral procedures, there is no way out from crises.[23]

Toward the end of the year he devoted a lengthy speech to the subject of the constituency electoral system, which he had supported in the very first debate in the cabinet on the first Knesset elections.

> The [then] minister of the interior, a native of Poland like myself, thought that what is done in Poland must be done throughout the world and proposed proportional representation. I opposed this but remained in the minority.[24]

The comment about Poland is not gratuitous, as is the comment on Diaspora mentality in the previous citation. Ben

Gurion saw himself as indigenous, Israeli, springing full-grown from the brow of authentic, rooted Jewish statehood. The others, the hair-splitters and carping petty critics, had not authenticated their Israeliness; they were imports. This ties in with his Israelocentrism in general, and his rejection of Diaspora Zionism and of imported sociological terminology (socialism).

It was an acrimonious debate with interruptions coming left, right and center. Ben Gurion was speaking in support of a proposal by Yosef Almogi, one of his loyal followers in Mapai, that there should be a plebiscite on the question of constituency elections. The proposal failed. In 1959, he convinced Mapai to adopt the change in its electoral platform.[25] In the ensuing crises of 1960-61, the issue died out, never to be revived during his tenure.

The coalition system had led to deep and bitter feeling on Ben Gurion's part. So much so, that he was accused in 1959 of having people in his entourage who had suggested a *putsch* as the way out. Ben Gurion denied the allegation, published in a popular afternoon daily.[26] In spite of the great provocation and his own achievement-oriented (bitzu'a) approach, it is clear that Ben Gurion's criticism of the existing electoral system was directed at proportional representation. Whether or not the *putsch* was proferred, it was not in Ben Gurion's style or way-of-thought.

Ben Gurion could not bend the party and particularly the smaller parties to support electoral reform. The system was imbedded too deeply in the basic interests of the Mapai central command as well. The constant friction and negotiations, with the religious (described in Chapter 6) and with the left (Chapter 10), led to disenchantment and weariness. Ben Gurion grew tired of the strife; the public tired of it too. The switch from a right-leaning cabinet (1949-1955) to a left-leaning government (1956-1963) made matters no easier; the contrary was true.

At any rate, there were 10 governments in office from the first one responsible to an elected Knesset in March 1949 to June 1963 when Ben Gurion resigned finally.[27] Including the provisional government the number is 11. In other words the average life per government was about 16 months. The crises not leading to the formation of new cabinets were even more frequent. When one adds to this the deteriorating relations with the party, Ben Gurion's waning popularity and loss of will become even clearer.

CHAPTER THIRTEEN

Party and State:
The Bond Which Cracked

STATE (MAMLAKHTIYUT) VERSUS THE PARTY

Ben Gurion's view of state management de-emphasized the party as a basis for power and gave the central thrust of policy to the state machinery. This can be seen in his attempt to depoliticize the army, and education, and his lack of day-to-day interest in, and control of, the party machine. With the growth in population, Mapai, which had always seen itself as a mass party, continued to attract larger and larger numbers. The intimacy and ideological orientation gave way to a bureaucratic party machine, manipulating ethnic and interest groups, and tightly managed by a small central body. A noted Israeli political scientist has with some hyperbole said that "the Israel Labor Party seems a combination of Narodnik ideology and Bolshevik organization."[1] The latter relates, of course, to a way of thinking rather than a form of organization or of central totalitarian control. The founders and moving spirits of the labor movement came overwhelmingly from Russia or Russian Poland. The party became one of mass mobilization, but at its apex an almost incestuous network of family-linked and quasi-family (kibbutz and land settlement leaders) relationships pervaded the structure. Entry into this top echelon was slow and measured.

The utopian "movement-oriented" ideology (or rather spirit — ideology is an overly rational term) combined with a shrewd use of power to control key positions at all levels of government, the Histadrut, labor councils and municipalities. Though the party went through all the democratic procedures of elections from the grass-roots upwards, blocs and alliances within the branches and on the national level gave preferment to "reliable" members, enforcing a relatively strict non-totalitarian democratic centralism which often made the electoral choices from above. The Central Committee, the Secretariat and Politbureau, ostensibly delegated to wield power by the larger elected bodies, became the determining force in party life, which thus took its lead from above. The power of these bodies to control nominations and appointments was magnified by the professionalization of public life: few political figures were independent financially. They depended on the party for jobs and positions of power which provided rather modest salaries, but salaries nonetheless, and that elixir of the aspiring — a measure of fame, or at least publicity and recognition.[2]

In spite of all this, the party never became an absolute rubber stamp, and within the limits of the chosen, free debate and even acrimony were the rule rather than the exception. Pressure groups and aspiring politicians also became adept at using the press, through calculated leak and managed news, to advance a point-of-view or obtain public support. Thus the party was never completely in anyone's pocket. Even the most important of all decisions, that on the proclamation of statehood, a few days before May 15, 1948, was far from unanimous, and one-third of Mapai then opposed Ben Gurion on this issue.[3]

With the success of the War of Independence, Ben Gurion's prestige was enormous, and his authority heightened. However, factionalism in Mapai and the limits of the coalition system crimped his charisma. Although this charisma had been routinized to a great extent in the military and in certain echelons of the state bureaucracy, the countervailing influence of ministries controlled by other parties, and competing policies proposed by party colleagues, such as Sharett, effectively limited this heightened authority and crimped his style.

Ben Gurion was aware of his party's weaknesses. In summer 1949, he said, "There are lights and shadows among all peoples, including ourselves . . . the Israel Worker's Party (Mapai) has not only lights but shadows, and they are heavy."[4] Against the background of Ben Gurion's almost total absorption in matters of defense and foreign policy, and his stress on mamlakhtiyut, the party management was left in the generally loyal hands of functionaries. However, in his capacity as *stratēgos* and head of government, Ben Gurion built up about him a small *élite* in both decision-making and policy-executing roles. Outstanding were Shimon Peres (whose independent foreign service in the securing of arms purchases and production brought him into continuing conflict with the foreign minister, be it Moshe Sharett or Golda Meir), and the popular Moshe Dayan. Their advancement had been in the shade of Ben Gurion rather than through the "long and numbing apprenticeship" of progress "through the party machine."[5] Policy differences, the age gap, the implied threat in the eventual battle for succession, and the unorthodox path of preferment served to reinforce the suspicions and fears of the "Old Guard" — whose public style was ideological rather than pragmatic, and whose loyalty to the state was often mediated through the machine.

The so-called "Young Ones" *(ha-tze'irim)* had made an abortive attempt to form a party power bloc as far back as 1950. In 1957, a further attempt was made, with somewhat greater impact.[6] After the 1959 elections, Dayan entered the cabinet, and Peres was made a member of Knesset and deputy minister of defense, marking his elevation from bureaucracy to politics. Two other "young" ministers were appointed, the late Dr. Giora Josephthal, and Abba Eban. All four supported Ben Gurion at the time and on into mid-1961.[7] Peres and Dayan remained Ben Gurion supporters beyond that time as well.

The veteran leadership, Mrs. Meir, Pinḥas Sapir, Zalman Aranne and to a more limited extent, Levi Eshkol, recognized that the lines were drawn, not yet on a pro- and anti-Ben Gurion basis, but on a "close" and "closer" to Ben Gurion pattern. The ideological and sentimental proximity of this veteran element to Aḥdut ha-'Avodah, former colleagues in Mapai of a period antedating the "Young Ones," was reinforced. Their search for allies outside the party confines, i.e., Aḥdut ha-'Avodah, was intensified in a number of policy issues: relations with Germany, the conflict with the National Religious Party, and the Lavon Affair. In the end, these conflicts wore Ben Gurion down, and led to his resignation, and to the eventual rift in Mapai in 1965.

Policy differences in the cabinet were developing simultaneously. The religious issue was perhaps the least important, but it was pervasive and permanent. The price Ben Gurion was willing to pay to the religious parties for their support in major foreign policy decisions did not appeal to Aḥdut ha-'Avodah, or to many secularist anti-orthodox figures in Mapai. Not being in the ultimate decision-making role, these elements especially could permit themselves the luxury of more open criticism and could give vent to feelings which Ben Gurion had to file away and ignore. Aranne was the most ideologically motivated and equipped of the so-called "Old Guard," and his secularism combined with a deep commitment to his variant of Jewishness had led to clashes in his administration of the nation's educational system. Mrs. Meir's views on orthodoxy were close to Aranne's.

The "Who is a Jew? " issue came to a head because of the new administrative rulings of an Aḥdut ha-'Avodah minister of the interior. A closer Mapai—Aḥdut ha-'Avodah axis would increase the labor strength to 54 in a Knesset of 120 members (figures for the 1959 elections), i.e., close enough to make a coalition without the orthodox a definite temptation. To digress briefly, the fact that such a coalition has not been attempted in the past decade indicates that Eshkol, who negotiated the 1961 cabinet (for Ben Gurion) and the 1965 coalition, and Mrs. Meir, who negotiated the 1969 government, had, when inheriting Ben Gurion's role, accepted his analysis as well. Better the compromise with the orthodox within the government than a clash with them from without, avoiding the consequent internal

Kulturkampf and the concomitant mobilization of Jewish public opinion overseas to take sides in an uncivil war. To return to the "Old Guard"—Aḥdut ha-'Avodah axis, the anti-religious factor was not sufficient in itself to lead to rapprochement between the two groups, but did help to create and maintain the atmosphere.

More potent was the issue of Germany. Here the personal convictions of Mrs. Meir, then foreign minister, were reinforced by the clash of institutional interests between her ministry and Peres' ministry of defense.[8] Peres was busily building his "European orientation" and had negotiated a number of successful agreements with Germany as well as France. Although in his book Peres carefully omits the dates of his German contacts, they seem to have begun after the Sinai withdrawal in 1957 and continued, often in great secrecy, into the 1960s with direct communications between the two ministries of defense.[9] (See Chapter 10.)

A new element was introduced into the Arab-Israel arms race in May 1962, when Egypt launched three trial military rockets of varying ranges. The Egyptian rocket development was conducted by West German scientists, and the Israeli security services took steps to induce the Germans to cease working for Egypt. In March 1963, an Israeli agent and an Austrian citizen were arrested in Switzerland for threatening the daughter of one of these scientists. The subsequent trial and publicity attracted great attention in Israel. Mrs. Meir phrased a sharp attack on "the German people [which] will not be able to free itself of responsibility for the continuation of this criminal activity."[10]

The issue brought to a head the clash between the pro-rapprochement forces, led by Ben Gurion and Peres, who feared that the public campaign against Germany would endanger the evolving relationship, which involved large quantities of arms (estimated by varying sources from about $175 million and up, but probably worth about $275 million) and the anti-German Mrs. Meir and the chief of Israeli intelligence and espionage services, Isser Harel. The latter two had at that time evolved a close liaison, though Harel was responsible directly to Ben Gurion. He and Harel held contrary estimates of the efficacy and potential danger of the Egyptian missile development, and the line toward Germany. Harel resigned rather than bow to Ben Gurion's demand to back down from this position at a meeting of the Knesset Foreign Affairs and Security Committee.[11] The clash increased Ben Gurion's isolation within his own party, showed a growing lack of control over a vital state organ (the security services) and naturally led to a tactical concert between Mrs. Meir, her veteran Mapai colleagues and Aḥdut ha-'Avodah, which long had spearheaded the anti-German wing in government.

THE SECOND LAVON AFFAIR

In the wings during the last half of the 1950s stood Pinḥas Lavon, the man who in the first years of statehood was seen by many as a potential replacement for Ben Gurion, if and when the latter would depart from the political scene. In the period of Ben Gurion's first retirement (December 1953 — February 1955) Lavon had served as minister of defense, a position which in Israel carries more weight perhaps than any other ministry. In his period of service, relations within the defense establisment deteriorated. There also arose "a dispute . . . over responsibility for an abortive act of sabotage . . . that Israel's military intelligence organized."[12] (See Chapter 7.) The lack of confidence between Lavon and the establishment Ben Gurion had built was aggravated by the strained relations between Lavon and his prime minister, Moshe Sharett. Sharett appointed an enquiry commission, its two members selected for their expected impartiality and high public status: Justice Yitzḥak Olshan of the Israeli Supreme Court and the first chief of staff, General Ya'akov Dori. Their investigation led to a stalemate over the issue of responsibility for the failure of the actions in Egypt, in dispute between the chief of military intelligence (labeled the Senior Officer) and Defense Minister Lavon:

> We cannot say anything except that we were not
> convinced beyond all possible doubt that the Senior

Officer did not receive the order from the minister of defense. At the same time, we are not certain that the minister of defense did in fact give the order.[13]

Thus ended the first Lavon Affair, whose details were kept from the public until the second affair began in mid-1960. In the meantime, Lavon became secretary-general of the Histadrut, a post which Ben Gurion had once held. As the key figure in the party, Ben Gurion certainly would have had to give his agreement to the nomination. Lavon effectively rid the Histadrut executive of his opponents and kept its doors closed to the younger protegés of Ben Gurion.[14] Late in the course of his stewardship of the Histadrut, Lavon had differed with Ben Gurion on the role of the labor establishment and the state (*étatism* vs. voluntarism, or mamlakhtiyut vs. class interests, depending on the point of view; see Chapter 5).

The second Lavon Affair began following a closed-door trial of a reserve intelligence officer, who shed new light on the original mishap. Lavon made this information available to Ben Gurion, who ordered his chief of staff to appoint a committee "to investigate thoroughly rumors of falsification and withholding of documents" in the first Lavon Affair.[15] The entire story of the affair has occasioned considerable heat, and light has been shed on it in a number of books; obviously considerations of space do not permit its full recounting.[16] In brief, Lavon opposed the appointment of a fresh committee, headed by another Supreme Court Justice, on grounds of bias. He leaked his story to *Ma'ariv*, a popular afternoon paper, then pursuing a strong anti-Ben Gurion line. Essentially, Lavon sought rehabilitation by cabinet decision. "Mr. Lavon . . . is no longer interested in further inquiries and will be satisfied by a statement from the cabinet and the Knesset Foreign Affairs and Security Committee that an injustice had been perpetrated against him, and that there was no basis for the accusations mounted against him, and therefore there were no grounds for the demand that he resign."[17]

The affair exploded into a major public issue, which embroiled Mapai and eventually the entire nation in a grand debate. Sides were taken on whether a judicial inquiry should be held, as Ben Gurion wanted, or whether another disposition of the matter could be found. Public confidence in the defense establishment was shaken by Lavon's claims at the Knesset Foreign Affairs and Security Committee, duly made available to the press, concerning an organized plot against him and an establishment-inspired campaign of character assassination. The august committee was called the "little Knesset" and in effect was the supreme legislative body for defense matters, since the Knesset plenum included Communist and Arab delegates which obviated closed parliamentary sessions as practiced in British procedure. These were excluded from the committee. The leakages from the secret committee sessions deeply angered the Ben Gurion forces. Naturally, public washing of the defense establishment's dirty laundry touched to the quick both Ben Gurion and the establishment he had created, and which he viewed as the crowning glory of Israel. Eshkol referred to the spectacle as "opening Pandora's box."[18]

The Lavon forces mounted a vigorous press and public information campaign against Ben Gurion. Opposition and quasi-opposition coalition partners — people Ben Gurion had ruthlessly shunted aside, bypassed or offended — joined the cacaphony. Over the long years of his leadership, Ben Gurion had made enemies. This was their golden opportunity. The resentment within the party was to some extent checked by Mapai politicians who were appalled at the "political earthquake" which shook the country.[19] They and their allies from other parties in the coalition decided to propose the appointment of a ministerial committee, instead of a judicial committee which Ben Gurion favored. The committee, according to a response from its chairman, the Progressive Party minister of justice, Pinḥas Rosen, to a query from Ben Gurion, was to deal with "procedural matters" relating to the handling of the affair. Rosen and Eshkol, Ben Gurion's devoted lieutenant and the strong man in the seven-member ministerial committee, saw their function to rid the state of the affair, to disembarrass the party and government of an issue which could destroy morale and faith in the defense forces. They hoped Ben Gurion would accept their findings — perhaps unwillingly and ungraciously — but even so, they would find a way out of the ugly chapter.

Not without internal difficulty did the cabinet appoint the "Committee of Seven" toward the end of October 1960, and at the end of December it reported back that "on the basis of material at its disposal . . . Lavon did not give the direct order for the 1954 security mishap." It further ruled that none of the people named in connection with the mishap, except the Senior Officer (the chief of intelligence in 1954) and the reserve officer (whose 1960 trial had reopened the affair), bore any responsibility.[20] The findings had cleared Lavon.

At best, the committee was to have smoothed away the crisis. At worst, and this cannot (yet?) be documented, some elements in or outside of Mapai might have hoped that this would lead to a confrontation with Ben Gurion, and this indeed is what happened. At the cabinet meeting which approved the findings, Ben Gurion, who had consistently fought for the concept of collective responsibility, announced that he was no longer a party to this responsibility, "either for the appointment of the committee, for its findings, or for the cabinet decision . . . ."[21]

He notified the cabinet that he would resign immediately were it not for the World Zionist Congress, forthcoming that week, and for another reason which he did not detail. This probably was the pressure being brought to bear from the United States regarding the nuclear reactor at Dimona. Immediately following the cabinet session, he took an extended vacation from his positions which lasted close to three months. During this period, he tendered his resignation to the president. In his letter of resignation, he claimed that the second Lavon Affair should have been clarified by a court of law or judicial inquiry which "would give both sides equal opportunity" to testify. He ended with these words:

> The campaign of detraction waged against me recently . . .
> did not affect me . . . . Democracy . . . involves separation
> of powers: executive, legislative and judicial. My
> resignation . . . comes out of an imperative of conscience
> and of concern for law and justice in the state.[22]

The resignation took effect on January 31, 1961. In the preceding month, various ministers had threatened to resign, including Mrs. Meir and the chairman of the ill-starred Committee of Seven, Pinḥas Rosen.[23]

The tensions within Mapai, already in evidence at the beginning of the affair, heightened as the passions around the affair mounted. For years Ben Gurion had sat at the apex, like a lid on a pot, or a great rock on a volcano. Finally the mounting pressures would force him off, the party would break asunder, the succession issue would come to a head, and Ben Gurion would increasingly isolate himself from both colleagues and public opinion, until the day some two years later, in June 1963, when he would tender his final resignation. The stress on international statecraft had coincided with a palling interest in politics: the statesman had lost his political base.

This, as the story-tellers write, is to anticipate. Ben Gurion's resignation in January 1961 over the Committee of Seven's rehabilitation of Lavon, must first be explained and the intervening steps described. Why did the findings so affect Ben Gurion? First, the fact that his colleagues, in his opinion, led him astray as to the true terms of reference of the committee (originally to have been procedural rather than substantive). Second, he challenged the admissibility of some evidence presented to the committee, and its barring of other evidence and testimony. Third, the actual findings, in clearing Lavon, thereby implicated a senior army officer and the army staff, tarnishing the image of the IDF, more than anything Ben Gurion's chief pride and greatest joy. Fourth, by stating that only the Senior Officer and the reserve officer were involved —

and no one else — there was an implicit clearing of Ben Gurion, as if to say, "If anyone believes that Ben Gurion was pulling hidden wires from Sde Boker in 1954, the committee hereby denies this unequivocally."

From being a reasonably neutral spectator when the affair reopened in mid-1960, Ben Gurion had suddenly been so put on the defensive that such gratuitous clearance angered him all the more.[24] This is borne out by a member of the Knesset Foreign Affairs and Security Committee of the time, who recalled the insinuations of the Communist spokesman in parliament, and a subsequent challenge by Ben Gurion to name names, in order to file a libel suit. "And there are other examples [which show] that these hints enraged Ben Gurion more than any other factor."[25]

Ben Gurion's resignation threw the country and his party into a turmoil which lasted off and on until the split in Mapai in 1965 and cast him in a role which tarnished his public authority and image to a great extent. It is therefore important to trace the subsequent phases of the crisis, which illustrate the steady erosion of his public authority and of his power within the party. The waning of his charisma was paralleled by a loss of his drive and will to govern.

About a month after his resignation, the press began carrying reports that Ben Gurion was willing to step down and hand over the reins of government to Levi Eshkol. [26] The inner circle of the party proposed that Eshkol become prime minister and that Ben Gurion remain as minister of defense, a situation similar to that which had briefly and unhappily obtained with Sharett half-a-decade earlier. Ben Gurion agreed that Eshkol assume the prime minister's role, but is said to have originally proposed Shimon Peres, Moshe Dayan or Yigael Yadin (the noted archaeologist who had been chief of operations during the 1948 War) as minister of defense. The proposals were incorporated in a first draft of a letter to the party but were deleted from the final draft.[27] This undoubtedly increased the suspicions within Mapai concerning the succession issue and the fostering of the younger elements. In the letter Ben Gurion said he would leave office, but put himself at the government's disposal to lead a pioneering drive to settle the Negev and attract young professionals or pioneering immigrants from Western countries to take part in building Israel.[28]

The country see-sawed in this fashion for some months, until finally elections were held in mid-August 1961. In the interim, two more occurrences further weakened Ben Gurion's position. The hapless Eshkol, wishing to defuse the possibility of Ben Gurion's abdication and restore some measure of unity to the party, proposed that Mapai's Central Committee should withdraw its mandate from Lavon as secretary-general of the Histadrut. This was interpreted by the public as Ben Gurion exacting revenge. It would seem, however, that although Ben Gurion was indeed pleased, he would have preferred a more formal "investigation" or "trial" by a party committee which would have given a moral basis to the action. Even on this issue, Mapai was far from unanimous; the vote was 159 in favor, 96 opposed and 5 abstained.[29] The opposition included figures like Golda Meir, Moshe Sharett, Zalman Aranne and Pinḥas Sapir. It should be noted that Sharett had become, in the apt description of an analyst of Mapai's split, "the permanent bearer of silent dissent."[30] This opposition within the party was strengthened and given a new wide public dimension when Professor Nathan Rotenstreich, a member of the Central Committee at that time and a close supporter of Lavon, served as a focal point for a group of intellectuals who organized public statements attacking Ben Gurion on the Lavon issue. The leaders of the group were some of the outstanding professors in Israel's oldest and at that time only university; they thus played a role far weightier than that of the American university protest of recent years. Their status was closer to that of keepers of the public conscience and their previous lack of intervention in politics lent an air of objectivity to their action. The group included Rotenstreich and Professor Jacob Katz, both later rectors, i.e., chief academic officers of the Hebrew University; heads of departments and such figures in academia as Professors S. N. Eisenstadt, Jacob Talmon, Joshua Prawer,

Don Patinkin, A. Uhrbach, Y. Arieli and close to 150 more, as well as the aged Martin Buber, though the latter's influence was greater outside of Israel than within.[31]

This measure of lack of confidence in Ben Gurion shook the public even more. It also deeply wounded Ben Gurion. As an autodidact whose speeches and writings embraced history, historiography and Bible, and who had taken an increasing interest in philosophy, he undoubtedly saw himself as no less a "man of the spirit" than his detractors at the University. His isolation increased and he felt it all the more when the professional intellectuals whose approbation he valued turned their backs on him.

Added to this opposition within and without the party was a compromise decision by the party leadership which further increased Ben Gurion's isolation. Prior to the mid-summer election, Mapai decided to "to take leave of the affair" — an alliterative Hebrew phrase *(lifrosh min ha-parasha)* — which meant that it would cease debating the issue and attempt to reduce its role in the election campaign. By shelving the issue, in effect the party further demonstrated its lack of support for the man who was its candidate for prime minister; this hardly strengthened Ben Gurion's image nor did it bode well for Mapai in the future. In the August 1961 elections, Mapai dropped by about 10 percent: from 47 to 42 mandates in the 120-member Knesset. The strained relations within Mapai were further complicated by the consequent increased weight of the four coalition partners, Aḥdut ha-'Avodah, Mapam, the Progressives and the National Religious Party.

These developments provide the background for the decision taken by the Knesset at its last session before the 1961 elections, at which these parties voted for a motion stating that "the resignation of the government and . . . the prime minister do not cancel the decisions of the government," i.e., the findings of the Committee of Seven which had cleared Lavon.[32] In spite of this, Ben Gurion continued to claim he was not bound by the committee's decision. He did so even after the elections, in the Knesset address introducing the new government, but later contented himself with private fulminations on the issue until it exploded again in 1964, a period not in the purview of this study.[33]

The negotiations preceding the establishment of the new government were so complicated, and Ben Gurion's relations with the potential partners so strained, that Mapai made Eshkol its chief negotiator, another symbol of the leader's loosening grip on the party. He would have preferred a coalition with the General Zionists in place of his two left-labor partner-rivals, for reasons both of foreign policy and internal politics. But the veteran party element, perhaps even then seeing a merger with Ahdut ha-'Avodah as a way of strengthening their position vis-à-vis the younger Ben Gurion protegés, continued in the policy of *aperatura a sinistra.*

The troubled government held office for less than two years. Slowly Ben Gurion tired of the routine, of the policy disputes over Germany, of the growing isolation he felt, and the strained relations and mounting suspicions among his close and formerly most loyal colleagues. In the years since the establishment of the state he had let his grip on the apparatus weaken, almost carelessly or even willfully. He resembled a locomotive conductor running ahead of his train, seldom looking behind to see if the cars were still attached, confident of the strength of the couplings and his own motive power.

The built-in limits of the coalition system slowly showed Ben Gurion (as well as the coalition partners) the boundaries within which the country's political life could operate and sustain itself. In the process, Ben Gurion's failure to maintain personal control of the party machine, his underestimation of the crisis Lavon occasioned, and the growing concern over the succession, as well as the mounting resentment of his power, led to his resignation, this time final, on June 16, 1963. The combined interests of the interlocked parts of the system, and the many enemies he had made en route, outweighed the authority, fame, and power, the charisma of the individual.[34]

A student of Asian Communism has pointed to the relation between the charismatic leader and the institutions he builds. In his view, "Nation-building . . . is a task not easily accomplished by institutional means alone even when highly efficient Communist organizational techniques are applied." Alongside of these is the charisma of a supreme leader. Thus, two systems co-exist: one is institutional, collective, impersonal, and routinized; the other is personal, individual, emotional and dynamic. [35]

The clash between the two in Israel ended in victory for the routinized institutions. "The . . . ideal and *also material* interests of the . . . disciples or other followers of the charismatic leader in continuing their relationship," as one scholar has put it, or continuing their power, is one of the principal motives in routinizing charisma. [36] Ben Gurion threatened too many entrenched interests, engendered too much conflict. Under the stress of these conflicts, and the strains on Ben Gurion of policy issues at home and abroad, the charisma faded. In the process, as in Lear: "Love cools, friendship falls off, brothers divide . . . . In countries, discord; in palaces, treason; and the bond crack'd." [37]

CHAPTER FOURTEEN

Retrospect

If anything has been shown in the preceding chapters, it is that Ben Gurion had an articulated set of principles. These hinged on ensuring the survival and growth of the Jewish settlement in Palestine, and the enhancement of state power in order to achieve his urgent aims of increasing Israel's population and raising its technical and scientific level. From the point of view of this overriding principle, everything he did was consonant with the aim. On specific issues, his principles however were not always susceptible of implementation. They can therefore be "measured" along a principles–pragmatism continuum. The latter means simply adjusting to situations which one cannot control: doing what is practical. The word "measured" is bound in quotation marks because, at this stage, such a measurement is qualitative, and an art, rather than quantitative and a science. To review the peaks of Ben Gurion's state-building achievements to the extent they have been indicated in the preceding study is the purpose of this chapter. It is an attempt to focus the diffuse and generalize from the particular.

With statehood a number of institutions underwent a transformation of roles. Within a few months, Ben Gurion disbanded the various armed groups, particularly Etzel and the Palmaḥ which could have served as rival loci of military and political challenge. In the case of Etzel, legitimation was relatively easy, both because Etzel's political aim of Jewish statehood had been achieved, though not the historic boundaries, and because the broad public base of support in Israel and in the Jewish Diaspora frowned on its separatism. In the case of the Palmaḥ, the difficulties were greater because of its obvious loyalty to the "legitimate" (Jewish Agency—State) mechanism and its weight in the labor constituency which supported Ben Gurion. Its danger as a political rival was all the greater. It was an arm of Mapam which had an alternate world strategy oriented toward the Soviet Union and a home ideological appeal of "purer" socialism. Ben Gurion exercised his state-building aim to the end: he unified the armed forces under a central and unitary command, answerable to him and the cabinet. It was also depoliticized. The center derived its legitimation from the electorate and Knesset; even though the office-holders were political, they were not illegitimate and sectarian or particularistic. The army then was not only unified but depoliticized. Its allegiance was to the government, through Ben Gurion first as an individual and eventually, with routinization after the Lavon interlude, as minister of defense. The principle was fully achieved in practice.

To a lesser extent, Ben Gurion was able to unify and depoliticize education. Here, in effect, he created one educational system for the "secular" or non-orthodox trends. He was unable, even if he so desired, to get the orthodox and non-orthodox to form one state educational system. Not only did the orthodox maintain a state-religious system, but a smaller parallel tolerated system existed alongside it. In this case, pragmatic recognition of social and traditional forces made compromise a necessity, which Ben Gurion made into a virtue. To delay "ultimate decisions" on the nature of Israel's society and religion's role in it became a principle. Ben Gurion violated his own delaying principle in the "Who is a Jew?" controversy, i.e., personal principle overrode the pragmatic compromise which he had made into a state principle. In this case Ben Gurion the ideologue was vanquished by Ben Gurion the state-builder. His principles of compromise over ultimates defeated his own anti-halakhic bias.

The labor movement had already lost part of its functions as a rival to the state when the labor educational trend was merged with the general trend. Further functions were transferred to the state when national labor exchanges replaced those of the Histadrut, and when the water system was nationalized. But the Histadrut and in this sense its beneficiary, Mapai, would not cede their hold on membership by nationalizing the sick fund or health insurance system. Furthermore, Ben Gurion was unable to induce all kibbutzim to abandon their own doctrine which prohibited the employment of hired laborers. In this sense, the two orthodox establishments which involved both a system of beliefs and a way of life, one orthodox religious, one orthodox socialist, proved stronger than the state. Perhaps this shows that in a democratic state like Israel, the combination both of belief and action in closed communities is stronger than the center. This may even be true in totalitarian regimes, though obviously to a lesser extent if the center uses both terror and atomization. At any rate, state primacy was asserted but implemented to a limited extent only.

On the principle—pragmatism continuum, the principle of the centrality of the labor movement was weakened; the capitalist sector was fostered in the name of rapid state-building. The pragmatic situation then became a principle: that of economic pluralism, to the extent of dropping the very term "socialism." This too was the fate of the word "Zionism." The principle was expressed by Ben Gurion as well or better than any other leader. He couched it in millennial and messianic terms, leaning on Isaiah. But impatient with the Zionists' implementation of their aims and pressed to carry out these aims without the weight of the movement and its loyalties to its own tradition and organization, he was content to force it to recognize its secondary role to the state and then to abandon it for broader horizons. Pragmatism forced its initial acceptance in the earliest years of the state; pragmatism led to its abandonment later. That later pragmatism became again a principle he had espoused forty years earlier, when he had said that after the state would be established, the movement would no longer be necessary.

In this process, the state, from being a means to realizing Zionism, became an end in itself: Zionism reified. There are those who would claim that this was because of Ben Gurion's identification with the state, a kind of "Moi, c'est l'état." This is a crude and uncharitable interpretation. Ben Gurion was indeed the personification of the state and of its defense forces, and zealously guarded his power as he did theirs. But that is a situation of role maintenance expected of every state leader and political figure. If Ben Gurion was motivated by aggrandizement, it was neither pecuniary nor trivial: it was historic and explains his drive better than any other single factor.

The defense of Israel also became a sanctified end. This meant according secondary place to the question of how to deal with Israeli Arabs. On the regional scene, it was an acting out of the principle of peace through superior strength. From that vantage point, any arms supplier was better than no arms supplier. If this meant covert receipt of US arms through a Germany which sent them free, so be it. The principle of Jewish survival and eventual peace for Israel, as perceived by Ben Gurion, overrode other, "Jewish" principles. It also took primacy over the pragmatic internal need of bowing to his leftist and rightist opposition. The German issue rankled and helped topple Ben Gurion, when added to a series of internal crises. Similarly, latching on to British and French interests against Egypt strengthened Israel militarily vis-à-vis its southern neighbor and produced immediate advantages. Both the left in Israel and the so-called New Left irrationalism outside of it have reckoned this for a sin. In all of these cases, state power was maximized and Israel's staying power enhanced, regardless of "lesser" or other considerations of internal or external popularity.

It has been argued that ours is a non-ideological age. Certainly Ben Gurion retreated from ideologies — social and international — and made his ideological thrust revolve around one theme: Messianic Israel. His Israelocentrism as a historic expression of the great periods of the Jewish past and the road to a great Jewish future had no room for detailed social programs. This pragmatic and principle adhesion to Israel's security and growth left Israel without a defined post-state social ideology, and the effects are visible in today's groping for redefinitions of the ultimates, though still screened to some extent by absorption with defense and borders.

Ben Gurion's total preoccupation with maximizing state power, especially in the area of defense and foreign relations, in general his desire to formulate state primacy (mamlakhtiyut) over all areas led to his neglect of the party machine. He took its loyalty as a given, and misread the importance of the machine. He perceived it as secondary to his state roles. At this point, a word about charisma and leadership is in place. Both concepts have lost some of their charisma, so to speak, particularly for the quantifiers in the social sciences. For example, the following: "The concept of leadership, like that of general intelligence, has lost its value for the social sciences, although it remains indispensable to general discourse."[1] In this sense a leader "is one who is repeatedly perceived to perform acts of leading."[2] This tautology does not advance one in any particular direction, but does show the state of the art. More useful is the sociological link of leadership with power.

> Leadership is the exercise of power or influence in social
> collectivities . . . [for] establishing the goals . . . creating
> the structures through which the purposes of the
> collectivity are fulfilled; and maintaining or enhancing
> these structures.[3]

These roles Ben Gurion filled; and did so with full legitimation until 1961. What were the sources of this legitimation, or in other words, from which sources did Ben Gurion derive his authority, on what bases did his power rest? The classic Weberian classification is trinitarian: traditional, rational-legal and charismatic.[4] Ben Gurion's blend of power rested on all three foundations. Weber's use of "traditional" implied the continuation of ascriptive roles, embodied in the traditional social and power relations of the community. In the Jewish communities of the Diaspora, there were usually three models of leadership and power: a) the rabbinate, and by extension, the intellectual and ideological leaders of the non-religious movements; b) the moneyed classes or rather individuals, who were given preeminence in the community because they could finance the institutions of the community: the synagogue, schools and talmudical academies, as well as other community funds — these men were often known as *parnassim* (provider — leader); and c) the mediator with the outside community or non-Jewish rulers, the *shtadlan*. Sometimes the second and third roles — financier and intervenor — overlapped, for obvious reasons.

Ben Gurion was never motivated to amass wealth, and during his ministry, usually left the budgetary side of dispensing state wealth to colleagues or underlings.[5] On the other hand, even in the revolutionary movements in Eastern European Jewry, the intellectual leader often filled the role of *rebbi*, of spiritual guide and doctrinal counsellor of his followers. Ben Gurion, as preacher and interpreter of doctrine, derived some of his authority from the deeply imbedded attitude of Jews in general, and of Eastern European Jews in particular, toward the rabbi, interpreter or symbol manipulator. He had few rivals in the Palestinian labor movement. His close collaborator and friend, Berl Katznelson, was dead before statehood. His one-time friend and rival Yitzḥak Tabenkin had gone off at a tangent with the minority of Mapai in 1944, and his lack of pragmatism and his dedicated doctrinal purity made him a sectarian rather than a national leader. Ben Gurion stood alone as an ideologue and "spiritual" guide. Though this caused irritation among the professional intellectuals and spiritual leaders, the people accepted the role naturally. In this sense, considering the unique Jewish position of statelessness and the historic precedents thus evolved, part of his authority stems from tradition.

Ben Gurion, the political spokesman, the man who dealt with

High Commissioners, cabinet ministers, and other figures of power, also filled the image of the new-style intercessor, but one who derived his plenipotentiary role from modern "democratic" procedures. The role was well-known, well-worn, so to speak, in Jewish history. Thus, in this sense as well, Ben Gurion derived authority from the realm of the traditional.

However, when one views Ben Gurion's career from the time of his election to the editorial board of *Ha-Aḥdut* until the creation of Israel, the rational-legal element of his preferment stands out. His was a step-by-step advancement from central positions in the various labor parties which eventually constituted Mapai, to the key role in the Histadrut, in the Jewish Agency—Zionist Executive, and from there to head the provisional government and become prime minister. His understanding of the byways of political power stood him in good stead. As far back as 1917, he had foreseen the need to build a strong workers' movement and have that movement become the motive force in the Yishuv and the World Zionist Organization. The organizational milieu, the committee work and the bureaucratic nuances of power-wielding in its so-called rational-legal (more legal than rational, one would think) framework — these were as well known to Ben Gurion as the very roads of Palestine which he and his comrades had trudged before cars were plentiful and fashionable.

Charisma presents problems. There are some scholars who tend to question its existence, or its validity.[6] The term though is certainly useful in "general discourse" and since this study usually eschews over-professional code words, charisma as a quality and term is indeed useful. It is a follower-leader quality, a product of interaction and mutual relations. Max Weber has written:

> In the case of charismatic authority, it is the
> charismatically qualified leader as such who is obeyed by
> virtue of personal trust in him and his revelation, his
> heroism, or his exemplary qualities as far as they fall
> within the scope of the individual's belief in his charisma.[7]

A reinterpretation of this is found in a recent journal article by David C. McClelland.

> [The leader] does not force [the followers] to submit and follow him by the sheer overwhelming magic of his personality and persuasive powers . . . . Max Weber . . . recognized that charismatic leaders obtained their effect through *Begeisterung,* a word which means "inspiration" rather than its usual translation as "enthusiasm" . . . . His role is to clarify which goals the group should achieve and then to create the confidence in its members that they can achieve them.[8]

There can be no doubt that Ben Gurion fulfilled these definitions of charismatic leadership. Nor should one forget the added "charisma of the office" or for that matter the charisma of the state, and of the post-revolutionary leader.

To such an extent is the above true, that Ben Gurion, and particularly his followers after the split in Mapai, have been accused of falling victim to the cult of personality. This charge might better be left in the realm of polemics for the time being. It would be reasonable to view Ben Gurion as a charismatic personality enhanced by the new statehood and the ensuing victory. Zalman Shazar had the ability to express what many others felt, if on occasion his style was rather full-blown. On Ben Gurion's seventieth birthday, he wrote:

> It is superfluous to recall what has not been, will not ever be forgotten — your role in our people's great time of decision, in the years of 1947, 1948 and thereafter . . . . It was not only well-balanced judgment or acute power of analysis that made of your decisions the turning point in our people's destiny, it was rather your unerring historical instinct and along with it the power of your will and your unshrinking courage.

Shazar continued, and even making allowances for the style,

his image-laden language evokes a possible definition of charisma.

> You seemed to look through dangers and past them. You
> were like a man overpowered by a hidden but luminous
> mission. The fire concealed within you consumed all the
> openly revealed doubts round about you. With its aid
> you went to strike like a sledgehammer at a great rock.
> And the rock was shattered.[9]

Shazar's not-so-obscure reference to Moses smiting the rock is telling: Moses is, after all, *the* overwhelming Jewish figure, and the person who led the Jews (Israelites) out of bondage.

Ben Gurion was surrounded, or surrounded himself, with young and, in a way, awe-struck disciples. Their names are a part of the roster of Israel's establishment: Dayan, Peres, Kollek, Navon, as well as many lesser-known but extremely competent and devoted men. Eshkol, the disciple who in Ben Gurion's eyes "failed," was under Ben Gurion's spell until the end. Though the love and admiration may have turned to something far different, even during the most strained and bitter days of poisoned relations, the disciple had a certain sense of awe and respect for the leader, surpassing that of an incumbent for his predecessor.[10]

How did he lose the sceptre of leadership and how did this charisma wane? Eisenstadt has offered a general explanation of the waning of charismatic innovations which in part explains the process.

> Once an innovation is accepted it may as a result become
> routine, "deflated," more and more removed from its
> original impetus. Those who participate in its perpetuation
> — its originators and their initial close collaborators —
> tend to become less interested in it; indeed their whole
> relation to these main springs of creativity may become
> attenuated.[11]

This attenuation was increased by the almost constant

friction of the years 1957-1959, over German arms and "Who is a Jew? ", and from 1960-1963 over the second Lavon Affair. In the month of December 1960, the press shows the following "crises" or major issues occupying the government and Ben Gurion: the Lavon Affair; US disclosure of the Dimona reactor; the Zionist Congress and Ben Gurion's views on Zionism; the ongoing Eichmann trial.[12] For Ben Gurion, the ground work for his policies had been laid, and the party strife was a burden. For his own party, the succession difficulties had begun: the machine was transferring its loyalties to the routinized leadership. Ben Gurion had effectively transferred his charisma to it.

The constant friction in the Knesset, the coalition and the party had its effect. Ben Gurion's waspishness in debate increased. In 1958, in an acrimonious debate over the religious crisis, Ben Gurion revealed his evaluation of himself and his life in a biting and sarcastic fashion. It is both revealing for its content as well as for the tone of impatience which became all the sharper as time passed. Ben Gurion had been accused of political maneuvering. He "confessed" that he had been engaged in

> . . . such maneuvers over 52 years, and more than 52 years
> ago, I made a maneuver and did not follow the Zionists of
> Helsingfors [a Zionist Congress held in that city which
> decided to increase efforts in the Diaspora] . . . but I
> immigrated to the Land [of Israel]. Again I maneuvered,
> and went to work the land and became an armed
> watchman . . . . I made a further maneuver and
> volunteered for the first Hebrew Legion of our
> day . . . . Out of a maneuver, I devoted myself for 13 years
> to the Histadrut [in order to build a laboring class of
> state-founders] . . . . As a maneuver, I . . . assumed the
> mission in 1933 to head the election campaign for the
> Zionist Congress which defeated [the Revisionists] and
> transformed the pioneering movement into the major force
> in the Zionist movement. Out of a maneuver, I

worked . . . 15 years in the Zionist Executive, and fought, when I learned that the Mandate would not last . . . for the immediate creation of the Jewish State. By a maneuver, I pushed the Yishuv and the Zionist General Council into proclaiming the Jewish State in 1948. Out of maneuvers, I organized and equipped the IDF as an army responsible solely to the state and undid the attempt by Herut to maintain an army of a political party . . . . [13]

The strife increased, the routinization grew, the personal loyalties diminished and Ben Gurion's interest and energies lagged. In June 1963, after an unwilling two years in office, he resigned, this time for good.

COMPARISON WITH OTHER LEADERS

It was my intention at the inception of this study to devote some attention to a comparison of Ben Gurion with other post-revolutionary leaders, such as Lenin, Nehru and possibly Nasser, as well as with leaders profoundly impelled by a sense of history, such as Churchill and De Gaulle. Further study and reflection raise a number of principle and methodological questions. For example, the given situation in Bolshevik Russia in 1917-1923, or in post-1947 India, are so vastly different from that of Israel in almost every way: size, stage of development, historic memories, economic problems, international constellation. The making of a leader relates to all of these and to his party. Beyond this, the inherited pattern of the past is both significant, and at the present stage of scholarship, insusceptible of measurement.

Nonetheless even if only from the humanist point of view, some lines of similarity suggest themselves with regard to Ben Gurion. With the exception of Nasser, who was limited in his historic and intellectual grasp, men like Lenin and Nehru had developed ideological frameworks and historic vision. The Russian Bolshevik obviously had a much more detailed ideology from which to work than the Indian socialist. Nonetheless, both were great pragmatists, able to yield, at least for longer or shorter "temporary periods," their sacred tenets for purposes of maintaining or consolidating power, national cohesion, or avoiding economic chaos and collapse. Both Lenin and Nehru were ready to accept partition of the homeland, and Nehru did in fact do so. The simple cliche that half, or at least part, of a loaf is better than starving in ideological purity was not wasted on either Lenin, Nehru or Ben Gurion.[14] All three departed from the socialist ideal: Ben Gurion eventually abandoning the term totally, Nehru putting off its application, and Lenin foregoing it at least during NEP. (The examples lead one to wonder whether socialism is at all possible in the early stages of a developing economy.)

Lenin had early evolved the idea of an *élite* band of revolutionaries. Ben Gurion's concept of ḥalutzim, though usually viewed beyond narrow party frameworks, bears comparisons: both are bands of men wedded to their ideal, monastic and monistic. An astute Israeli author has drawn a comparison between Ben Gurion and Lenin. Ben Gurion wrote of Lenin, in 1923:

> Indeed, this man is great. His glance penetrates and sees reality through a transparent glass. There is no formula, saying, cliche or binding example for it. For the man is graced with the quality of genius to look life in the face, to think not in concepts and in words but in basic facts of reality. The man possesses courage and heroism of thought, which do not falter before the inertia of accepted and common concepts; he has a long-viewing eye, which breaks through and penetrates into the complications of reality and draws upon those forces which are destined to rule. But the fixed aim also determines the road for this master tactician, from which he does not depart to the right or left, but knows how to reach it by various paths, according to the situation. For there is one road for him — that which leads to the aim.[15]

"The enthusiatic description reads today," Amos Elon has written, "almost as an unconscious self-portrait of Ben Gurion, or a personal program of himself for himself."[16]

The attitude toward words, especially those spoken by people outside of the home base, is similar. Lenin wrote in 1915:

> Half a century of Russian political emigration (and thirty years of *Social Democratic* organization) have . . . proved that all declarations, conferences, etc. abroad are powerless, unimportant, fictitious, if they are not supported by a lasting movement of a definite social stratum in Russia.[17]

How often does Ben Gurion in his Palestinocentric announcements cited throughout this work express similar sentiments. So too, both leaders spent time in exile carefully briefing themselves on their countries.

The roles of Lenin in 1917 and of Ben Gurion in 1948 were crucial for their respective revolutions. Their roles were central after the change of government in the two countries. However, on a conscious level, Ben Gurion identified more with Churchill. It is quite possible that the young Ben Gurion saw in Lenin a model which the later Ben Gurion replaced with national war-time leaders. In a sense, he thus bears comparison with both Churchill and De Gaulle. Both were war-time leaders with an overriding sense of history and both were also master tacticians. Churchill's famous pact with the devil (Stalin) and De Gaulle's stated policy on Algeria compared with the policies he adopted on achieving power may suffice as examples of this. Of the two, Ben Gurion idolized Churchill and seems to have patterned himself after him. In general, he was an Anglophile, as evidenced by his over-evaluation of British democracy and its party system.

De Gaulle, Ben Gurion has said, is "cast in a majestic mold . . . . He is fearless in politics as he was in war. His confidence is supreme and his power of decision utterly unfaltering . . . he shapes events." But in regard to Churchill, Ben Gurion, who as a matter of course ruthlessly slashed superlatives in drafts submitted by his staff with the Greek *"Mēden agan"* (nothing in excess), waxed lyrical.[18] The lengthy panegyric merits reproduction in full. It may very well be as accurate an evaluation of its author as of its subject.

> How can Churchill be described in ordinary terms? He was unique. Not only was he the greatest leader Britain ever produced but he was certainly among the greatest statesmen of all time. And who in history can match his varied adventures, the facets to his character, his many-sided talents? What he did in 1940 was a rare feat in history: he lifted an entire nation out of the depths of humiliation and defeat, instilled in them the strength to hold fast against heavy odds, and eventually roused them to efforts which ensured victory. He did this in a democracy, where his basic weapon to get a united nation behind him was his own power of persuasion. He was able to do so by his unique combination of qualities — magnetic leadership, powerful eloquence, contagious courage, supreme self-confidence, a sense of history and an unshakable faith in the destiny of his people. His shoulders were broad enough to bear the heaviest possible responsibility and there was nothing dilatory about his decision-making. I am sure he knew he was the only man at the time who could save Britain. And he did. I know the age-old discussion about whether a man produces the hour or the hour the man. I think it is quite on the cards that if not for Churchill, England would have gone down — with all the implications for the world if that had happened. History would have been quite different if there had been no Churchill.[19]

In both evaluations, it is the man who shapes events, and this was the Ben Gurion model. Indeed "history would have been quite different" if there had been no Ben Gurion. More time and distance are required before a full evaluation may be made of his role in history. Shortcomings or flaws in his historic and social vision will have to be weighed against the critical decisions he made affecting both the course of events and the institutional and ideational framework of the state and the Jewish people. Ben Gurion's great strength lay in his blending of the pragmatic with his principles, with his overall aims. This may be the test of every outstanding national leader; by this measure, he ranks high indeed.

I the Lord have called thee in righteousness,   אני ה' קראתיך בצדק

and have taken hold of thy hand,   ואחזק בידך ואצרך

and kept thee, and set thee for   ואתנך לברית עם לאור גוים

a covenant of the people, a light unto the nations.   Isaiah 42:6

Postscript

It is the day of David Ben Gurion's funeral. In sunlit Jerusalem, its red roofs dwarfed by the Knesset's hilltop where stood the bier, the nation of Israel bowed its head before the creator of its independence. Borne on the shoulders and the wings of the defense forces he created and welded, his body has been interred, next to his loyal and loving Paula, at Sde Boker, a man-made oasis in the midst of the Wilderness of Zin whose hills and haunted, desolate moonscape he loved and wished to bring to life.

The end of a great man, "If you seek his monument, look about you." It is the end of an era.

* * *

As fortune would have it, I completed reading the proofs of this book the day before Ben Gurion died. I had not set out to trace the full story of this man, so aptly called David. I proposed to study part of his life and thought and influence and impact. The strained attempt at limitation of the book's scope and at objectivity of analysis has perhaps clouded the vision and sweep of this David's historic stature.

In the first years of statehood, at — symbolically — a tree-

290

planting ceremony, Ben Gurion said: "This is a *Zionist* state, which is commanded to perform acts of creation — of Genesis. The task is two-fold: ingathering the exiles and building the wasteland." His words on that occasion end with Job:

> For there is hope for a tree,
> if it be cut down, it may sprout again;
> its tender branch will not cease.
> Though its root should age in the earth,
> and in the dust its stock should die,
> from the scent of water it will blossom,
> and put forth boughs like a plant.
> But man grows weak and dies,
> and when he has perished, where is he?

He opened the address with Ezekiel's parable of the uprooted tree of Israel being replanted and coming again to life.

> Thus saith the Lord God:
> I will take the lofty top of the cedar . . .
> from the topmost of its young twigs a tender one. . . .
> On a mountain high of Israel will I plant it.
> It shall bring forth boughs and bear fruit,
> under it shall dwell all birds of wing.
> In the shade of its branches shall they dwell.

In Ben Gurion's shade, I believe, Israel will dwell for years to come, and Israel will indeed know where he is.

Jerusalem, Israel
8 Kislev, 5734
December 3, 1973

Notes

CHAPTER ONE

1   Y.L. (Yeshayahu Leibowitz), "David Ben Gurion," *Ha-Encyclopedia ha-'Ivrit* [The Hebrew Encyclopedia] (Tel Aviv: 1966), addenda vol. to vols. 1—16.
2   Speech to 20th Zionist Congress. David Ben Gurion, *Ba-Ma'arakhah* [In the Struggle] (Tel Aviv: Am Oved, 1957), vol. 1, p. 239.
3   *Ibid.*, pp. 249, 256.
4   *Ibid.*, vol. 4, p. 15.
5   A useful bibliography can be found in *International Encyclopedia of the Social Sciences* (Macmillan and The Free Press, 1968), vol. 9, pp. 100—101, 105—107 and 113. See also Cecil A. Gibb, "Leadership," in Gardner Lindzey (ed.), *Handbook of Social Psychology* (Cambridge, Mass.: Addison-Wesley, 1954), vol. 2, pp. 877—920; Lewis J. Edinger (ed.), *Political Leadership in Industrialized Societies* (New York: Wiley, 1967); S.N. Eisenstadt (ed.), *Max Weber on Charisma* (Chicago: University of Chicago Press, 1968); Dankwart Rustow (ed.), *Philosophers and Kings* (New York: Braziller, 1970); *Journal of International Affairs*, vol. 24, 1(1970), entire issue devoted to "Leadership: The Psychology of Political Men."
6   Lewis D. Edinger, *Kurt Schumacher : A Study in Personality and Political Behavior* (Stanford: Stanford University Press, 1965). Also Erik H. Erikson, *Young Man Luther* (New York: Norton, 1962); *Ghandi's Truth* (New York: Norton, 1960). See also Michael Brecher, *Nehru, A Political Biography* (London: Oxford University Press, 1959) for a classic example of the biographical genre; as well as studies of Lenin, Stalin and Trotsky, etc.

CHAPTER TWO

1   Brakha Habas, *David Ben Gurion ve-Doro* [David Ben Gurion and His Generation] (Tel Aviv: Massada, 1952), p. 3.

2   An authoritative and carefully researched biography of Ben Gurion has yet to be written. The data given here are those generally accepted by a number of authors, based on reminiscences by Ben Gurion and fellow townsmen from Plonsk. They are therefore rather subjective. Biographical information is available in Brakha Habas, *op. cit.;* Michael Bar-Zohar, *Ben Gurion. The Armed Prophet* (Englewood Cliffs, N.J.: Prentice-Hall, 1968); Barnet Litvinoff, *Ben Gurion of Israel* (New York: Praeger, 1954); and Robert St. John, *Ben Gurion* (London: Jarrolds, 1959). Ben Gurion's *Zikhronot* [Memoirs], 2 vols. (Tel Aviv: Am Oved, 1971), contains valuable sources or reminiscences; see also Amos Elon, "The Monument Writes about Himself," *Ha-'Aretz,* April 9, 1971 for a critical — highly critical — review of *Zikhronot.*

3   Ben Halpern, *The Idea of the Jewish State* (Cambridge: Harvard University Press, 1961), provides an excellent framework for his subject and for the study. Much of the sociological and ideological background here has been based on his book.

4   Cf. Alfred Nossig (ed.), *Jüdische Statistik* (Berlin: Jüdische Verlag, 1903), p. 299.

5   Jewish Colonisation Association, *Recueil des Materiaux I* (Paris: 1906), pp. 189, 206.

6   Halpern, *op. cit.,* pp. 15–16.

7   Ben Gurion, in a Knesset address on women's rights, referred to his mother as having died when he was "about ten" (*Ḥazon ve-Derekh* [Vision and Way] (Tel Aviv: Mapai, 1952), vol. 3, p. 166, July 2, 1951). His biographer, in the original article on him in *Ha-Encyclopedia ha-Ivrit* [The Hebrew Encyclopedia], vol. 9, p. 53, wrote that he lost his mother at the age of 11. The writer of the article, Yehuda Erez, collected and helped publish most of Ben Gurion's writings and speeches, and may very well be correct. Erez has been extremely kind and helpful to the writer of the present study.

8   Halpern, *op. cit.,* pp. 56 ff., 82.

9   The word was used in the new sense in 1881, see *Ha-Encyclopedia ha-Ivrit,* vol. 17, p. 480.

10   Halpern, *op. cit.,* p. 29.

11   Zvi Even-Shoshan (Rosenberg), *Toldot Tenu'at ha-Po'alim be-Eretz Yisra'el* [The History of the Labor Movement in the Land of Israel] (Tel Aviv: Am Oved, 1963), vol. 1, pp. 66–67.

12   *Ibid.,* pp. 71–72.

13   *Ibid.,* pp. 92–93.

14   *Ibid.,* p. 93.

15   Besides appearing in *Ha-Aḥdut,* a number of choice articles from the periodical have been assembled in David Ben Gurion, *Ketavim*

Rishonim [Early Writings] (Tel Aviv: 1952), published on the occasion of Ben Gurion's 75th birthday.

16 Litvinoff, *op. cit.*, p. 67.

17 Interview at Sde Boker, April 7, 1968.

18 *Idem.*

19 Litvinoff, *op. cit.*, p. 75. The name is hyphenated in the original.

20 *Ben Gurion Looks Back in Talks with Moshe Pearlman* (New York: Simon and Schuster, 1965), chapter 5, pp. 50—51.

21 Even-Shoshan, *op. cit.*, p. 317. The material in the preceding and following passages is based on pp. 310—320; 430—447.

22 *Ibid.*, p. 432.

23 David Ben Gurion, *Mi-Ma'amad le-'Am* [From Class to Nation] (Tel Aviv: Aiyanot, 1956), p. 45 (below — *Mi-Ma'amad.*)

24 *Ibid.*, p. 176.

25 *Ibid.*, p. 143.

26 *Ibid.*, p. 271.

27 Interview of April 7, 1968.

28 *Palestine: A Study of Jewish, Arab and British Policies*, published for the Esco Foundation for Palestine, Inc. (New York: Yale University Press, 1947), 2 vols., vol. 2, pp. 664—665. Referred to as *Esco* below.

29 Cf. Great Britain, Palestine Royal Commission Report, Cmd. 5479, 1937, p. 86.

30 See especially J.C. Hurewitz, *The Struggle for Palestine* (New York: Norton & Co., 1950), chapter 3, particularly p. 38 ff.

31 *Ibid.*, p. 43.

32 *Mi-Ma'amad*, pp. 281, 329.

33 Great Britain, Palestine Royal Commission Report, Cmd. 5479, 1937, col. 129, pp. 120—121.

34 Interview of April 7, 1968.

35 Litvinoff, *op. cit.*, p. 127.

36 *Ibid.*, p. 128.

37 Hurewitz, *op. cit.*, pp. 77—78.

38 *Ibid.*, p. 93.

39 *Ba-Ma'arakhah* [In the Struggle] (Tel Aviv: Mapai, 1948), vol. 3, p. 18.

40 *Ibid.*, p. 14; emphasis in the original.

41 Hurewitz, *op. cit.*, p. 158.

42 *Ba-Ma'arakhah* vol. 4, pp. 22—23, October, 1941.

43 Biltmore resolution cited in *Esco*, vol. 2, p. 1085.

44 Meyer Weisgal, a dedicated partisan of Weizmann and critic of Ben Gurion, discussed this at length in an interview on January 1, 1970.

45 Hurewitz, *op. cit.*, p. 159.

46 *Ibid.*, pp. 201—203.

47 See Yehuda Bauer, *Flight and Rescue; Brichah* (New York: Random House, 1970).

48 See Ze'ev Sharef, *Three Days* (New York: Doubleday, Garden City, 1962); see also *The Autobiography of Nahum Goldmann* (New York: Holt, Rinehart and Winston, 1969), pp. 246—297.

CHAPTER THREE

1   Michael Brecher, *The Foreign Policy System of Israel: Setting, Image, Process* (London: Oxford University Press, 1972), p. 220. Professor Brecher has been extremely kind and encouraging and graciously permitted access to his study while it was still in manuscript and proof stages.

2   Press Conference, Tel Aviv, February 20, 1959, Government Press Office, cited by Brecher, *op. cit.*, p. 230.

3   David Ben Gurion, "Yisra'el ba-'Amim" [Israel Among the Nations], in *Netzaḥ Yisra'el* [Eternity of Israel] (Tel Aviv: Aiyanot, n.d.), p. 127.

4   *Netzaḥ Yisra'el*, p. 13.

5   *Ḥazon ve-Derekh* [Vision and Way] (Tel Aviv: Mapai, 1951), vol. 1, pp. 199–200 (below — *Ḥazon*).

6   David Ben Gurion, *Mi-Ma'amad le 'Am* [From Class to Nation] (Tel Aviv: Aiyanot, 1956), pp. 58–59 (below — *Mi-Ma'amad*).

7   *Netzaḥ Yisra'el*, pp. 144–145.

8   *Ḥazon*, vol. 4, p. 115, also p. 305.

9   *Netzaḥ Yisra'el*, p. 77; *Ḥazon*, vol. 1, p. 46.

10   *Ḥazon*, vol. 2, pp. 154–155.

11   *Ibid.*, vol. 3, pp. 18–35.

12   *Ibid.*, vol. 2, p. 167.

13   See *Netzaḥ Yisra'el*, p. 23, for a description of "spiritual Diaspora" or "Diaspora of the soul."

14   "Zionism and Pseudo-Zionism" in *Forum for the Problems of Zionism, Jewry and the State of Israel*, Proceedings of the Jerusalem Ideological Conference (of August 1957) (Jerusalem: World Zionist Organization, 1959), pp. 149–150.

15   *Ḥazon*, vol. 2, p. 167; *Jewish Agency Digest*, Jerusalem, II(32), May 5, 1950, p. 1294.

16   *Ḥazon*, vol. 2, p. 48.

17   *Ibid.*, vol. 4, p. 302.

18   *Ibid.*, vol. 2, p. 177.

19   *Ibid.*, p. 169.

20   A conversation in the home of his daughter, Dr. Renana Ben Gurion, herself a biologist, in the late 1950s.

21   Deuteronomy 7:7–8, translated by Avi-hai; the essay it heads is called "Mission and Purpose," and was originally given as a lecture to Israel's High Command in 1950. The second citation which is the companion of the above is from Isaiah 43:5–6, foretelling the ingathering of the Jews from the four points of the compass.

22   *Ma'arekhet Sinai* [The Sinai Campaign] (Tel Aviv: Am Oved, 1964), p. 105.

23   *Ibid.*, pp. 241, 265.

24   See Dankwart Rustow, *A World of Nations* (Washington: Brookings Institute, 1968), p. 40.

25   See particularly Ben Gurion's lecture to the Israel Defense Forces

(IDF) High Command on April 6, 1950, Ḥazon, vol. 2, pp. 42—47.

26   Lecture at Beit Berl, Israel, to a "task force" of the Labor Party on relations between state and religion, May 2, 1971. Zalman Shazar in Davar, September 21, 1956, called Ben Gurion a deeply religious personality.

27   Ben Gurion Looks Back in Talks with Moshe Pearlman (New York: Simon and Schuster, 1965), pp. 216—217. Interview of December 25, 1969 at Sde Boker. Though the quotations of Ben Gurion are usually from the period under consideration (1948—1963), these exceptions are in place since they deal not with the recollection of an event but with a tenet, held consistently over a long period.

28   In a more recent interview with Avis Shulman in Sde Boker on July 1, 1971, he said twice that he "believes in God."

29   Ḥazon, vol. 1, pp. 33—34; emphasis in original.

30   Robert Jay Lifton, Revolutionary Immortality (Middlesex: Penguin Books, 1970), has written an essay on Maoism and the search for immortality which is an interesting development in historiography and historic interpretation.

31   Ḥazon, vol. 2, p. 171.

32   Ibid., vol. 1, p. 43.

33   Re the Greek and Spanish, conversations with Ben Gurion's aides, various dates; Burma visit, The Jerusalem Post, December, 1961.

34   Isaiah 2: 2—4; Micah 4:1—3.

35   At a session of the General Assembly of the Reconstituted Jewish Agency, Jerusalem, June 23, 1971.

36   Ḥazon, vol. 1, pp. 276—277.

37   Ibid., p. 278.

38   Divrei ha-Knesset [Knesset Proceedings], vol. 3, p. 128, November 21, 1949.

39   Ḥazon, vol. 3, pp. 134—135.

40   Ibid., vol. 1, p. 183. (See also Netzaḥ Yisra'el, p. 28.)

41   Ibid., vol. 3, p. 203. It is interesting to note that Ben Gurion's successor, Levi Eshkol, did not use the "light" terminology. In part, the ambitiousness of the idea did not reflect Eshkol's more modest view of the world and himself, and in part, rejection of his predecessor's language may have been a conscious or unconscious attempt to establish his own style and identity. (Source — personal observations, 1963—1965.) Ben Gurion's use of messianism and of the "light" idea had occasioned much criticism. See Min ha-Yesod (Tel Aviv: Amikam, 1962), esp. Professor Nathan Rotenstreich's article, pp. 17—31. The theme of "light unto the nations" was not always viewed positively in Ben Gurion's earlier thoughts. In 1933, speaking of the Jewish right to exist in Europe or any place as an elemental right of life, not dependent on any special sense of mission, he said:

> We say: Behold we are like unto all nations. We live where we live. We are an end unto ourselves just as Persia and Germany are ends unto themselves. Our right to

> existence is in our existence. We *did not undertake any contract to be a light unto the nations,* to do anyone a favor.
>
> (*Mi-Ma'amad la-'Am,* p. 159)

However, the rejection is of an ideological mission in the Diaspora — either socialist or Communist — to convert the masses in Europe. This he believed was not needed to justify Jewish existence. But in Israel, at a later stage, the mission is not merely to justify the state's existence, but to give it the ultimate consonance with its "original" prophetic roots.

42   *Ḥazon,* vol. 1, p. 8.

43   *Divrei ha-Knesset,* vol. 3, p. 443, January 4, 1950.

44   *Netzaḥ Yisra'el,* p. 28.

45   *Ḥazon,* vol. 1, p. 191. This idea was repeated in an address on "Science and Ethics" at Brandeis University, March 9, 1960. The sentence preceding this part on that occasion, as cited in Brecher, *op. cit.,* p. 242, reads: "I do not hold that we are a chosen people." In context this probably means that Israel is not the *only* chosen people, since the next statement is "Every people, to some extent, is a chosen people — in its own eyes at any rate." See also note 41 above.

46   *Ibid.,* vol. 2, p. 178.

47   *Ibid.,* vol. 5, pp. 77–81, 92–96.

48   *Ibid.,* p. 87.

49   *Netzaḥ Yisra'el,* p. 27.

50   Cited by Henry Steele Commager in "Is Freedom in America Dying," *Look,* 34(14), July 14, 1970.

51   *Netzaḥ Yisra'el,* p. 27.

52   *Ḥazon,* vol. 1, p. 117.

53   *Ibid.,* vol. 2, pp. 177–178.

54   *Ibid.,* p. 171.

55   *The Jerusalem Post,* September 30, 1966, translated from *Davar,* September, 1956; mistakenly given in the *Post* as October 21.

56   *Divrei ha-Knesset,* vol. 5, p. 1589, May 31, 1950.

57   Interview at Sde Boker, December 25, 1969.

58   *Netzaḥ Yisra'el,* p. 8.

59   Though many sources over the years claim to have heard Ben Gurion say this, including the present author, Michael Brecher found three "ear-witnesses" to the remark made at the Independence Day Rally at the Ramat Gan stadium in 1955. Brecher, *op. cit.,* p. 231. After much searching, the original was uncovered, indeed on that occasion, April 27, 1955: "Our future does not depend on what the *nations (goyim)* say, but what the *Jews* do" (*Ḥazon,* vol. 4, p. 171).

60   *Ḥazon,* vol. 3, p. 22, freely translated.

61   *Ba-Ma'arakha,* vol. 4, pp. 137, 315. On strategy and tactics see *Ben Gurion Looks Backs . . . ,* p. 125.

62   *Ḥazon,* vol. 3, pp. 21–22.

63   *Divrei ha-Knesset*, vol. 3, p. 5, November 7, 1949.

64   *Ḥazon*, vol. 1, p. 233.

65   *Ibid.*, p. 193.

66   *Ibid.*, vol. 5, p. 277. The entire quotation has oratorical effect:

> I cannot say that this year I learned new things . . . but
> it seems I saw things with greater clarity than it is
> possible to see from the confinements of an office. And
> I shall tell you briefly what I saw:
> Too much desert and wasteland,
>   and too little settlement and development,
> Too much concentration and crowding in the towns . . .
>   and too little population on the borders;
> Too many debaters and servants,
>   and too few productive workers;
> Too much pursuit of comfort, luxury and richness,
>   and too little productivity and pioneering initia-
>   tive;
> Too many splits and quarrels,
>   and too little joint effort and overall responsi-
>   bility;
> Too many phrases about Jewish unity and brotherhood,
>   and too little real help to the newcomers;
> Too many demands from the state,
>   and too few demands from [ourselves]
> Too many requests for rights,
>   and too little fulfilling of responsibilities.

67   *Ibid.*, vol. 2, p. 66. See also vol. 1, p. 71 for the stress on science and technology.

68   *Ibid.*, vol. 1, pp. 219.

69   Recollections of the writer.

70   Rabbi Richard G. Hirsch, Director of the Religious Action Center of the Union of American Hebrew Congregations (Reform), in *The Jerusalem Post*, January 1, 1970.

71   Arthur Hertzberg, historian and rabbi, at a lecture in the President of Israel's Study Circle on Contemporary Jewry, March 1, 1970.

72   The paragraphs preceding this reference in the text present an interesting methodological point. The best "scientific" method to establish all the above would probably be an analysis of the proceedings and decisions of Jewish organizations as well as a survey of attitudes among Jews in Israel and elsewhere. This would indeed be an ambitious undertaking and is obviously beyond the scope of this work. On the other hand, the conclusions arrived at are based on careful personal observation over close to two decades and extensive contacts in Israel and overseas; they are conclusion which are qualitatively correct and the quantitative measures mentioned above would only bear out their precise extent and numerical applicability.

CHAPTER FOUR

1   See J.C. Hurewitz, *The Struggle for Palestine* (New York: Norton & Co., 1950), especially Chapter 3.

2   Leonard J. Fein, *Politics in Israel* (Boston: Little, Brown & Co., 1967), p. 68.

3   *Ibid.*, pp. 68 ff; Michael Brecher, *The Foreign Policy System of Israel* (London: Oxford University Press, 1972), Chapter 6, pp. 117—133. The commonly accepted academic bases for study of Israel's politics are works by S.N. Eisenstadt, Benjamin Akzin, Emanuel Gutmann and Martin Selinger of the Hebrew University, as well as those of A. Antonovsky of Jerusalem and A. Arian of Tel Aviv University.

4   Brecher, *loc. cit.*

5   *Hazon ve-Derekh* [Vision and Way] (Tel Aviv: Mapai, 1951), vol. 1, p. 51 (below — *Hazon*).

6   *Sefer ha-Hukim* [Legal Statutes], no. 540; August 21, 1968, p. 226. This was the practice before officially legislated.

7   *Hazon*, vol. 5, p. 12.

CHAPTER FIVE

1   Introduction to David Ben Gurion, *Mi-Ma'amad la-'Am* [From Class to Nation] (Tel Aviv: Aiyanot, 1956), p. 9 (below — *Mi-Ma'amad*).

2   *Ha-Ve'idah ha-Shevi'it shel ha-Histadrut* [The Seventh Convention of the Histadrut] (Tel Aviv: Histadrut, 1949), p. xi.

3   *Ibid.*, p. viii.

4   David Ben Gurion, *Ha-Histadrut veha-Medinah* [The Histadrut and the State] (Tel Aviv: Histadrut, 1956), pp. 20—27.

5   *Sefer ha-Hukim*, [Legal Statutes], 5719, (Jerusalem: Government of Israel, 1959), pp. 32 ff.

6   See Ervin Birnbaum, *The Politics of Compromise: State and Religion in Israel* (Rutherford: Fairleigh Dickinson Press, 1970), esp. pp. 201—210.

7   *Divrei ha-Knesset* [Knesset Proceedings], vol. 14, p. 1486, June 3, 1953.

8   *Sefer ha-Hukim*, 5714, pp. 2 ff.

9   Address at Histadrut Convention, May 29, 1949 in *Ha-Ve'idah ha-Shevi'it . . .*, pp. 306—320, also in David Ben Gurion, *Hazon ve-Derekh* [Vision and Way] (Tel Aviv: Mapai, 1951), vol. 1, p. 174 (below — *Hazon*). The citations following are from pp. 168—174.

10   *Ibid.*, p. 176. Ben Gurion's relations with the left kibbutzim were at that time strained because of general political differences as well as defense matters, e.g., the absorption of the Palmah into the Israel Defence Forces.

11   Numbers 32:17, 20. The word was used by "enlighteners" in the

Hebrew press in Europe. Professor S. Ettinger of the Hebrew University kindly pointed this out. In 1881, a group of Rumanian Zionists called themselves *He-Ḥalutz* (*Encyclopedia Ivrit*, vol. 17, p. 480).

12   *Ḥazon*, vol. 1, p. 100, speech of April 8, 1949.

13   *Ibid.*, p. 101.

14   *Ibid.*, vol. 5, p. 229, speech of July 19, 1954, referring to an earlier address, June 10, 1954, pp. 210–213.

15   *Ibid.*, p. 253, speech of October 17, 1954.

16   *Ibid.*, vol. 4, p. 254, August 5, 1953, study day of pro-Mapai Kibbutz Federation.

17   For a brief biography of Borochov and excerpts from his writings, see Borochov, *Nationalism and the Class Struggle* (New York: Po'alei Tziyyon, 1937). The introduction by Abraham Ducker is particularly succinct and useful.

18   Ha-Shomer ha-Tza'ir had its origins in Zionist scout movements in Galicia, Poland and Austria around World War I and took on its Marxist coloration in the 'twenties. See Elkanah Margalit, *Ha-Shomer ha-Tza'ir: Me-'Adat Ne'urim le-Marxism Mehapkhani 1913–1936* [Ha-Shomer ha-Tza'ir: From Youth Group to Revolutionary Marxism], (Tel Aviv: Tel Aviv University and Ha-Kibbutz ha-Me'uḥad Press, 1971); and Zvi Even-Shoshan, *Toldot Tenu'at ha-Po'alim b'Eretz Yisra'el* [History of the Labor Movement in the Land of Israel] (Tel Aviv: Am Oved, 1966), vol. 1, pp. 376–379 and vol. 2, pp. 162–166. Mapam is the acronym of *Mifleget ha-Po'alim ha-Me'uḥedet*, the United Workers' Party; see Chapter 4.

19   Ben Gurion, *Ha-Histadrut veha-Medinah*, p. 50.

20   *Ibid.*, p. 31.

21   *Ḥazon*, vol. 3, p. 108, speech to National Council of Mapai: April 29, 1951.

22   *Ibid.*, p. 135.

23   Published by Mapai, Tel Aviv, 1953. Originally in *Davar*, January 23, 30; February 6, 13, 20, 27; March 6, 13, 1953. Yitzḥak Navon, Mr. Ben Gurion's secretary at the time, notes that Ben Gurion never admitted authorship, though his grandson's name was well known. His humor would show in references to S.S. Yariv, with whom, Ben Gurion said, he was in great agreement. Ben Gurion, referring to coalition negotiations, informed the Knesset he "had consulted with S.S. Yariv . . . and taken his advice." (*Divrei ha-Knesset* 19, p. 283, November 3, 1955.)

24   *On the Communism . . .* , p. 52.

25   *Ibid.*, p. 112.

26   Interview of April 7, 1968.

27   *Ḥazon*, vol. 2, p. 249, address at Mapai Convention, August 16, 1950.

28   Ben Gurion, *Ha-Histadrut veha-Medinah*, p. 33.

29   *Ḥazon*, vol 3, p. 22, April 7, 1950.

30   *Mi-Ma'amad*, p. 141.

31   *Ḥazon*, vol. 1, p. 66. The word "cooperative" stands in no relation

to the rest of the point and was probably added as a sop to balance-conscious laborites.

32   *Ibid.*, vol. 1, p. 255.

33   *Ibid.*, vol. 3, p. 54.

34   *Ibid.*, vol. 3, p. 57.

35   Government Printer, *Israel Government Yearbook* 5711 (1950/51) (Tel Aviv: 1950). Encouragement of Capital Investment Law, p. 99; subsequent Yearbooks also.

36   *Hazon*, vol. 5, p. 228. The original midrash is in *Genesis Rabbah* 9; *Ecclesiastes Rabbah* 3.

37   To an Israel Bond Mission, summer 1957, recorded by the writer.

38   *The Jerusalem Post*, December 13, 1960.

39   Pinhas Lavon, *Derekh ha-Histadrut be-Medinah*, [The Path of the Histadrut in the State] (Tel Aviv: Histadrut, 1959), pp. 7—8. Also discussions with specialists in Histadrut affairs in September 1971.

40   *The Jerusalem Post*, December 13, 1960.

41   *Idem.*

42   Pinhas Lavon, *Hevrat ha-'Avodah* [A Labor Society] (Tel Aviv: Mif'alei Tarbut Vehinuch, 1968), pp. 201—202.

43   See *Kovetz min ha-Yesod* [Collection of articles by the Lavonist *Min ha-Yesod* group] (Tel Aviv: Amikam, 1962).

44   *Davar*, December 16, 1960.

45   *Hazon*, vol. 3, p. 133.

46   Y. Becker, *Mishnato shel David Ben Gurion* [The Teachings of David Ben Gurion] (Tel Aviv: Yavneh, 1958), vol. 2, p. 492.

CHAPTER SIX

1   Eliezer Goldman, *Religious Issues in Israel's Political Life* (Jerusalem: World Zionist Organization, 1964), p. 17.

2   The discussion of school "trends" comes later in this chapter. The letter referred to is dated June 19, 1947 (Zionist Archives, Jerusalem).

3   David Ben Gurion, *Netzah Yisra'el* [The Eternity of Israel] (Tel Aviv: Aiyanot, 1958), p.154.

4   *Ibid.*, pp. 156, 158.

5   The discussion of this and other points in this work has been supplemented by information assembled by Ervin Birnbaum, *The Politics of Compromise, State and Religion in Israel* (Rutherford: Fairleigh Dickinson Press, 1970), particularly pp. 82—86.

6   A leading "secularist," the late minister of education, Zalman Aranne, once observed in a private gathering convened by Levi Eshkol to discuss state and religion that he favored the operation of buses on the Sabbath, but not of trains. The comment, noted by the writer at that time, shows just how "illogical" any compromise may be, a fact which did not escape Aranne's humorous attention at the time.

7   *Ben Gurion Looks Back in Talks with Moshe Pearlman* (New York: Simon and Schuster, 1965), p. 219. The talks took place in 1964, the year after Ben Gurion's resignation. The point of view is consonant with his attitude while in office.

8   *Ibid.*, p. 220.

9   M. Loewenstein in *Divrei ha-Knesset* [Knesset Proceedings], vol. 4, p. 744, February 7, 1950.

10 *Divrei ha-Knesset*, pp. 714–720, 726–740. The Kohn draft constitution and the salient points in the debate are quoted in E. Gutmann and Y. Dror (eds.), *Mishtar Medinat Yisra'el* [The Government of the State of Israel] (Jerusalem: The Hebrew University, 1967), pp. 57–79. See also Eliezer Goldman, *op. cit.*, Chapter 3, pp. 47–74. On the broader constitutional questions, see Emanuel Rackman, *Israel's Emerging Constitution, 1948–51* (New York: Columbia University Press, 1955).

11 *Divrei ha-Knesset*, vol. 5, p. 1743, June 13, 1950. English from Yehezkiel Dror and Emanuel Gutmann, *The Government of Israel* (Jerusalem: Hebrew University, 1961).

12 David Ben Gurion, *Ḥazon ve-Derekh* [Vision and Way] Vol. 3, p. 57 (below – *Ḥazon*).

13 *Ibid.*, vol. 3, p. 59. The entire controversy is summarized on pp. 60–74.

14 *Divrei ha-Knesset*, vol. 8, p. 1103, February 14, 1951.

15 *Ibid.*, vol. 10, p. 198, October 7, 1951.

16 *Ibid.*, pp. 248–254, October 8, 1951.

17 Oscar Kraines, *Government and Politics of Israel* (Boston: Houghton Mifflin, 1961), pp. 114, 118. Ervin Birnbaum, *op. cit.*, pp. 159–162.

18 *Divrei ha-Knesset*, vol. 8, p. 1103, February 14, 1951; emphasis added.

19 *Sefer ha-Ḥukim* [Legal Statutes], 5703 (1953), pp. 137 ff. Also E. Gutmann and Y. Dror (eds.), *op. cit.*, pp. 563–565. The operative paragraph is number 11.

20 *Netzaḥ Yisra'el* p. 158.

21 *Sefer ha-Ḥukim*, 5710 (1949–50), p. 114; translation from Gutmann and Dror (eds.), *op. cit.*, p. 105.

22 Goldman, *op. cit.* p. 67.

23 *Divrei ha-Knesset*, vol. 24, 2201, July 1, 1958

24 *Ibid.*, pp. 2230–2232, July 7, 1958, speech of M. H. Shapiro.

25 *Ibid.*, p. 2314, July 15, 1958.

26 *Mi Yehudi* [Who is a Jew], a reader (Jerusalem: n.p., 5729–1969), pp. a–c. See also *Jewish Identity*, A documentary compilation by Baruch Litvin, ed. S.B. Hoenig (New York: Feldheim, 1965).

27 *Divrei ha-Knesset*, vol. 25, p. 377, December 1, 1958; speech of Yitzḥak Raphael.

28 *Ibid.*, pp. 380–381.

29 *Ibid.*, vol. 28, p. 21, December 16, 1959.

30 *Ibid.*, vol. 19, p. 230, November 2, 1955.

31   *Ḥazon*, vol. 3, p. 213.
32   *Divrei ha-Knesset*, vol. 28, p. 91, December 16, 1959; emphasis added.
33   Conversation of February 27, 1972.

CHAPTER SEVEN

1   Israel Beer, *The Security of Israel* (Tel Aviv: Amikam, 1966), p. 129. The English book is part of a larger work originally published in Hebrew under a similar title. Beer was arrested and convicted on charges of espionage in 1961 and died in prison. Whether he was a planted foreign agent or a misguided leftist patriot is an unanswered question.

2   Ben Gurion in the introduction to *Toldot Milḥemet ha-Komemiut* [History of the War of Liberation] (Tel Aviv: Maʿarakhot, 1959), pp. 67—72 ff., (below—*Toldot*). The Haganah had 420 men on its payroll, the Palmaḥ totaled 1,500, Jewish Settlement Police about 1,800. The rest were reserves, at varying stages of training, including women. Regarding Etzel, it would seem that the name was already in use in 1931. See unpublished doctorate, Daniel Levine, *David Raziel, The Man and his Times*, Yeshiva University, 1971.

3   David Ben Gurion, *Medinat Yisra'el ha-Meḥudeshet* [The Restored State of Israel], (Tel Aviv: Am Oved, 1969), vol. 1, pp. 85—86. The book is a collection of diary entries and notes apparently written at the time, letters, and other original matter. Emphasis added.

4   *Ibid.*, vol. 1, p. 142.

5   Netanel Lorch, *The Edge of the Sword* (New York: Putnam, 1961), pp. 238—239.

6   Ben Gurion in the introduction to the official *Toldot*, p. 55.

7   See Lorch, *op. cit.*, pp. 255—256; and Ben Gurion, *Medinat Yisra'el ha-Meḥudeshet*, *op. cit.*, vol. 1, pp. 179—191; for the Etzel view see Menaḥem Begin, *Ha-Mered* [The Revolt] (Jerusalem: Achiasaf, 1950), pp. 211—216, 242—251.

8   David Ben Gurion, *Medinat Yisra'el ha-Meḥudeshet*, *op. cit.*, vol. 1, p. 184, emphasis added.

9   H.H. Gerth and C. Wright Mills, *From Max Weber* (London: Oxford University Press, 1946), p. 78, emphasis added.

10   Ben Gurion in *Toldot*, p. 55. In *Medinat Yisra'el ha-Meḥudeshet*, vol. 1, p. 285, the wording is the same, but the order slightly different.

11   Lorch, *op. cit.*, pp. 324—325.

12   See Yehuda Bauer, *Diplomatia u-Maḥteret* [Diplomacy and Underground in Zionism, 1939—1945] (Tel Aviv: Sifriat Poalim, 1966), for analysis of the Palmaḥ development as well as the interplay of Haganah, Palmaḥ and Etzel.

13   Ben Gurion in *Toldot*, p. 55.

14 Ben Gurion, *Medinat Yisra'el ha-Meḥudeshet, op. cit.*, vol. 1, p. 276.

15 Lorch, *op. cit.*, pp. 395–397, Ben Gurion, *Medinat Yisra'el ha-Meḥudeshet*, vol. 1, pp. 267–280.

16 Lorch, *op. cit.*, pp. 396–397.

17 *Davar*, July 29, 1948; cited in Ben Gurion, *Medinat Yisra'el ha-Meḥudeshet*, p. 269.

18 Conversation with a former General Staff officer, who requested anonymity; fall, 1971. Death intervened in arranging an interview with the late Agudah leader, Rabbi Yitzḥak Meir Levine. See Lorch, *op. cit.*, p. 292: "... well over two-thirds of the 'Orthodox' company of the Palmaḥ [were killed at Latrun in July 1948. This] was one of the factors which henceforth prevailed against constitution of formations on a religious basis."

19 The unification of command was also not simple, though the complications were not political but personal, leading to the resignation of air force commander Aharon Remez. (Recollected by Moshe Pearlman, May 18, 1971.) See *Ben Gurion Looks Back* ... (New York: Simon and Schuster, 1965), p. 144 and Yigael Yadin in Yigal Allon, *The Making of Israel's Army* (London: Vallentine, Mitchell, 1970), p. 223. Ben Gurion's firm control of policy is shown by the resignation of one chief of staff, Yadin, over budget priorities. See Pearlman, *op. cit.*, p. 126 and *Ḥazon ve-Derekh* [Vision and Way] (Tel Aviv: Mapai, 1951–57), 5 vols., vol. 1, p. 307; also Yadin interview on 1948 war, *Ma'ariv*, May 7, 1973. Professor Yehoshua Arieli kindly brought to the writer's attention the need to deal, however briefly, with the question of political approach raised in the article.

20 *Sefer ha-Ḥukim* [Legal Statutes], 5709 (1949), pp. 271–273.

21 *Divrei ha-Knesset*, vol. 2, p. 1337; August 15, 1949.

22 This period was shortened for men over 26; by amendment the period of service has changed in keeping with political and military developments. At the time of writing, fall 1973, the term for men was three years, and for women twenty months.

23 *Ḥazon*, vol. 1, p. 218. *Divrei ha-Knesset*, vol. 2, p. 1339, August 15, 1949.

24 See J.C. Hurewitz, *Middle East Politics: The Military Dimension* (New York: Praeger, 1969), pp. 373–378.

25 By parliamentary maneuver, this powerful committee constituted a nonpartisan secret forum for the government and Zionist opposition, since it excluded the Communists and Arab members of the Knesset.

26 *Ḥazon*, vol. 1, p. 221. *Divrei ha-Knesset*, vol. 2, p. 1340, August 15, 1949.

27 In 1950, the minister of defense was empowered by an amendment of the law to defer execution of the agricultural service. Ben Gurion, in a conversation with the writer on December 25, 1969, explained this as a need to bow to the needs of expertise and modern techniques in training. Evidence bears this out. The amendment crops up regularly in the Knesset and the farm service provision is still on the books.

28   *Divrei ha-Knesset*, vol. 2, p. 1338, August 15, 1949.

29   Y. Riftin, M.K., and I. Galili, M.K., *Divrei ha-Knesset*, vol. 2, pp. 1438 and 1457, August 29 and 30, 1949.

30   *Ibid.*, p. 1439, August 29, 1949.

31   *Ibid.*, p. 1572, September 5, 1949.

32   *Ibid.*, p. 1564, September 5, 1949.

33   Dan Horowitz and Eliyahu Hasin, *Ha-Parashah* [The Affair] (Tel Aviv: Am Hassefer, 1961). The book was written in defense of Lavon. One of the major criticisms of the Lavon Affair of 1960 by the followers of Ben Gurion was that for the first time proceedings of the Knesset Foreign Affairs and Security Committee were leaked. The report is apparently based on an account of the committee's sessions.

34   Moshe Dayan, *Diary of the Sinai Campaign* (New York: Harper and Row, 1966), pp. 12–13.

35   Conversation of December 25, 1969.

36   *Medinat Yisra'el ha-Meḥudeshet*, vol. 1, p. 288.

37   Cited in *Ha-'Aretz*, May 21, 1970. The problem may not be civil-military only. Dayan speaks of two cases during the Sinai Campaign in which local commanders either jumped the gun, once by as much as 24 hours, or by sending a patrol, which had been approved, but actually cloaking under this name a full combat unit. It may be that the considerable latitude permitted lower level officers is partly responsible for this, as well as the lack of firm tradition beyond initiative and voluntarism.

38   *Ḥazon*, vol. 1, p. 11.

39   *Ibid.*, vol. 1, p. 326, and vol. 5, p. 302.

40   David Ben Gurion, *Netzaḥ Yisra'el* [The Eternity of Israel] (Tel Aviv: Aiyanot, 1954), p. 417.

41   For other years: the numbers of killed and wounded were:
1952 — 147
1953 — 162
1954 — 180
1955 — 258
Ma'arekhet Sinai, p. 39.

42   On this point see Ben Gurion's defense of the Kinneret action of December 1955: "The government of Israel is required to defend the life of a simple fisherman . . . .", *Divrei ha-Knesset*, vol. 19, p. 675, January 2, 1956.

43   *Ibid.*, p. 674, January 2, 1956.

44   Shlomo Aronson and Dan Horowitz, "The Strategy of Controlled Retaliation: The Israeli Case", a mimeographed article kindly made available by the authors.

45   *Divrei ha-Knesset*, vol. 19, p. 233, November 2, 1955, emphasis added.

46   *Ibid.*, vol. 9, p. 331, November 5, 1951.

47   To what extent the Arabs got the message is one question the Aronson and Horowitz study attempts to answer. On the whole they

agree with Nadav Safran, *From War to War, The Arab-Israeli Confrontation, 1948–1967* (New York: Pegasus, 1969), p. 45, who concludes that the raids were most effective against Jordan which "on the whole not only avoided sponsoring . . . infiltration itself but did all it could to prevent Palestinian refugees organized and armed by initiatives from outside Jordan from undertaking it." One wonders whether some Arabs grasped the subtlety of the retaliatory raids — that they were not due to past incidents, but intended for future results. The former Egyptian Minister of Information Muhammad Haykal refers in his *Memoirs* to the raids as "punishment raids," see *Ma'ariv*, September 12, 1971, p. 15.

48   The decision having been made by acting minister of defense, Pinḥas Lavon, Ben Gurion approved it. (Aronson and Horowitz, *op. cit.*)

49   *Ḥazon*, vol. 5, p. 126.

50   Aronson and Horowitz, *op. cit.*

51   Yigal Allon, *op. cit.*, p. 56.

52   Robert Anderson quoting Nasser in David Ben Gurion, *Ha-Masa u-Matan ha-Sodi* ["The Secret Negotiations"] *Ma'ariv*, July 2, 1971.

53   Shlomo Aronson, "Ben Gurion, Eshkol, Allon and Dayan: The Art of Priorities," Hebrew, mimeographed, n.d.

54   *Divrei ha-Knesset*, vol. 19, p. 285, November 3, 1955.

55   *The Record of Israel's Peace Offers to the Arab States, 1948–1963* (Jerusalem: Ministry for Foreign Affairs, 1963), p. 50, excerpt from an interview with the *Times* (London), July 26, 1955.

56   *Davar*, August 14, 1955.

57   Anderson, "We all understand that in the deal with Czechoslovakia, Egypt discovered a source of weapons which brings a new and dangerous element into the Middle East," in David Ben Gurion, *Ha-Masa u-Matan ha-Sodi*, *Ma'ariv*, July 2, 1971.

58   *Divrei ha-Knesset*, vol. 19, p. 232, November 2, 1955.

59   *Ma'arekhet Sinai*, p. 52, January 5, 1956, address at a labor meeting.

60   *Divrei ha-Knesset*, vol. 19, p. 676, January 2, 1956.

61   *Ibid.*, p. 233, November 2, 1955.

62   Moshe Dayan, *op. cit.*, pp. 14–15.

63   *Ma'arekhet Sinai*, pp. 51–52, January 5, 1956.

64   *Ibid.*, p. 148, August 26, 1956.

65   *The Jerusalem Post*, November 3, 1955.

66   *Divrei ha-Knesset*, vol. 21, p. 111, October 17, 1956.

67   Shimon Peres, *David's Sling* (London: Weidenfeld and Nicolson, 1970), p. 203.

68   J.C. Hurewitz, *op. cit.*, p. 363.

69   *Idem.*

70   *Ma'arekhet Sinai*, pp. 51–52, at a Labor Party conference.

71   Interviews with Ben Gurion in May 1968, Sde Boker, made available by Melville Mark of Israel Communications; mimeographed, p. 25.

72   *Ḥazon*, vol. 2, p. 164.

73   Beer, *op. cit.*, p. 87.

74   *Divrei ha-Knesset*, vol. 20, p. 2069, June 19, 1956.

75   *Ḥazon*, vol. 1, p. 204.
76   James G. McDonald, *My Mission to Israel*, (New York: Simon and Schuster, 1951), pp. 116—121.
77   Allon, *op. cit.*, pp. 42—43.
78   The citations are from *Divrei ha-Knesset*, vol. 22, pp. 1233—1242, March 5, 1957.
79   *Ibid.*, p. 1238. The point is important, considering the May 1967 developments and U Thant's action in withdrawing UN forces. Ben Gurion rather prophetically said, "This procedure will in my opinion give the UN the possibility to ensure that no hasty step will be taken which might lead to war activities." The memorandum was apparetly spelled out in greater detail by Hammarskjöld on August 5, 1957. General Dayan made reference to it in a speech "Between War and Peace," published by *The Jerusalem Post*, August 10, 1973.
80   *Ibid.*, pp. 1238—9; 1241.
81   *Ibid.*, p. 1241.
82   *Ba-Ma'arakhah*, vol. 5, pp. 318—319; emphasis in original.
83   *Divrei ha-Knesset*, vol. 5, p. 1794, June 20, 1950.
84   *Idem.*
85   Address at a Gadn'a conference, *Ḥazon*, vol. 3, p. 258.
86   Syd Applebaum, *Education in the IDF* (mimeographed) (Tel Aviv: Office of the Army Spokesman, 1960); Amos Perlmutter, *Military and Politics in Israel* (London: Cass & Co., 1969), p. 72.
87   See note 84 above, *Ḥazon*, vol. 3, p. 254.
88   See note 27.
89   To Avi-ḥai, December 25, 1969.
90   *Ḥazon*, vol. 1, p. 308; emphasis in original. The selection is not identified and may therefore have been a ministry of defense document.
91   *Ibid.*, vol. 3, p. 44.
92   *Divrei ha-Knesset*, vol. 2, p. 1341, August 15, 1949.
93   *Ibid.*, vol. 19, p. 674, January 2, 1956.
94   *Ibid.*, vol. 15, pp. 314—315, December 7, 1953; pp. 717—718, January 25, 1954; vol. 17, p. 859, February 21, 1955. Officially Ben Gurion remained in office until the new (Sharett) government was presented to the Knesset on January 25, 1954.
95   *Medinat Yisra'el ha-Meḥudeshet*, vol. 1, p. 448.
96   Letter to President Ben-Zvi; November 2, 1963; *Ḥazon*, vol. 5, p. 10; *Medinat Yisra'el ha-Meḥudeshet*, vol. 1, pp. 425—426.
97   *Ḥazon*, vol. 5, p. 11.
98   Source not at liberty to divulge private documents seen; Perlmutter, *op. cit.*, p. 85, suggests the same conflict over "border raids."
99   Michael Brecher, *The Foreign Policy System of Israel: Setting, Image, Process* (London: Oxford University Press, 1972), p. 402.
100   *The Jerusalem Post*, October 31, 1965.
101   To Avi-ḥai, January 17, 1971.
102   To Avi-ḥai, December 25, 1969.
103   Perlmutter, *op. cit.*, p. 89. This author errs in the date of Ben

Gurion's return; cf. note 94, last reference to *Divrei ha-Knesset.*

104   See note 33.

105   The original committee dates were provided by the Israel cabinet secretary, Michael Arnon, in a conversation on July 15, 1970.

106   E.A. Bayne, *American University Field Staff Reports Service,* vol. 10, no. 3 (Israel) May 1961, p. 7. The details of the committee's work, its terms of reference, even the fact that it has met, are kept secret.

CHAPTER EIGHT

1   Government Printer, *Shnaton ha-Memshalah* [Israel Government Yearbook] 5710 (1949/1950) (Tel Aviv: 1949), p. 303. The number of Jews for the same period rose from 759,000 to 1,014,000. Cf. *ibid.*, 5711 (1950), p. 362.

2   Ben Gurion, *Ba-Ma'arakhah* [In the Struggle] (Tel Aviv: Am Oved, 1957), 5 vols; vol. 1, p. 143, *inter alia.* (Below — *Ba-Ma'arakhah.*)

3   Jewish Agency for Palestine, *The Jewish Case before the Anglo-American Committee of Inquiry on Palestine* (Jerusalem, 1947), cited in D. Peretz, *Israel and the Palestine Arabs* (Washington: Middle East Institute, 1958), p. 93.

4   Yehezkiel Dror and Emanuel Gutmann, *The Government of Israel* (Jerusalem: Hebrew University, 1961), pp. 33–34.

5   David Ben Gurion, *Mi-Ma'amad la-'Am* [From Class to Nation] (Tel Aviv: Aiyanot, 1956), pp. 107–108. (Below—*Mi-Ma'amad.*)

6   *Ha-'Aretz,* January 6, 1949.

7   *Divrei ha-Knesset,* vol. 10, p. 330, November 5, 1951.

8   See note 2 above.

9   *Sefer ha-Ḥukim* [Legal Statutes] 5712 (1951/52), p. 146. Cf. D. Peretz, "The Arab Minority in Israel," *Middle East Journal,* vol. 8 (Spring 1954), p. 146. The law was an instrument in eliminating clandestine repatriation of Arab refugees.

10   Ben Gurion, *Ḥazon,* vol. 1, pp. 93–94.

11   *Divrei ha-Knesset,* vol. 22, p. 2194, April 19, 1957.

12   Radio address on first anniversary of Israel's independence (1949), *Ḥazon,* vol. 1, p. 114.

13   Dror and Gutmann, *op. cit.,* p. 675.

14   D. Peretz, "The Arab Minority of Israel," *Middle East Journal,* vol. 8 (Spring, 1954), p. 141.

15   *Idem.* Such a fate befell Ikrit, Sha'b, Birwa, Bir-'Am, Um-al-Faraj, Majdal Gad.

16   *Divrei ha-Knesset,* vol. 9, p. 1787, May 16, 1951.

17   *Ibid.,* vol. 10, pp. 234, 246, 258, October 8, 1951.

18   *Ibid.,* vol. 33, p. 1314, February 20, 1962.

19   Sneh referred to an interview in *Figaro,* January 6, 1962.

20   *Ibid.,* pp. 1316, 1321, February 20, 1962.

21   D. Peretz, "The Arab Minority of Israel," *op. cit.*, p. 143.

22   *Divrei ha-Knesset*, vol. 8, p. 735, January 9, 1951.

23   *Ibid.*, vol. 10, pp. 620–621, December 11, 1951. Shortly thereafter, the Knesset's Security and Foreign Affairs Committee echoed this position, resolving: "As long as the present security situation continues and the relations between Israel and its neighbors have not changed, the military administration should continue to guard the security of the state." *Davar*, February 13, 1952.

24   *Davar*, February 7, 1960.

25   *Divrei ha-Knesset*, vol. 33, pp. 1323–1324, February 20, 1962.

26   *Ibid.*, vol. 33, p. 1327, February 20, 1962.

27   *Ibid.*, vol. 33, pp. 1323–1324, February 20, 1962.

28   Sabri Gerais, *Ha-'Aravim be- Yisra'el* [The Arabs in Israel] (Haifa: Al-Teahad, 1966), p. 61.

29   *Divrei ha-Knesset*, vol. 6, p. 2153, July 11, 1950. Cf: Peretz, "The Arab Minority of Israel," *op. cit.*, p. 147.

30   *Sefer ha-Ḥukim*, 5712 (1951/52), p. 146.

31   The higher number is that given by the UN-appointed Clapp Mission, end of 1948. Cf: Peretz, *Israel and the Palestine Arabs* p. 70. The lower is from Walter Pinner, *How Many Arab Refugees* (London: 1959).

32   Peretz, *Israel and the Palestine Arabs*, pp. 37–39.

33   James G. McDonald, *My Mission to Israel* (New York: Simon and Schuster, 1951), pp. 181–182.

34   Cf. M. Sharett's speech, *Divrei ha-Knesset*, vol. 1, p. 722, June 15, 1949.

35   Peretz, *Israel and the Palestine Arabs*, pp. 39, 43.

36   Other than the Shiloaḥ factor, Sharett's speech of June 15, 1949, in which he rejected *in toto* admission of any refugees, suggests that he was not responsible for the 100,000 proposal. Sharett, however, enunciated the withdrawal of the offer in a speech on August 1, 1949, when he said repatriation would not be considered before peace came with the Arab states.

37   Nadav Safran, *The United States and Israel* (Cambridge, Mass.: Harvard University Press, 1963), p. 18.

38   Simḥa Flapan, "The Kennesset (sic) Votes on the Refugee Problem," *New Outlook*, vol. 4, p. 9; December 1961.

39   *Divrei ha-Knesset*, vol. 32, p. 87, October 11, 1961.

40   *Idem.*

41   Registration Disposal of Property: "(Emergency Regulations) Deserted Property," *'Iton Rishmi* [Official Gazette], no. 6, sup. 2, p. 11, June 23, 1948. Definition of Abandoned Areas: "Ordinance for Abandoned Areas, 1948," *'Iton Rishmi*, no. 7, p. 19, June 30, 1948. A legal discussion of the law is found in S. Yifraḥ, *Dinei ha-Apotropus* [Laws of the Custodian] (Tel Aviv: 1953), pp. 5–7.

42   Minister of Agriculture: "Emergency Regulations (Cultivation of Waste Lands)," *'Iton Rishmi*, no. 27, sup. 2, p. 3, October 15, 1948. Custodian: Regulation 40 in "Emergency Regulations in the Matter

of Abandoned Property," *'Iton Rishmi*, No. 37, p. 14, December 12, 1948. Absentee Property Regulations, *ibid.* Cf: *Sefer ha-Ḥukim*, vol. 1, (5709) (1949), pp. 57, 269. S. Yifraḥ, *op. cit.*, pp. 8—11.

43   *Davar*, November 20, 1959. The meeting took place in an Arab village.

44   *Idem.*

45   Oscar Kraines, *Government and Politics in Israel* (Boston: Houghton Mifflin,, 1961), p. 193.

46   *Ha-'Aretz*, April 30, 1958.

47   Ernest Stock, *From Conflict to Understanding* (New York: Institute of Human Relations, 1968), p. 43.

48   Not only Arab members of the Knesset, but also Communists, whose party opposed the idea of the Jewish state, have been consistently excluded from the Knesset Committee on Security and Foreign Affairs.

49   Stock, *op. cit.*, pp. 26—29.

50   *Ibid.*, p. 27.

51   *Ibid.*, p. 28.

52   *Divrei ha-Knesset*, vol. 21, p. 462, December 12, 1956.

53   *Idem.*

54   Cf. *Ben Gurion Looks Back . . .* (New York: Simon and Schuster, 1965), pp. 120—121.

55   *Ha-'Aretz*, May 4, 1958 and week of April 28—May 2, 1958.

56   *Davar*, June 3, 1958.

57   *Divrei ha-Knesset*, vol. 33, p. 1323, February 20, 1962, emphasis added.

58   Ben Gurion, *Ba-Ma'arakhah*, vol. 2, p. 286, April 6, 1948.

59   *Divrei ha-Knesset*, vol. 13, p. 331, December 23, 1952.

60   No doubt another unit under Ben Gurion, the General Security Service (*Sherut ha-Bitaḥon ha-Kelalli*, the so-called *shin-bet* or internal security agency) performed a role in regard to the Arab minority, but available information is necessarily scanty.

61   Government Printer, *Israel Government Yearbook*, 5711 (1950/51) (Tel Aviv: 1950), p. 73.

62   Cf. *The Jerusalem Post*, November 27, 1961.

63   Radio address, *Ḥazon*, vol. 1, p. 113, May 3, 1949; vol. 2, p. 241, June 8, 1953.

64   *Davar*, February 13, 1952.

65   *Idem.*

66   *Divrei ha-Knesset*, vol. 22, p. 2398, July 15, 1957.

67   *Ibid.*, vol. 33, p. 1325, February 20, 1962.

CHAPTER NINE

1   Ben Gurion, at Mapai council, January 12, 1949, *Ḥazon ve-Derekh* [Vision and Way] (Tel Aviv: Mapai, 1951—57), 5 vols.; vol. 1, p. 21.

2   *Divrei ha-Knesset*, vol. 10, p. 621, December 11, 1951.

3   Ben Gurion, *Mi-Ma'amad le-'Am* [From Class to Nation] (Tel Aviv: Aiyanot, 1956), p. 105. The change from this policy to the one cited at the beginning of the previous chapter (Israel is *in* but not *of* the Middle East) occurs in 1948–1951.

4   Ben Gurion, "Speech to the Assembly of Representatives, October 2, 1947," cited in *La Paix dans le Moyen-Orient* (Jerusalem: Etat d'Israel, Ministère des Affaires Etrangères, 1955), p. 20.

5   Ben Gurion, "Speech to the Knesset, March 8, 1949," cited in *La Paix*, etc.

6   The free port in Haifa was a basis of the late 1949 secret negotiations with King 'Abdallah of Jordan. See James G. McDonald, *My Mission to Israel*, (New York: Simon and Schuster, 1951), p. 213. Offers to Egypt were made sporadically, sometimes openly, sometimes secretly in the early 1950s and as late as 1956 when Ben Gurion repeated them to Nasser via a secret emissary (Robert Anderson): see David Ben Gurion, *Ha-Masa u-Matan ha-Sodi bein Yisra'el le-Nasir* [The Secret Negotiations Between Israel and Nasser], part 2, *Ma'ariv*, July 9, 1971. For water exploitation, see below.

7   See note 1, also cf. "Declaration of the Zionist General Council (April 12, 1948)" in *La Paix, op. cit.*, p. 20, which reads in part "We [the Jews] are a peaceful people and we have come here [Palestine] to build in peace"; a later version of the same idea is found in Ben Gurion's 1956 words to Anderson, "in order to concentrate on this project [settlement of the Negev] and the absorption of immigrants . . . . We require peace." (Ben Gurion, *Ha-Masa u-Matan ha-Sodi*, pt. 1, *Ma'ariv*, July 2, 1971, p. 9.)

8   Ben Gurion, *Hazon*, vol. 1, pp. 93–94.

9   *Idem.*

10   *Ibid.*, p. 135. A more complete and literary form of the island in the sea metaphor occurs in Ben Gurion's speech to the Zionist Congress, April 24, 1956, "Israel is a small island surrounded by a large Arab sea which spreads over two continents," Ben Gurion, *Ma'arekhet Sinai*, [The Sinai Campaign] (Tel Aviv: Aiyanot, 1964). p. 105.

11   Ben Gurion, *Mi-Ma'amad, op. cit.*, p. 39, emphasis in the original.

12   The Egyptians faced with the anihilation of their army signed on February 24, 1949: Lebanon signed in March, Jordan in April, Syria in July. The Iraqis folded their tents and silently stole away. The Jordanians under their armistice were responsible to prevent an Iraq re-entry.

13   See Nadav Safran, *From War to War* (New York: Pegasus, 1968), especially pp. 36–56. His brief and trenchant analysis has been a useful framework for this work in trying to show how the failure of the peace efforts formed Ben Gurion's security complex.

14   See Safran, *op. cit.*, pp. 36–42 for an analysis of the Lausanne failure.

15   Ben Gurion, *Hazon*, vol. 3, pp. 162–166, June 17, 1951.

16   *Divrei ha-Knesset,* vol. 10, p. 331, November 5, 1951; cf: *Ma'arekhet Sinai,* p. 40, August 18, 1952; p. 107, April 24, 1956.

17   Naguib: Ben Gurion, *Ḥazon,* vol. 4, p. 77, August 18, 1952; Nasser: *Ma'arekhet Sinai,* p. 53, January 5, 1956. Cf: Ben Gurion, *Ha-Masa u-Matan ha-Sodi,* part 1, *Maariv,* July 2, 1971.

18   Ben Gurion, *Ḥazon,* vol. 3, p. 166, June 17, 1951.

19   Cf. Safran, *op. cit.,* p. 48.

20   *Divrei ha-Knesset,* vol. 5, p. 1588, May 31, 1950.

21   See Nadav Safran, *The United States and Israel* (Cambridge: Harvard University Press, 1963), pp. 220, 225.

22   Safran, *From War to War,* p. 43.

23   Leopold Laufer, *Israel and the Developing Countries* (New York: Twentieth Century Fund, 1967), p. 21.

24   *Divrei ha-Knesset,* vol. 20, p. 1683, April 22, 1956.

25   *Ibid.,* p. 1685.

26   *Ḥazon,* vol. 5, p. 130, May 6, 1954.

27   *Ibid.,* pp. 130–132, May 6, 1954.

28   *Ibid.,* p. 135.

29   *Divrei ha-Knesset,* vol. 12, p. 2985, August 18, 1952.

30   See Ben Gurion, *Ha-Masa u-Matan ha-Sodi,* cited. Ben Gurion in 1956 told Anderson: "We knew the internal problems of Egypt . . . . We were ready to help. We made contacts with Naguib. He asked us to wait."

31   *Divrei ha-Knesset,* vol. 12, p. 2985, August 18, 1952. Although he did not mention the presence of 80,000 British troops in the Canal Zone as another factor separating Egypt from Israel, Ben Gurion must have taken it into account. The idea of the separation from Egypt was sounded a year earlier. See *Ḥazon,* vol. 3, p. 164, June 17 1951.

32   See *The Jerusalem Post,* November 6–13, 1955.

33   *Ibid.,* November 16, 1955; *The Record of Israel's Peace Offers to the Arab States, 1948–1963* (Jerusalem: Ministry for Foreign Affairs, 1963), p. 55. (Below — *The Record.*)

34   *The Jerusalem Post,* November 19, 1955.

35   *Divrei ha-Knesset,* vol. 19, p. 672–673, January 2, 1956.

36   See end of Chapter 10.

37   Yitzhak Navon, interview of January 6, 1971.

38   Michael Brecher, *The Foreign Policy System of Israel: Setting, Image, Process* (London: Oxford University Press, 1972), p. 253. I am very grateful to Professor Brecher for generously permitting me to see this section of his work while yet in the galley stage.

39   *Ibid.,* pp. 281–282.

40   *Ma'arekhet Sinai,* pp. 24, 36, 214.

41   *The Jerusalem Post,* October 18, 1966, quoted in Brecher, *op. cit.,* pp. 285–288. The original lecture was given in 1957.

42   *The Record of Israel's Peace Offers, op. cit.,* p. 44, September 17, 1954.

43   *Divrei ha-Knesset,* vol. 10, p. 331, November 5, 1951.

44   *Ha-Congress ha-Tziyyoni ha-Kaf-Dalet, Din ve-Ḥeshbon Steno-graphi* [The Twenty-fourth Zionist Congress, Stenographic Record] (Jerusalem: Zionist Executive, 1956–57), p. 135, April 26, 1956.

45   Ben Gurion, *Ha-Masa u-Matan ha-Sodi, Ma'ariv*, July 2, 1971, p. 10.

46   *The Record*, p. 58.

47   Safran, *The United States and Israel*, p. 218.

48   *Ha-Mizraḥ he-Ḥadash* [The New Orient], vol. 5 (Winter 1954), p. 106.

49   *Ha-'Aretz*, October 20, 1953.

50   Simḥa Flapan, "Dispute over the Jordan," *New Outlook*, 3(4), February, 1960.

51   Ben Gurion, *Ha-Masa u-Matan ha-Sodi, Maariv*, July 9, 1971.

52   *Ma'arekhet Sinai*, pp. 90–91, March 20, 1956.

53   Extract from Michael Bar-Zohar, *The Armed Prophet* in *The Jerusalem Post*, Friday, September 30, 1966.

54   *The Jerusalem Post*, February 3, 1958.

55   *The Jerusalem Post*, February 16, 1958.

56   *The Jerusalem Post*, July 22, 1958.

57   The leftists in the cabinet protested vehemently and urged Israel not to become involved in competition between the blocs, but refrained from causing a coalition crisis on the matter.

58   *The Jerusalem Post*, February 2, 1960.

59   *The Jerusalem Post*, February 29, 1960. The Egyptians had moved in on February 26.

CHAPTER TEN

1   David Ben Gurion, *Ḥazon ve-Derekh* [Vision and Way] (Tel Aviv: Mapai, 1951–57), 5 vols.; vol. 2, p. 30.

2   *Divrei ha-Knesset*, vol. 5, p. 1589, May 31, 1950.

3   *Toldot Milḥemet ha-Komemiyut* [History of the War of Liberation] (Tel Aviv: Ma'arakhot, 1959) (below—*Toldot*), p. 78; *Ḥazon*, vol. 2, p. 350.

4   Leonard Slater, *The Pledge* (New York: Simon and Schuster, 1970), especially pp. 21–120.

5   *Divrei ha-Knesset*, vol. 10, p. 326, November 5, 1951.

6   Netanel Lorch, *The Edge of the Sword* (New York: Putnam, 1961), p. 153.

7   Nadav Safran, *The United States and Israel*, (Cambridge: Harvard University Press, 1963), p. 220.

8   *Divrei ha-Knesset*, vol. 10, p. 327, November 5, 1951.

9   *Medinat Yisra'el ha-Meḥudeshet* [The Restored State of Israel] (Tel Aviv: Am Oved, 1969), vol. 1, p. 517.

10   Moshe Dayan, *Diary of the Sinai Campaign* (New York: Harper and Row, 1966), pp. 12—13. See Chapter 7.

11   *Divrei ha-Knesset*, vol. 20, p. 1687, April 27, 1956.

12   *Medinat Yisra'el ha-Mehudeshet*, vol. 1, p. 510.

13   *Divrei ha-Knesset*, vol. 20, p. 2071, June 19, 1956.

14   *Medinat Yisra'el ha-Mehudeshet*, vol. 1, p. 516.

15   Shimon Peres, *David's Sling* (London: Weidenfeld and Nicolson, 1970), pp. 200—205.

16   Peres, in an interview on January 17, 1971, particularly mentioned Dulles' reaction.

17   *Divrei ha-Knesset*, vol. 10. p. 896, January 7, 1952.

18   *Ibid.*, p. 897, January 7, 1952. The biblical reference is to I Kings 21:19.

19   *Herut*, January 8, 1952.

20   *Hazon*, vol. 3, p. 278. The reference to political murder may allude to the accusations by labor leaders concerning the death of Chaim Arlozoroff, the head of the Jewish Agency Political Department, in 1933. The Revisionists tried for the murder were found not guilty, but the recriminations occasionally surface decades later.

21   *Ibid.*, p. 280.

22   *The Jerusalem Post*, September 11, 1952.

23   Peres, *op. cit.*, p. 66.

24   *Ha-Encyclopedia ha-'Ivrit*, addenda vol., p. 520.

25   Peres, *op. cit.*, p. 66. His point was that arms sales and arms purchases were two sides of one coin; increased production increased the economic viability of the Israel arms industry.

26   *Divrei ha-Knesset*, vol. 29, p. 2408, July 1, 1959. Trial shipments are the usual commercial procedure.

27   *Ibid.*, p. 2415.

28   *Ibid.*, vol. 18, pp. 107, 109, November 16, 1954. The Mapai-sponsored resolution was aimed at heading off Communist and Mapam resolutions. It expressed "deep concern over the rearmament of East and West Germany," and conjured up the possible recurrence for "the world and the Jewish people" of a future catastrophe.

29   *Divrei ha-Knesset*, vol. 27, pp. 2406—2407, July 1, 1959.

30   Oscar Kraines, *Government and Politics of Israel* (Boston: Houghton Mifflin, 1961), p. 93.

31   *Divrei ha-Knesset*, vol. 23, p. 482, December 24, 1957.

32   Interviews with Yitzhak Navon, formerly Ben Gurion's *chef de cabinet*, on January 6, 1971, and Peres, January 17, 1971.

33   Peres, *op. cit.*, pp. 63—65, 75, 100. (In the interview with Peres, he referred, in reply to a question regarding the German deal, to the published figure of IL500 million. When asked if this was not dollars (instead of Israel pounds) he repeated "pounds" and remarked that the Israel pound was then worth IL1.80 per dollar.)

34   *Ibid.*, pp. 109—110.

35   *Divrei ha-Knesset*, vol. 2, p. 1337, August 15, 1949.

36   *Ibid.*, vol. 1, p. 57, March 8, 1949.

37   J.C. Hurewitz, *Middle East Politics: The Military Dimension* (New York: Praeger, 1969), p. 360.

38   Peres, interview.

39   *The Jerusalem Post,* July 10, 1961.

40   E.D. Bergmann in *Encyclopedia of Zionism and Israel* (New York: Herzl Press and McGraw Hill, 1971), vol. 1, p. 89.

41   *The Jerusalem Post,* December 26, 1960. The decision was taken about two years earlier, Ben Gurion told the cabinet.

42   *Idem.*

43   *Divrei ha-Knesset,* vol. 30, p. 545, December 21, 1960.

44   Bergmann, *op. cit., idem.*

45   Nadav Safran, *From War to War* (New York: Pegasus, 1968), p. 47.

46   *The Jerusalem Post,* September 10, 1969 (denying a NBC report) and July 19, 1970 (denying a *New York Times* story); both using the same language: "speculative, unauthorized and . . . inaccurate."

47   *Ibid.,* February 10, 1963.

48   There has been some conjecture that one of Ben Gurion's reasons for the 1963 "final" resignation was that he had found himself in a blind alley regarding Dimona and US demands for inspection. (Source — a former high-ranking Israeli foreign service officer.) However, Navon told me on January 6, 1971, that this was absolutely not the case and the problem had been solved. Considering Navon's frankness in the interview, and his access to all sources of information reaching Ben Gurion at the time, it would be reasonable to accept his version. Obviously, none of the diplomatic documents are available.

49   Peres, *op. cit.,* pp. 44—63.

50   Abel Thomas, then Director-General of the French ministry of the interior (under Bourgès-Manoury), cited in Peres, p. 57.

51   *Divrei ha-Knesset,* vol. 19, p. 671, January 2, 1956.

52   *Ibid.,* vol. 20, pp. 2042—2043, June 18, 1956.

53   *Ibid.,* p. 2067, June 19, 1956.

54   Peres, *op. cit.,* p. 71.

55   See especially Michael Brecher's two volumes: *The Foreign Policy System of Israel* (London: Oxford University Press, 1972), and *Decisions in Israel's Foreign Policy* (London: Oxford University Press, 1974).

56   *Mo'etzet ha-Medinah ha-Zemanit* [Provisional State Council Proceedings], Third Session, June 3, 1948.

57   *Ibid.,* Sixth Session, p. 21, June 24, 1948.

58   *Idem.*

59   Yifrah, *Dinei ha-Apotropos* [Laws of the Custodian]. On the Jerusalem siege see Dov Joseph, *The Faithful City* (Tel Aviv: Schocken, 1950).

60   J.C. Hurewitz, *Diplomacy in the Near and Middle East, A Documentary Record* (Princeton: Van Nostrand, 1956), vol. 2, p. 292. General Assembly Resolution 181 (II).

61   *Divrei ha-Knesset,* vol. 3, p. 221, December 13, 1949.
62   *Idem.*
63   *Ibid.,* p. 281, December 13, 1949.
64   The citation is in more frequent use as Ben Gurion ages. On June 15, 1971, he used it at a meeting of the Reconstituted Jewish Agency, and in a newspaper article in *Ma'ariv* on July 2, 1971.

CHAPTER ELEVEN

1   Membership figures are always an inexact science. From 1946 to 1951, the World Zionist Organization enrolled over 2,150,000 due-paying members (purchases of *shekalim*) or contributors to "national funds." Voters for the Twenty-Third World Zionist Congress delegates cast almost 575,000 ballots. (Source — stenographic record of report to 23rd Zionist Congress, October 30, 1951.)
2   *Mi-Ma'amad Le-'Am* [From Class to Nation] (Tel Aviv: Aiyanot, 1956), p. 43. Written on November 25, 1917, in New York. (Below — *Mi-Ma'amad.*)
3   *Ḥazon ve-Derekh* [Vision and Way] (Tel Aviv: Mapai, 1951—57), 5 vols; vol. 2, p. 175. (Below — *Ḥazon*).
4   *Mi-Ma'amad,* p. 43. He had on occasion spoken of the need for a continued Zionist movement after the state (cf. *Divrei ha-Knesset,* vol. 13, p. 58, November 5, 1952, referring to his position in 1937 and 1952).
5   D. Ben Gurion, *Ba-Ma'arakha* [In the Struggle] (Tel Aviv: Am Oved, 1957), vol. 1, pp. 282—285.
6   *Ḥazon,* vol. 1, pp. 119-133, May 5, 1949.
7   *Ibid.* p. 126.
8   *Ibid.,* p. 128.
9   *Ba-Ma'arakhah,* vol. 1, pp. 283—285; cited also in *Ḥazon,* vol. 4, pp. 112—114 from Knesset speech noted above (note 4).
10   On the latter point, see an unpublished doctoral dissertation by Rabbi Joseph Heckelman, *What If? An attempt to assess the significance and participation of overseas volunteers in Israel's War of Independence* (New York: Jewish Theological Seminary of America, 1970).
11   *Sessions of the Zionist General Council,* April 19—28, 1950 (Jerusalem: Zionist Executive of Jerusalem, n.d.) (Below — *Sessions.*)
12   *Idem.;* April 24, 1950, also *Ḥazon,* vol. 2, pp. 167—169.
13   I. Harari, at the Zionist General Council, *Sessions,* p. 52.
14   *Ibid.,* p. 18.
15   Resolutions of Zionist General Council, in *Sessions,* p. 185.
16   *Divrei ha-Knesset,* vol. 5, p. 1367, May 15, 1950.
17   Memos by Dr. A.L. Lauterbach, of April 11 and May 4, 1950. Central Zionist Archives, Jerusalem, File Z5/T1126.

18   The Z5 series of files (minutes of the Jewish Agency Executive in New York) in the Zionist Archives show Silver's growing irritation, the show-down with Jerusalem and with the proponents of increasing community representation in the US fund-raising campaigns. The leaders of the drive for a changed representation in UJA leadership were Henry Morgenthau, Jr., secretary of the treasury under FDR, and Henry Montor. Silver told the executive on November 1, 1948 (file Z5/4) "If B.G. and Kaplan [then minister of finance] want to work on the American scene . . . they should say so, then we will quit."

19   *Ḥazon*, vol. 2, p. 165. Somewhat further in this speech (April 25, 1950 at the General Council) Ben Gurion inveighed against "outside overseers," overseas Zionists who would supervise the people of Israel, pp. 175–176.

20   Moshe Brilliant (later of the *Times* of London and *New York Times*) in *The Jerusalem Post*, August 19, 1951. Italics added.

21   *Divrei ha-Knesset*, vol. 11, p. 1187, May 5, 1952.

22   *Ibid.*, p. 1890.

23   *Ibid.*, p. 1924, May 6, 1952. The Zionist proposals may be found in the Zionist Archives, Jerusalem, File Z5/T1125 and 1126.

24   *Ibid.*, vol. 13, p. 56, November 4, 1952.

25   *Ibid.*, p. 59.

26   *Ibid.*, pp. 60–61.

27   R. Gid'on (ed.), *Ḥukei Medinat Yisra'el* [Laws of the State of Israel] vol. 9, pp. 2505–2506 (Tel Aviv: 1959).

28   *Ibid.*, p. 3181, signed on July 26, 1954.

29   *Ḥazon*, vol. 4, p. 304; originally the introduction to Israel Government Year Book, 5714, published November, 1953.

30   *The Jerusalem Post*, July 12, 1957; July 28, 1958; December 26, 1959; December 14, 1960.

31   *Ibid.*, December 30, 1957.

32   *Ibid.*, August 5, 1958.

33   *Ibid.*, December 29, 1953. Goldmann replied that he could not agree to the form and manner in which Ben Gurion expressed himself (*Idem*). The text of Ben Gurion's letter is in *Ḥazon*, vol. 5, p. 33–40.

34   The Twenty-Fourth Zionist Congress, Stenographic Record, Jerusalem, April 24 – May 7, 1946 (Jerusalem: Zionist Executive, 1956), p. 16, April 24, 1956 (Hebrew).

35   *Ha-Histadrut veha-Medinah* [The Histadrut and the State] (Tel Aviv: Histadrut, 1956), p. 58.

36   The interpretation is cited in *The Jerusalem Post* August 19, 1957. The address is given in *Forum for the Problems of Zionism, Jewry and the State of Israel*, Proceedings of the Jerusalem Ideological Conference of August 1957 (Jerusalem: Zionist Organization, 1959). A careful scrutiny of the speeches does not show that Ben Gurion flatly denied being a Zionist, but the point is clear from the citation. Ben Gurion referred to his stance at the 1957 Conference in an

interview on April 7, 1968 and gave his position as "I am a Jew and not a Zionist."

37   The Twenty-Fifth Zionist Congress, Stenographic Record, Jerusalem, December 27, 1960 – January 11, 1961 (Jerusalem: Zionist Executive, 1961), pp. 47–61, December 28, 1960 (Hebrew).

38   *Davar*, April 29, 1961, cited in *The Jerusalem Post*, May 5, 1961. The term 'agreed lie' is *sheker muskam* in Hebrew. Conventional lie would be a better translation. Moshe Kohn, literary editor of the *Jerusalem Post*, pointed out to the author that the term was the title of Max Nordau's book, *Conventionelle Lügen der Kulturmenschheit* (Leipzig: 1883), translated as *Conventional Lies of Our Civilization* (London: 1895).

39   *The Jerusalem Post*, May 5, 1961.

40   *The Autobiography of Nahum Goldmann* (New York: Holt, Rinehart and Winston, 1969), pp. 318–319.

41   *Ḥazon*, vol. 2, p. 174.

42   *Ibid.*, vol. 1, p. 175.

43   *Ibid.*, vol. 2, p. 179; he used the English word publicity, rather than a Hebrew equivalent.

44   *In Vigilant Brotherhood*, The American Jewish Committee's Relationship to Palestine and Israel (New York: AJC, 1964), p. 53. For a scholarly treatment of the subject, see Samuel Halperin, *The Political World of American Zionism* (Detroit: Wayne University Press, 1961).

45   *In Vigilant Brotherhood*, p. 53.

46   *Ibid.*, p. 54.

47   *Ibid.*, pp. 64–66, Blaustein's response is on pp. 66–69. It is not cited, being irrelevant to the main purpose of this chapter. However as a document reflecting the thinking of an important segment of US Jewry, it merits study. The statements were made on August 23, 1950.

48   Note that the statement is phrased both positively and negatively, to leave no room for doubt: US Jews owe political allegiance only to the US and none to Israel. The phrase "Israel speaks only on behalf of its own citizens" appeared in the draft Law on the Status of the World Zionist Organization and was dropped.

49   Personal recollection of author.

50   *In Vigilant Brotherhood*, p. 57. For details of the foreign ministry reaction to the swastika incidents, see Michael Brecher, *The Foreign Policy System of Israel: Setting, Image, Process* (London: Oxford University Press, 1972), pp. 237–238.

51   *The Jerusalem Post*, December 5, 1960, reports the cabinet decision limiting Ben Gurion's appearance at the Council.

52   *Ḥazon*, vol. 2, p. 177.

53   *In Vigilant Brotherhood*, p. 57.

54   *Idem.*

55   *Idem.*

56   *Ibid.*, p. 70.

57   *The Jerusalem Post,* undated press release in Goldmann file.
58   *Ḥazon,* vol. 2, pp. 349–368; vol. 3, pp. 160–162.
59   Official Gazette, no. 1, May 14, 1948; cited in Yehezkiel Dror and Emanuel Gutmann, *The Government of Israel* (Jerusalem: Hebrew University, 1961), pp. 33–34.
60   *Divrei ha-Knesset,* vol. 6, pp. 2036–2037, July 3, 1950.
61   Dror and Gutmann, *op. cit.,* p. 105. The companion law on Nationality confers Israeli citizenship on the 'oleh (p. 107).
62   *Ḥazon,* vol. 2, p. 231.
63   *Ibid.,* vol. 1, p. 126. In May 1949, Ben Gurion spoke of 200,000 immigrants a year, which would near double the Jewish population at statehood in less than four years. In vol. 3, p. 291, he recalls the four-year aim.
64   *Ibid.,* vol. 1, p. 127.
65   *Ibid.,* vol. 2, p. 359. King David Hotel speech of September 3, 1950.
66   *Divrei ha-Knesset,* vol. 11, p. 1316, February 13, 1952.
67   *Ibid.,* p. 1400, February 20, 1952.
68   *Ḥazon,* vol. 2, pp. 180 ff.
69   Dankwart A. Rustow, *A World of Nations* (Washington, D.C.: The Brookings Institution, 1967), p. 61.
70   Private communication with the appointee, Syd Applebaum.
71   *'Am Yisra'el u-Medinat Yisra'el, ha-Ve'ida ha-'Olamit ha-Rishonah shel ha-No'ar ha-Yehudi* [The Jewish People and the State of Israel, The First World Conference of Jewish Youth] (Jerusalem: The Jewish Agency, 1958), p. 198.
72   *Ḥazon,* vol. 2. pp. 157–161.
73   *Ibid.,* vol. 1, p. 8.
74   See above in this chapter.
75   Michael Brecher, *The Foreign Policy System of Israel* (London: Oxford University Press, 1972), p. 237.
76   *The Jerusalem Post,* May 30, 1960. The term volunteers appears in the ambassador's *note verbale* delivered in the Argentine foreign ministry on June 3, 1960: see *The Israel Digest,* June 24, 1960.
77   *The Israel Digest,* June 24, 1960.
78   *Idem.*
79   Brecher, *op. cit.,* p. 232.
80   *Divrei ha-Knesset,* vol. 13, p. 60, November 5, 1952.

CHAPTER TWELVE

1   Cited in Oscar Kraines, *Government and Politics of Israel* (Boston: Houghton Mifflin, 1961), p. 27.
2   See Emanuel Rackman, *Israel's Emerging Constitution 1948–1951* (New York: Columbia University Press, 1955) for a discussion of the broad constitutional issues. The Kohn draft constitution is cited in

Emanuel Gutmann and Yehezkiel Dror (eds.), *Mishtar Medinat Yisra'el* [The Government of the State of Israel](Jerusalem: Hebrew University, 1969), pp. 57—64.

3   M. Loewenstein in *Divrei ha-Knesset*, vol. 4, p. 744, February 7, 1950.

4   *Ibid.*, pp. 714—720; 726—740.

5   *Ibid.*, pp. 779—780, February 13, 1950 and vol. 5, June 13, 1950.

6   *Ibid.*, vol. 4, p. 819, February 20, 1950.

7   *Ḥazon, ve-Derekh* [Vision and Way] (Tel Aviv: Mapai, 1951—57), 5 vols.; vol. 3, p. 57 (below — *Ḥazon*).

8   See Dan Horowitz and Moshe Lissak, *Mi-Yishuv le-Medinah* [From Yishuv to State] (Jerusalem: Hebrew University, 1972).

9   *Ḥazon*, vol. 1, p. 51; the other three were on foreign policy, labor majority in the coalition and full civil equality of women.

10   *Sefer ha-Ḥukim* (5709—1949), p. 1.

11   *Divrei ha-Knesset*, vol. 1, p. 54, March 9, 1949.

12   *Ibid.*, vol. 7, p. 33, October 17, 1950.

13   *Idem.*

14   *Ibid.*, vol. 23, pp. 563—564, January 7, 1958.

15   *Ibid.*, vol. 28, p. 88, December 16, 1959.

16   *Ibid.*, vol. 19, p. 283, November 3, 1955.

17   *Divrei ha-Knesset*, vol. 2, p. 1564, September 5, 1949.

18   *Ḥazon*, vol. 4, p. 273—274.

19   *Divrei ha-Knesset*, vol. 5, pp. 1790—1791, June 20, 1950.

20   *Medinat Yisra'el ha-Meḥudeshet* [The Restored State of Israel] (Tel Aviv: Am Oved), vol. 2, p. 578.

21   *Ibid.*, pp. 578—579.

22   Ervin Birnbaum, *The Politics of Compromise: State and Religion in Israel* (Rutherford: Fairleigh Dickinson Press, 1970), Appendix 4.

23   *Divrei ha-Knesset*, vol. 23, p. 1134, March 4, 1958; citing vol. 23, p. 587, January 7, 1958 and p. 647, January 15, 1958.

24   *Ibid.*, vol. 25, p. 488, December 9, 1958.

25   Kraines, *op. cit.*, p. 95.

26   *Ma'ariv*, January 2, 1959. *Divrei ha-Knesset*, vol. 25, p. 795, January 7, 1959.

27   Birnbaum, *loc. cit.* footnote 20.

CHAPTER THIRTEEN

1   Professor Shlomo Avineri in a lecture to the American Jewish Committee Faculty Seminar, Jerusalem, December 23, 1970.

2   Cf. Alan Arian, *Ideological Change in Israel* (Cleveland: The Press of Case Western Reserve University, 1968), p. 175: "Advancement in key decision making positions was almost certainly determined by the length and loyalty of party service . . . the socialization of the political leadership [of Mapai] took place in party headquarters," etc.

3   Michael Bar-Zohar, *Ben Gurion: The Armed Prophet* (Englewood Cliffs, N.J.: Prentice Hall, 1968), pp. 124–126.

4   *Ḥazon ve-Derekh* [Vision and Way] (Tel Aviv: Mapai, 1951–57), 5 vols.; vol. 1, p. 191.

5   Arian, *op. cit.*, p. 175.

6   Natan Yannai, *Ker'a ba-Tzameret* [Split at the Top] (Tel Aviv: Levin-Epstein, 1969), pp. 103–109.

7   *Ibid.*, pp. 109–110.

8   Interviews with Peres, January 17, 1971 and Navon, January 5, 1971.

9   Shimon Peres, *David's Sling* (London: Weidenfeld and Nicolson, 1970), esp. pp. 67–74. Peres writes that German Defense Minister Strauss "showed great interest in the Sinai Campaign" (p. 71), which still must have been reasonably fresh in world interest (1957). Peres also describes a secret meeting between Ben Gurion, then visiting France, and the German defense minister in Paris, early in 1961 (p. 72). Strauss was defense minister from 1956–1962.

10   Yannai, *Ker'a ba-Tzameret, op. cit.*, pp. 39–40.

11   American intelligence sources have told the writer that Ben Gurion's information was correct and that the Israeli overreaction in attempting to influence US arms supply policies tended to discredit Israel intelligence estimates in Washington for a number of years after the 1963 German scientists crisis.

12   J.C. Hurewitz, *Middle East Politics: The Military Dimension* (New York: Praeger, 1969), p. 375. The entire story of the "abortive art of sabotage" has never been officially published, and its details are not relevant to this work. Hurewitz refers to its taking place "in Cairo" but there are sources which also mention Alexandria and there were perhaps related actions or attempts in other Arab countries. Amos Perlmutter in *Military and Politics in Israel* (London: Cass, 1969), pp. 87–88, also mentions Syria. He shelters behind "security reasons" for not giving details of the operations "which led to several fiascos" but denigrates various journalistic reports as near-fictional. E.A. Bayne in *American Universities Field Staff Reports Service, X, 3*, 1961 "Israel's Affair" reported with his usual sobriety and balance, although one may assume that even Bayne was not privy to all the information. Hurewitz's reference to the chief of Israeli military intelligence as Gavli is an error in transliteration. The Hebrew is Givly, but often pronounced Jibly, the form Perlmutter uses. As stated, the details are not relevant to this chapter and Hurewitz's one statement is the pithiest description.

13   From the Olshan-Dori Report, extract published in *The Jerusalem Post*. December 26, 1960. A full discussion of the Lavon Affair may be found in D. Horowitz, and E. Hasin *Ha-Parashah* [The Affair] (Tel Aviv: Am Hassefer, 1961). The book, is written in defense of Lavon. Ben Gurion's *Devarim Kehavayatam* [Things as They Happened] (Tel Aviv: Am Hassefer, 1965) is a review of the affair from his vantage-point.

14   Yannai, *Ker'a*, cited, p. 16. A more recent secretary-general of the Histadrut, Yitzḥak Ben Aharon, waged a similar battle for control of the Labor appointments to the Executive. In this sense, the problem is institutional: control by Labor oligarchy at the center or the intra-party "coalition" on the one hand, or by the chief party representative in the institution.

15   *Ibid.*, p. 17.

16   The books are Ḥasin and Horwitz, *Ha-Parashah;* D. Ben Gurion, *Devarim Kehavayatam*, both cited above, note 13. Haggai Eshed, *Mi Natan et ha-Hora'ah?*, ["Who Gave the Order? "], was severely censored and never published in book form.

17   *Ma'ariv*, September 23, 1960; cited, *Ker'a*, p. 19.

18   Recollection of Avraham Avi-ḥai.

19   The felicitous phrase in quotation marks is from *Ker'a*, p. 20. Yannai's summary seems to be pithy and reasonably objective.

20   *The Jerusalem Post*, December 22, 1960. Difficulties in appointing the seven-man committee, consisting of a Progressive Party chairman (Pinḥas Rosen), 2 Mapai members (Levi Eshkol and Bekhor Shitreet), 1 Aḥdut ha-'Avodah (Yitzḥak Ben Aharon), 1 Mapam (Israel Barzilai), 1 National Religious Party (Hayyim Moshe Shapiro), 1 Po'alei Agudah (Binyamin Mintz), began when only a five-man group was proposed. (*The Jerusalem Post*, October 24, 31, and November 1, 1960.)

21   *Ker'a*, p. 23. Dayan, Josephtal and Eban abstained on the vote, as did Dr. Yosef Burg of the National Religious Party. *The Jerusalem Post* December 26, 1960 and *Ker'a*, p. 25.

22   *Medinat Yisra'el ha-Meḥudeshet* [The Restored State of Israel] (Tel Aviv: Am Oved, 1969), vol. 2, p. 639.

23   *The Jerusalem Post*, December 28, 1960; January 23 and February 1, 1961.

24   This point was elucidated by Yitzḥak Navon, Ben Gurion's former chèf de cabinet in an interview on January 6, 1971.

25   Moshe Unna, "Twenty Years in the Knesset," *'Amudim* (The Magazine of ha-Kibbutz ha-Dati), vol. 19, 6, (no. 303), p. 198. Mr. Yisrael Zvi Weinberg called the article to the attention of the writer.

26   *The Jerusalem Post*, February 28, 1961.

27   *Ker'a*, pp. 32–33.

28   *The Jerusalem Post*, March 6, 1961.

29   Yannai, *Ker'a*, p. 27.

30   *Ibid.*, pp. 34–35.

31   *Ibid.*, p. 29.

32   *Ibid.*, p. 31.

33   *Ibid.*, p. 34.

34   Two illustrations of the resentment felt toward Ben Gurion follow. In one case, the reason is due to his personal attitudes toward the Zionist movement, which he had severely criticized (see Chapter 11). The cabinet decided that "unless the Prime Minister was prepared to express the majority view of the government concerning the Zionist

movement, he should not make the opening address, and moreover, should make it clear he was expressing his personal views . . . ." (*The Jerusalem Post*, December 5, 1960). The proponent, Minister of Justice Pinḥas Rosen, had been a close supporter of Ben Gurion, but the old relationship had cooled at that very period due to Rosen's role as chairman of the Committee of Seven. Second, Moshe Sharett told Michael Brecher in July 1960, "Since 1957, Ben Gurion has had carte blanche in foreign policy; the party never debates these issues any longer" (Brecher, cited, Chapter 16). The inherent bitterness comes through quite clearly.

35   Robert A. Scalapino, "The New Role of Nationalism," *Problems of Communism*, XX(1–2), January-April, 1972, pp. 11–12.

36   S.N. Eisenstadt (ed.), *Max Weber on Charisma and Institution Building* (Chicago: University of Chicago Press, 1968), p. 54.

37   William Shakespeare, *King Lear*, Act I, Scene 2.

CHAPTER FOURTEEN

1   Cecil A. Gibb, "Leadership: Psychological Aspects," *International Encyclopedia of the Social Sciences* (The Macmillan Company and The Free Press, 1968), vol. 9, p. 91.

2   *Idem.*

3   Arnold S. Tannenbaum, "Leadership: Sociological Aspects," *International Encyclopedia, op. cit.*, p. 101.

4   H.H. Gerth and C. Wright Mills, *From Max Weber* (London: Oxford University Press, 1946), pp. 78–79.

5   One of Ben Gurion's aides related that when he was offered the sum of $100,000 for his memoirs, he asked, in all sincerity: "What would I do with so much money? "

6   See the instructive article by David E. Apter, "Nkrumah, Charisma and the Coup," in Dankwart D. Rustow (ed.), *Philosophers and Kings* (New York: Braziller, 1970), pp. 117–120.

7   S.N. Eisenstadt (ed.), *Max Weber on Charisma and Institution Building, and Social Transformation* (Chicago: University of Chicago Press, 1968), p. 47.

8   David C. McClelland, "The Two Faces of Power," *Journal of International Affairs*, 24(1), 1970, p. 38.

9   *The Jerusalem Post*, September 30, 1966, translated from *Davar*, September 21, 1956; see note 55, Chapter 3.

10   Observation by one of Eshkol's aides in 1963–65.

11   Eisenstadt, *op. cit.*, Introduction, p. xvii.

12   *The Jerusalem Post*, December 1960.

13   *Divrei ha-Knesset*, vol. 25, p. 434, December 3, 1958.

14   For Lenin on territorial flexibility, Hayim Greenberg, *The Inner Eye* (New York: Jewish Frontier, 1953), pp. 281 ff. On Nehru, the standard work is Michael Brecher, *Nehru, A Political Biography*

(London: Oxford University Press, 1959).

15   Ben Gurion, *Zikhronot* [Memoirs] (Tel Aviv: Am Oved, 1971), 2 vols.; vol. 1, pp. 254—255.

16   *Ha-'Aretz*, April 9, 1971.

17   Christopher Hill, *Lenin and the Russian Revolution* (Middlesex: Penguin Books, 1971), p. 60.

18   One of his aides to Avi-ḥai.

19   *Ben Gurion Looks Back in Talks with Moshe Pearlman* (New York: Simon and Schuster, 1965), p. 99.

Bibliography

HEBREW

'Am Yisra'el u-Medinat Yisra'el, ha-Ve'ida ha-'Olamit ha-Rishonah shel
ha-No'ar ha-Yehudi (The Jewish People and the State of Israel, The
First World Conference of Jewish Youth). Jerusalem: The Jewish
Agency, 1958.

Bauer, Yehuda. Diplomatia u-Mahteret (Diplomacy and Underground in
Zionism, 1939—1945). 2nd edition. Tel Aviv: Sifriat Poalim, 1966.

Becker, Ya'akov. Mishnato shel David Ben Gurion (The Teachings of David
Ben Gurion). 2 volumes. Tel Aviv: Yavneh, 1958.

Beer, Israel. Bithon Yisra'el (The Security of Israel). Tel Aviv: Amikam,
1966.

Bein, Alex. Toldot ha-Hityashvut (History of Agricultural Settlement).
English abridged version: The Return to the Soil. Jerusalem: Zionist
Organization, 1952.

Begin, Menahem. Ha-Mered (The Revolt). Jerusalem: Achiasaf, 1950.

Ben Gurion, David. Anahnu u-Shheineinu (We and Our Neighbors). Tel
Aviv: Davar, 1929.

_____. Devarim le-'Iyun (Subjects for Study). Jerusalem: Zionist Organ-
ization, Youth Department, 1958.

_____. Devarim Kehavayatam (Things as They Happened). Tel Aviv: Am
Hassefer, 1965.

_____. Ha-Emet Kodemet la-Kol (Truth Above All). Tel Aviv: Mimeo,
1961.

_____. Hazon ve-Derekh   (Vision and Way). 5 volumes. Tel Aviv: Labor
Party (Mapai), 1951—1957.

_____. Be-Hilahem Yisra'el (When Israel Fought). 2nd edition. Tel Aviv:
Labor Party (Mapai), 1950.

_____. *Ha-Histadrut veha-Medinah* (The Histadrut and the State). Tel Aviv: Histadrut, 1956.

_____. *Ketavim Rishonim* (Early Writings). Tel Aviv: 1952.

_____. *Likrat he-'Atid le-She'ailat Eretz Yisra'el* (To the Future of the Palestine Problem).

_____. *Mi-Ma'amad le-'Am* (From Class to Nation). Tel Aviv: Aiyanot, 1956.

_____. *Ba-Ma'arakhah* (In the Struggle). 5 volumes. Tel Aviv: Am Oved, 1957.

_____. *Ma'arekhet Sinai* (The Sinai Campaign). Tel Aviv: Am Oved, 1964.

_____. *Medinat Yisra'el ha-Mehudeshet* (The Restored State of Israel). Tel Aviv: Am Oved, 1962.

_____. *Mikhtavim El Paula* (Letters to Paula). Tel Aviv: Am Oved: 1968.

_____. *Netzah Yisra'el* (The Eternity of Israel). Tel Aviv: Aiyanot, n.d.

_____. *Ha-Po'el ha-'Ivri ve-Histadruto* (The Hebrew Worker and His Organization). Tel Aviv: Histadrut, 1964.

_____. *Tenu'at ha-Po'alim veha-Revisionistim* (The Labor Movement and the Revisionists). Tel Aviv: League for Labor Palestine, 1933.

_____. *Zikhronot* (Memoirs).3 volumes. Tel Aviv: Am Oved, 1971–1973.

Ha-Congress ha-Tziyyoni ha-Kaf-Dalet, Din ve-Heshbon Stenographi (The Twenty-Fourth Zionist Congress, Stenographic Record). Jerusalem: Zionist Executive, 1956–1957.

Ha-Congress ha-Tziyyoni ha-Kaf-Heh, Din ve-Heshbon Stenographi (The Twenty-Fifth Zionist Congress, Stenographic Record). Jerusalem: Zionist Executive, 1961.

Even-Shoshan (Rosenberg), Zvi. *Toldot Tenu'at ha-Po'alim be-Eretz Yisra'el* (History of the Labor Movement in the Land of Israel). 3 volumes. Am Oved, 1963–1966.

Gerias, Sabri. *Ha-'Aravim be-Yisra'el* (The Arabs in Israel). Haifa: Al-Teahad, 1966.

Gid'on, R. (ed.), *Hukei Medinat Yisra'el* (Laws of the State of Israel). Tel Aviv: 1959.

Gordon, A.D. *Kitvei A.D. Gordon.* 5 volumes. Tel Aviv: Ha-Po'el ha-Tza'ir, 1925–1929.

Gutmann, Emanuel & Dror, Yehezkiel (eds.), *Mishtar Medinat Yisra'el* (The Government of the State of Israel). Jerusalem: The Hebrew University, 1969.

Habas, Brakha, *Ben Gurion ve-Doro* (Ben Gurion and His Generation). Tel Aviv: Massada, 1952.

Ha-Encyclopedia ha-'Ivrit (The Hebrew Encyclopedia). Jerusalem & Tel Aviv: Encyclopedia Publishing Co., 1966.

Herut. *Mi-Parashat Lavon le-Farashat Ben Gurion* (From the Lavon Affair to the Ben Gurion Affair). Tel Aviv: Herut Party, 1961.

Horowitz, Dan and Hasin, Eliyahu. *Ha-Parashah* (The Affair). Tel Aviv: Am Hassefer, 1961.

Horowitz, Dan and Lissak, Moshe. *Mi-Yishuv le-Medinah* (From Yishuv to State). Jerusalem: Hebrew University, 1972.

Jabotinsky, Vladimir. *Ne'umim* (Speeches). 2 volumes. Jerusalem: 1947—1948.

The Jewish Agency. *'Am Yisra'el u-Medinat Yisra'el,* ha-Ve'ida ha-'Olamit ha-Rishona shel ha-No'ar ha-Yehudi (The Jewish People and the State of Israel, The First World Conference of Jewish Youth). Jerusalem: The Jewish Agency, 1958.

Katznelson, Berl. *Kitvei Berl Katznelson* (Writings of Berl Katznelson). Tel Aviv: Mapai, 1946—1949.

Lachover, Shmuel. *Kitvei Ben Gurion* (The Writings of Ben Gurion — A Bibliography, 1910—1958). Tel Aviv: 1960.

Lavon, Pinhas. *Derekh ha-Histadrut be-Medinah* (The Path of the Histadrut in the State). Tel Aviv: Histadrut, 1959.

————. *Hevrat ha-'Avodah* (A Labor Society). Tel Aviv: Mifaley Tarbut Vehinuch, 1968.

Mi Yehudi (Who is a Jew). A reader, Jerusalem: 1969.

Pirkei ha-Po'el ha-Tza'ir (Chapters of ha-Po'el ha-Tza'ir). 9 volumes. Tel Aviv: Anthology Committee of ha-Po'el ha-Tza'ir, 1928—1937.

Kovetz min ha-Yesod (Collection of articles by the Lavonist Min ha-Yesod group). Tel Aviv: Amikam, 1962.

Sefer ha-Palmah (The Book of the Palmah). Tel Aviv: Ha-Kibbutz ha-Me'uhad, 1953.

Sharett, Moshe. *Be-Sha'ar ha-Umot* (At the Threshold of Statehood). Tel Aviv: Am Oved, 1966.

————. *Yoman Medini* (Making of Policy — The Diaries of Moshe Sharett). Tel Aviv: Am Oved, 1968.

Toldot Milhemet ha-Komemiut (History of the War of Liberation). Tel Aviv: Ma'arakhot (IDF), 1959.

Ha-Ve'ida ha-Shevi'it shel ha-Histadrut (The Seventh Convention of the Histadrut). Tel Aviv: Histadrut, 1949.

Yalkut Ahdut ha-'Avodah (Ahdut ha-'Avodah Anthology). 2 volumes. Tel Aviv: Zionist-Socialist Organization of Palestine Workers, 1929—1932.

Yannai, Natan. *Ker'a ba-Tzameret* (Split at the Top). Tel Aviv: Levin-Epstein, 1969.

Yifrah, S. *Dinei ha-Apotropos* (Laws of the Custodian). Tel Aviv: 1953.

Zisling, A. *David Ben Gurion: Emet ve-Selef* (David Ben Gurion: Truth and Falsehood). Tel Aviv: 1959.

NON—HEBREW

Allon, Yigal. *The Making of Israel's Army.* London: Vallentine and Mitchell, 1970.

American Jewish Committee. *In Vigilant Brotherhood.* The American Jewish Committee's Relationship to Palestine and Israel. New York: AJC, 1964.

Applebaum, Syd. *Education in the IDF* (mimeographed). Tel Aviv: Office of the Army Spokesman, 1960.

Arian, Alan. *Ideological Change in Israel.* Cleveland: The Press of Case Western Reserve University, 1968.

Aronson, Shlomo and Horowitz, Dan. *Aspects of the Israeli-Arab Conflict.* In preparation.

Bar-Zohar, Michael. *Ben Gurion. The Armed Prophet.* Englewood Cliffs, N.J.: Prentice-Hall, 1968.

Bauer, Yehuda. *Flight and Rescue; Brichah.* New York: Random House, 1970.

Beer, Israel. *The Security of Israel.* Tel Aviv: Amikam, 1966.

Bein, Alex. *Theodore Herzl.* New York, Philadelphia: Meridian, JPS, 1962.

Ben Gurion, David. *Ben Gurion Looks Back in Talks with Moshe Pearlman.* New York: Simon and Schuster, 1965.

———. *Israel: Years of Challenge.* New York: Holt, Rinehart and Winston, 1963.

———. *Jewish Labor.* Translated by E. Werbner and G. Cashman. London: Hechalutz, 1935.

———. *The Jews in Their Land.* Translated by M. Nurock and M. Louvish. New York: Doubleday, 1966.

Bernstein, Edvard. *Evolutionary Socialism.* New York: Schocken, 1961.

Bernstein, Marver H. *The Politics of Israel.* The First Decade of Statehood. Princeton: Princeton University Press, 1957.

Birnbaum, Ervin. *The Politics of Compromise: State and Religion in Israel.* Rutherford: Fairleigh Dickinson Press, 1970.

Borochov, Ber. *Nationalism and the Class Struggle.* New York: Poalei Zion, 1937.

Brecher, Michael. *The Foreign Policy System of Israel: Setting, Image, Process.* London: Oxford University Press, 1972.

———. *Nehru, A Political Biography.* London: Oxford University Press, 1959.

Buber, Martin. *Israel and Palestine: The History of an Idea.* New York: Farrar, Strauss and Young, 1952.

Burns, E.L.M. *Between Arab and Israeli.* London: Harrap, 1962.

Cohen, Israel. *A Short History of Zionism.* London: Muller, 1951.

———. *The Zionist Movement.* New York: Zionist Organization of America, 1946.

Dayan, Moshe. *Diary of the Sinai Campaign.* New York: Harper and Row, 1966.

Deutsch, Karl W. *Nationalism and Social Communication.* 2nd edition. Cambridge, Mass.: MIT Press, 1966.

Dror, Yeḥezkiel and Gutmann Emanuel. *The Government of Israel.* Jerusalem: Hebrew University, 1961.

Edinger, Lewis D. *Kurt Schumacher: A Study in Personality and Political Behavior.* Stanford: Stanford University Press, 1965.

———. (ed.). *Political Leadership in Industrialized Societies.* New York: Wiley, 1967.

Eisenstadt, S.N. (ed.). *Max Weber on Charisma and Institution Building and Social Transformation.* Chicago: University of Chicago Press, 1968.

Elon, Amos. *The Israelis: Founders and Sons.* London: Weidenfeld and Nicolson, 1971.
Encyclopedia of Zionism and Israel. New York: Herzl Press and McGraw Hill, 1971.
Erikson, Erik H. *Ghandi's Truth.* New York: Norton, 1960.
_____. *Young Man Luther.* New York: Norton, 1962.
Esco Foundation for Palestine, Inc. *Palestine.* A Study of Jewish, Arab and British Policies. 2 volumes. New Haven: Yale University Press, 1947.
Fein, Leonard J. *Politics in Israel.* Boston: Little, Brown & Co., 1967.
Forum for the Problems of Zionism, Jewry and the State of Israel. Proceedings of the Jerusalem Ideological Conference (of August, 1957). Jerusalem: World Zionist Organization, 1959.
Gerth, H.H. and Mills, C. Wright. *From Max Weber.* London: Oxford University Press, 1946.
Goldman, Eliezer. *Religious Issues in Israel's Political Life.* Jerusalem: The World Zionist Organization, Youth Department, Religious Section, 1964.
Goldmann, Naḥum. *The Autobiography of Nahum Goldmann.* New York: Holt, Rinehart and Winston, 1969.
Great Britain, Parliamentary Papers. Cmd. 3530. *Report of Commission of the Palestine Disturbances of August, 1929.* London: 1930.
_____. Cmd. 5479. *Palestine: Royal Commission Report.* London: 1938.
_____. Cmd. 5354. *Palestine: Partition Commission Report.* London: 1938.
_____. Cmd. 6019. *Palestine: Statement of Policy.* London: 1939.
Greenberg, Hayim. *The Inner Eye.* New York: Jewish Frontier, 1953.
Hadawi, S. *Israel and the Arab Minority.* Arab Information Centre, 1959.
Halperin, Samuel. *The Political World of American Zionism.* Detroit: Wayne University Press, 1961.
Halpern, Ben. *The Idea of the Jewish State.* Cambridge, Mass.: Harvard University Press, 1961.
Heckelman, Joseph. *What If?* An attempt to assess the significance and participation of overseas volunteers in Israel's War of Independence. New York: Jewish Theological Seminary of America, 1970 (unpublished thesis).
Heller, Joseph. *The Zionist Idea.* New York: Schocken, 1949.
Hertzberg, Arthur. *The Zionist Idea.* New York, Philadelphia: Meridian, JPS, 1960.
Hill, Christopher. *Lenin and the Russian Revolution.* Middlesex: Penguin Books, 1971.
Hurewitz, J.C. *Diplomacy in the Near and Middle East, A Documentary Record.* Princeton: Van Nostrand, 1956.
_____. *Middle East Politics: The Military Dimension.* New York: Praeger, 1969.
_____. *The Struggle for Palestine.* New York: Norton & Co., 1950.
International Encyclopedia of the Social Sciences. Macmillan and The Free Press, 1968.

Jewish Agency for Palestine. *The Jewish Case Before the Anglo-American Committee of Inquiry on Palestine.* Jerusalem: 1947.
Jewish Identity. A documentary compilation by Baruch Litvin, S.B. Hoenig (ed.). New York: Feldheim, 1965.
Joseph, Dov. *The Faithful City.* Tel Aviv: Schocken, 1950.
Kimche, Jon and David. *The Secret Roads.* New York: Farrar, Strauss, Cudahy, 1955.
Kraines, Oscar. *Government and Politics in Israel.* Boston: Houghton Mifflin, 1961.
Laufer, Leopold. *Israel and the Developing Countries.* New York: Twentieth Century Fund, 1967.
Lifton, Robert Jay. *Revolutionary Immortality.* Middlesex: Penguin Books, 1970.
Lindzey, Gardner (ed.). *Handbook of Social Psychology.* Cambridge, Mass.: Addison-Wesley, 1954.
Litvinoff, Barnet. *Ben Gurion of Israel.* New York: Praeger, 1954.
Lorch, Netanel. *The Edge of the Sword.* New York: Putnam, 1961.
McDonald, James G. *My Mission to Israel.* New York: Simon and Schuster, 1951.
Nossig, Alfred (ed.). *Jüdische Statistik.* Berlin: Jüdische Verlag, 1903.
O'Ballance, Edgar. *The Arab-Israeli War, 1948.* London: Faber, 1956.
La Paix dans le Moyen-Orient. Jerusalem: Etat d'Israël, Ministère des Affaires Etrangères, 1955.
Peres, Shimon. *David's Sling.* London: Weidenfeld and Nicolson, 1970.
Peretz, D. *Israel and the Palestine Arabs.* Washington: Middle East Institute, 1958.
Perlmutter, Amos. *Military and Politics in Israel.* London: Cass, 1969.
Rackman, Emanuel. *Israel's Emerging Constitution, 1948–1951.* New York: Columbia University Press, 1955.
The Record of Israel's Peace Offers to the Arab States, 1948–1963. Jerusalem: Ministry for Foreign Affairs, 1963.
Rustow, Dankwart. *A World of Nations.* Washington: Brookings Institute, 1968.
———— (ed.). *Philosophers and Kings.* New York: Braziller, 1970.
Safran, Nadav. *From War to War.* New York: Pegasus, 1968.
————. *The United States and Israel.* Cambridge: Harvard University Press, 1963.
St. John, Robert. *Ben Gurion.* London: Jarrolds, 1959.
Seligman, Lester G. *Leadership in a New Nation.* Political Development in Israel. New York: 1964.
Sessions of the Zionist General Council. April 19–28, 1950. Jerusalem: Zionist Executive of Jerusalem, n.d.
Sharef, Zeev. *Three Days.* Garden City, New York: Doubleday, 1962.
Slater, Leonard. *The Pledge.* New York: Simon and Schuster, 1970.
Stock, Ernest. *From Conflict to Understanding.* New York: Institute of Human Relations, 1968.
————. *Israel on the Road to Sinai, 1949–1956.* Ithaca: Cornell, 1967.

Sykes, Christopher. *Cross Roads to Israel.* Palestine from Balfour to Bevin. London: Collins, 1965.

Syrkin, Marie. *Nachman Syrkin.* New York: 1960.

Syrkin, Naḥman (Ben Elieser — pseud.). *Die Judenfrage und der Sozialistische Judenstaat.* Berne: 1898.

———. *Essays on Socialist Zionism.* 1935.

Taylor, Alan R. *Prelude to Israel,* An Analysis of Zionist Diplomacy 1897–1947. New York: Philosophical Library, 1959.

Weisgal, Meyer W. and Carmichael, Joel (eds.). *Chaim Weizmann.* A Biography by Several Hands. London: Weidenfeld and Nicolson, 1962.

Weizmann, Chaim. *Selected Speeches of Chaim Weizmann, A Tribute.* Edited by P. Goodman, 1945.

———. *Trial and Error.* New York: Harper and Brothers, 1949.

———. *The Jewish People in Palestine.* 1939.

Wise, Stephen. *Challenging Years.* (Autobiography). New York: 1949.

Wriggins, W. Howard. *The Ruler's Imperative: Strategies for Political Survival in Asia and Africa.* New York: Columbia University Press, 1969.

Zionist Organization. *Book of Documents Submitted to General Assembly of UN.* New York: 1947.

———. *Minutes (Protocols) of Zionist Congresses.*

———. *The Jewish Case Before the Anglo-American Committee.* Jerusalem: 1947.

———. *The Jewish Plan for Palestine.* Jerusalem: 1947.

———. *Reports of the Zionist Executive to Zionist Congresses.*

ARTICLES — HEBREW

Aronson, Shlomo. "Ben Gurion, Eshkol, Allon and Dayan: The Art of Priorities."

———. and Horowitz, Dan. "The Strategy of Controlled Retaliation: The Israeli Case," n.d.

Ben Gurion, David. "Ha-Masa u-Matan ha-Sodi" (The Secret Negotiations). *Ma'ariv,* July 2, 1971, July 9, 1971.

Unna, Moshe, "Twenty Years in the Knesset." *'Amudim* (The Magazine of ha-Kibbutz ha-Dati). XIX, 6.

ARTICLES — NON-HEBREW

Bayne, E.A. *American University Field Staff Reports Service.* 10(3), (Israel), May, 1961.

Commager, Henry Steele. "Is Freedom in America Dying? " *Look,* 34 (13), July 14, 1970.

Flapan, Simḥa. "Dispute Over the Jordan." *New Outlook*, 3(4), February, 1960.

———— . "The Kennesset (sic) Votes on the Refugee Problem." *New Outlook*, 4(9). December, 1961.

McClelland, David C. "The Two Faces of Power." *Journal of International Affairs*, 24 (1), 1970.

Peretz, D. "The Arab Minority in Israel." *Middle East Journal.* Spring, 1954.

Scalapino, Robert A. "The New Role of Nationalism." *Problems of Communism*, 20 (1–2). January–April, 1971.

KNESSET OR PROVISIONAL COUNCIL PROCEEDINGS

Mo'etzet ha-Medinah ha-Zemanit (Provisional State Council Proceedings).
Divrei ha-Knesset (Knesset Proceedings).

NEWSPAPERS

Ha-'Aretz. Independent (morning) daily. Tel Aviv.
The Jerusalem Post. Independent pro-government (morning) daily.
Davar. Labor (Histadrut) (morning) daily. Tel Aviv.
Ma'ariv. Independent (afternoon) daily. Tel Aviv.

Biographical Notes

October 16, 1886 (17 Tishrei, 5647) : born in Plonsk, Russian Poland, to Avigdor and Sheindel Green; educated in a modernized Hebrew-speaking ḥeder, privately tutored in secular subjects.

1900 : among the founders of 'Ezra, a local Zionist youth group.

1903 : joined Po'alei Tziyyon; organized party activities, particularly in Warsaw.

1906 : immigrated to Palestine, worked as agricultural laborer in Petaḥ Tikvah and Rishon le-Tziyyon.

1907 : elected to central committee of Po'alei Tziyyon, participated in party's third conference.

1907–1910 : agricultural worker in Sejera, Lower Galilee.

1910 : joined editorial staff of ha-Aḥdut, periodical of Po'alei Tziyyon.

1911 : delegate to 11th Zionist Congress, studied in Salonika.

1912–1914 : studied law in Istanbul, returning to Palestine on vacation, when World War I broke out.

1915 : exiled from Palestine; went to New York.

1915–1918 : in New York worked with Yitzḥak Ben-Zvi on studies of Palestine and the labor movement, helped organize Labor Zionist groups, propagandized for immigration to Palestine and urged formation of a Jewish Legion to serve in Middle East with British army.

1917 : married Paula Munweis.

1918 : returned to Palestine with British army.

1919 : attended 13th conference of Po'alei Tziyyon and later opened founding conference of Aḥdut ha-'Avodah, a merger of Po'alei Tziyyon and other labor groups.

1920–1921 : political bureau of Po'alei Tziyyon in London.

1921–1935 : secretary of Histadrut; advocated establishment of worker-based independent Jewish economy in Palestine and the role of Histadrut as instrument for building and development.

1930 : instrumental in merger of Aḥdut ha-'Avodah and Ha-Po'el ha-Tza'ir to form Mapai, the labour party which he was to lead to increasing strength.

1933 : attended 18th Zionist Congress; elected to Zionist and Jewish Agency executive committees, having helped make labor largest force in World Zionist Organization.

1935–1948 : chairman of Jewish Agency Executive in Jerusalem.

1935–1936 : attempted to launch negotiations about the future of Palestine with Arab nationalist leaders.

1937 : supported Peel (Royal Commission of Enquiry) plan calling for partition of Palestine.

1938–1939 : participated in London Round Table Talks; strenuously condemned British White Paper of 1939.

1942–1944 : helped formulate Biltmore Program of 1942, calling for opening of Palestine to Jewish immigration and stating that creation of a Jewish state ("commonwealth") was aim of the Zionist movement. Rallied Yishuv to support of Program at price of Mapai party unity.

1946–1948 : assumed responsibility for defense of Yishuv; initiated and directed development of Haganah military capability through arms purchases and support for illegal immigration.

May 14, 1948 : proclaimed independence of State of Israel; prime minister and defense minister in the Provisional Government. Created and unified Israel Defense Forces, the Haganah's successor, through enforced merging of competing military elements; during War of Independence, directed military strategy.

1949 : following first national elections, continued to hold posts of prime minister and minister of defense.

1949–1953 : declared Jerusalem to be capital of Israel in the face of international protest. Strove to unite new nation through development of army, rapid absorption of massive immigration and unification of the educational system. Urged reparation negotiations with West Germany, despite strong internal dissent.

December 1953 : retired from government, settling in Sde Boker.

1955 : returned to government as defense minister; pursued activist policy characterized by the series of reprisal raids. Following elections, became prime minister, retaining defense portfolio.

1956 : initiated, in collaboration with France and Britain, Sinai Campaign, in which Israel captured Sinai Peninsula and Gaza Strip, but within a few months withdrew in face of Soviet threats and US pressures. Subsequently stated that Campaign greatly improved security situation and opened Eilat to Israel-bound shipping.

1958 : Cabinet crises due to his advocacy and implementation of closer relations with West Germany and the "Who is a Jew? " issue.

1960—1961 : opposed verdict of government committee exonerating Pinḥas Lavon from responsibility for 1954 security mishap. Control of Mapai and his overall political support weakened due to Lavon controversy.

June 16, 1963 : resigned from government, naming Levi Eshkol as his successor.

1964 : demanded reopening of Lavon Affair, advocated electoral reform, opposed alignment between Mapai and Aḥdut ha-'Avodah, criticized Eshkol's policies.

1965 : organized new party, Rafi (Israel Labor List), which received only 10 seats in elections.

1968 : spurned Labor Party which Rafi joined, after Moshe Dayan had entered cabinet on eve of Six-Day War (June 1967).

1969 : again stood for Knesset heading State List — a splinter group of Rafi loyalists; party received only four seats.

1970 : resigned from Knesset and devoted himself to writing his memoirs and other works dealing with history of Israel.

1973 : died, December 1, 1973 (6 Kislev, 5734).

Glossary

Aggadah — name given to those sections of Talmud and Midrash containing homiletic expositions of the Bible, stories, legends, folklore, anecdotes, or maxims. In contradistinction to Halakhah.

Agudat Yisra'el — world organization of orthodox Jews, founded in 1912. Anti-Zionist for many years, it became more cooperative with Zionism following the Holocaust. In Israel, the party has contested all national elections and has even participated in government coalitions.

Aḥdut ha-'Avodah — Zionist Socialist Labor Party in Palestine founded in 1919. In 1930 this movement merged with Ha-Po'el ha-Tza'ir and formed Mapai. The name was taken by Si'ah Bet (Faction Two), the anti-partition and anti-Ben Gurion opposition in Mapai, when it formed a separate political party in 1944. In 1948, Aḥdut ha-'Avodah merged with ha-Shomer ha-Tza'ir to form Mapam. It split from Mapam in 1954 and in 1968, and merged with Mapai (and Rafi) to form the Israel Labor Party.

'Aliyah — (1) immigration to Eretz Yisra'el; (2) one of the waves of immigration to Eretz Yisra'el from the early 1880s. (Literally: going up, ascent.)

Asefat ha-Nivḥarim — representative assembly elected by Jews in Palestine during the period of the British Mandate (1920—48); referred to also as Assembly of Delegates. Its executive body was called Va'ad Le'umi (National Council).

Bilti-miflagtiim — non-party labor adherents who favored an encompassing labor movement in Israel and merged with Po'alei Tziyyon in 1919 to form Aḥdut ha-'Avodah.

Bitaḥon — security, defense. The stress on the primacy of defense considerations led to the coining of the term Bitḥonism and Bitḥonist.

Bitzu‘a — execution, implementation, carrying out; hence pragmatic. The hybrid Bitzu‘ist carries the sense of pragmatist and doer and may on occasion be pejorative.

Dati — religious, observant of the orthodox code of Jewish ritual and law.

Dayan (pl. **dayanim**) — member of the rabbinic court.

Eretz Yisra’el — Land of Israel; Palestine.

Etzel — (acronym for Irgun Tzeva’i Le’umi; "National Military Organization"), underground Jewish organization in Eretz Yisra’el founded in 1931, which engaged from 1937 in retaliatory acts against Arab attacks and later against the British Mandatory authorities.

Fidaiyun — literally "self-sacrificers"; Arab units often sponsored and backed by military intelligence (Egyptian and Syrian particularly) which undertook infiltration and marauding attacks and espionage activities within Israeli territory.

General Zionists — Zionist party, whose members were those who did not join the first Zionist political parties, and especially advocated private enterprise.

Goyim — literally, nations; later applied to non-Jews; cf. English "Gentile."

Haganah — clandestine Jewish organization for armed self-defense in Eretz Yisra’el under the British Mandate, which eventually evolved into a people’s militia and became the basis for the Israel Defense Forces.

Ha-Kibbutz ha-Artzi — a union of kibbutzim in Israel, founded in 1927 by the first collective settlements of ha-Shomer ha-Tza‘ir pioneers.

Ha-Kibbutz ha-Me’uḥad — federation of kibbutzim which favored large communes and the introduction of industry. It was the backbone of Si’ah Bet and then Aḥdut ha-‘Avodah. A minority of Mapai sympathizers ceded from some of its kibbutzim in the early 1950s.

Halakhah (adj. **halakhic**) — an accepted decision in rabbinic law. Also refers to those parts of the Talmud concerned with legal matters. In contradistinction to Aggadah.

Ḥalutz (pl. **ḥalutzim**) — pioneer, especially in agriculture, in Eretz Yisra’el.

Ḥalutziyut — pioneering.

Ḥannukah — eight-day celebration commemorating the victory of Judah Maccabee over the Syrian king Antiochus Epiphanes and the subsequent rededication of the Temple. Literally, Dedication; commonly known as the Feast of Lights, usually falling in December.

Ha-Po‘el ha-Mizrachi — religious pioneering and labor movement in Eretz Yisra’el founded in 1922 by young elements of Mizrachi.

Ha-Po'el ha-Tza'ir (Hebrew: The Young Workers) — Eretz Yisra'el labor party founded by the early pioneers of the Second 'Aliyah (1904–1914).

Ha-Shomer — organization of Jewish workers in Eretz Yisra'el founded in 1909 to defend Jewish settlements. Literally the Watchman or Guard.

Ha-Shomer ha-Tza'ir — Zionist youth organization and former Palestinian political party formed in Galicia in 1913, it participated in 1948 in the formation of Mapam; doctrinaire in ideology it strove for a merger of Zionism and Marxism.

Haskalah — "Enlightenment": movement for spreading modern European culture among Jews c. 1750–1880.

Ḥeder — (literally "room"), school for teaching children Jewish religious observance and basic texts, especially the prayer-book and Bible. ˙

Histadrut — (abbr. for Hebr. *Ha-Histadrut ha-Kelalit shel ha-'Ovedim ha-'Ivriyyim be-Eretz Yisra'el*), General Federation of Jewish Labor, founded in 1920; subsequently renamed *Histadrut Ha-'Ovedim be-Eretz Yisra'el.*

Ḥovevei Tziyyon — federation of *Ḥibbat Tziyyon*, early (pre-Herzl) Zionist movement in Russia. Literally, Lovers of Zion.

Jewish Agency — international nongovernment body, whose aims are to assist and encourage development and settlement in Eretz Yisra'el. Its executive and that of the World Zionist Organization usually were composed of the same members but in certain periods the Agency executive has included non-Zionist representatives.

Kaballah (adj. **kabbalistic**) — the Jewish mystical tradition.

Kashrut — Jewish dietary laws.

Kibbutz (pl. **kibbutzim**) — commune constituting a settlement in Eretz Yisra'el based mainly on agriculture but engaging also in industry.

Kishleh — prison in Turkish times in the Old City of Jerusalem. At present an Israel Police station.

Knesset — unicamenal parliament of the State of Israel.

Leḥi (abbr. for Heb. *Loḥamei Ḥerut Yisra'el*, "Fighters for the Freedom of Israel") — radically anti-British armed underground organization in Palestine, founded in 1940 by dissidents from Etzel).

Le'om — Nationality; ethnic group.

Mamlakhti — pertaining to the state or nation; non-sectoral.

Mamlakhtiyut — the placing of national interests above sectoral ones; giving the state primacy over sectoral interests or rival institutions. From the word *Mamlakha* — Kingdom (*melekh* — king), and therefore especially evocative.

Mapai — (initials of Heb. *Mifleget Po'alei Eretz Yisra'el*), also called Israel (formerly Palestine) Labor Party, founded in 1930 by the union of Aḥdut ha-'Avodah and Ha-Po'el ha-Tza'ir.

Mapam — left-wing Labor-Zionist Israel party formed in 1948 by the fusion of Ha-Shomer ha-Tza'ir and Aḥdut ha-'Avodah–Po'alei Tziyyon.

Maskilim — adherents of Haskalah ("Enlightenment") movement.

Midrash — method of interpreting Scripture to elucidate legal points (*Midrash Halakhah*) or to bring out lessons by stories or homiletics (*Midrash Aggadah*). Also the name for a collection of such rabbinic interpretations.

Mizrachi — religious Zionist movement, founded in 1902 as a religious faction of the World Zionist Organization.

Moshav (pl. **moshavim**) — smallholders' cooperative agricultural settlement in Israel.

'Oleh — personal noun from 'aliyah; an immigrant; literally one who goes up or ascends (to the Land of Israel).

Palmaḥ — (abbr. for Hebr. *pelugot maḥatz*; "shock companies"), striking arm of the Haganah.

Parnas (pl. **parnassim**) — chief synagogue functionary originally vested with both religious and administrative functions; subsequently an elected lay leader.

Po'alei Agudat Yisra'el — religious labor movement affiliate of Agudat Yisra'el founded in Poland 1922, active in Eretz Yisra'el from 1925.

Po'alei Tziyyon — political party whose ideology consisted of a combination of Zionism and Socialism founded in Russia toward the end of the 19th century.

Revisionists — movement of maximalist political Zionists founded in 1925 and led by Vladimir Jabotinsky.

Sabras — native-born Israelis.

Shabbat — the Jewish Sabbath which starts at sunset on Friday and ends at nightfall on Saturday. In orthodox procedure travel, kindling fire and other "work" are prohibited.

Shtadlan — Jewish representative or negotiator with access to dignitaries of state, active at royal courts, etc.

Sefardi (pl. **Sefardim**) — Jews of Spain and Portugal and their descendants, wherever resident, as constrasted with Ashkenazi(m); by extension Jews from Arabic-speaking, Middle Eastern or Oriental countries.

Si'ah Bet — opposition group within Mapai which was anti-partition and anti-Ben Gurion; formed Aḥdut ha-'Avodah in 1944.

Torah — Pentateuch or the Pentateuchal scroll for reading in synagogue; entire body of traditional Jewish teaching and literature.

Tze'irim — the younger non-establishment element in Mapai in 1950s and early '60s; identified with Ben Gurion in his struggle with the veteran Mapai leadership.

Va'ad Le'umi — National Council of Assembly of Delegates of the Jewish community in Eretz Yisra'el during the period of the British Mandate.

Yeshivah (pl. **yeshivot**) — Jewish traditional academy devoted primarily to study of rabbinic literature.

Yishuv — settlement: more specifically, the Jewish community of Eretz Yisra'el in the pre-state period.

Zionist Congress — regular world-wide conferences of representatives of the Zionist movement instituted by Theodor Herzl in 1897.

Index

'Abdallah, 24, 137, 138, 179,
185, 188—9
Abu Ghosh, 160
Aden, 48, 57
Adenauer, Konrad, 202—3, 208
Advisor on Arab Affairs, 169
Aggression, 128, 139, 188
Agriculture, agricultural, 14, 80,
85, 117, 119—20, 144, 211
Agudat Yisra'el, 60, 63, 93, 97,
99, 100, 101, 207
Aḥdut ha-'Avodah, 22, 61—2, 66,
102, 106, 108, 115, 158, 205,
206—7, 210, 254, 272, 273,
263—5
Al Ḥamah, 127
Allenby, General E.H., 20
Allon, Yigal, 124, 137
Almogi, Yosef, 258
Altalena, 113, 114, 203
America(n), (see also US), 20, 22,
33, 35, 40, 57, 106, 131, 137,
149, 161, 181—3, 192, 195,
199, 202, 208, 210—11, 226,
231—3, 235—9, 241—2
American Emergency Committee

for Zionist Affairs, 34
American Jewish Committee,
233—9
American Jewish Congress, 245
Amman, 24
Anderson, Robert, 131, 193
Anglo-American Committee on
Palestine, 151
Anglo-Egyptian Treaty, 28, 186
Anglo-Iraqi Treaty, 28
Anti-religious, 8, 97, 104, 106,
252
Anti-Semitism, anti-Semitic, 62,
83, 181, 236
Arab(s), 6, 20, 23—8, 30—2, 41,
45, 57, 68, 77, 98, 115,
125—31, 135, 139, 151—171,
176, 178, 180, 183—8, 192—7,
200, 207, 216, 218, 222, 251,
264, 267, 278
Arab Higher Committee, 30
Arabic language and culture, 119,
166, 170, 176
Arab League, 129
Arab refugees, 155—6, 160—1,
163—4, 178—9

342